D1271203

Caribbean Waves

BLACKS IN THE DIASPORA

Darlene Clark Hine, John McCluskey, Jr.,
and David Barry Gaspar
General Editors

CARIBBEAN WAVES

Relocating Claude McKay and Paule Marshall

Heather Hathaway

Indiana University Press

Bloomington and Indianapolis

This book is a publication of

Indiana University Press
601 North Morton Street
Bloomington, Indiana 47404-3797 USA

www.indiana.edu/~iupress

Telephone orders   800-842-6796
Fax orders   812-855-7931
Orders by e-mail   iuporder@indiana.edu

Library of Congress Cataloging-in-Publication Data

Hathaway, Heather.
Caribbean waves : relocating Claude McKay and Paule Marshall / Heather
Hathaway.
    p.   cm. — (Blacks in the diaspora)
Includes bibliographical references (p.   ) and index.
ISBN 0–253–33569–8 (cl : alk. paper)
  1. McKay, Claude, 1890–1948—Criticism and interpretation.
  2. American literature—Afro-American authors—History and
    criticism.   3. Marshall, Paule, 1929-   —Criticism and
interpretation.   4. American literature—West Indian influences.
  5. West Indian Americans—Intellectual life.   6. West Indian
Americans in literature.   7. Caribbean Area—In literature.
    8. Blacks in literature.   I. Title.   II. Series.
            PS3525.A24785Z69   1999
810.9′896073—dc21   99–13329

    1   2   3   4   5   04   03   02   01   00   99

To my parents and brothers,
who have supported me always.

Contents

Acknowledgments

M ANY PEOPLE HAVE facilitated the completion of this project. I am most directly indebted to Werner Sollors, whose intellectual stimulation and careful, critical eye have influenced this project enormously. I am also grateful for his wonderful sense of humor. Less directly, but no less importantly, I am indebted to James A. Miller, who has offered a constant supply of professional and personal support from the day I met him as an undergraduate. His ardent commitment to ethical education has deeply affected all areas of my teaching and research.

I am also indebted to a host of other teachers, scholars, and institutions. For introducing me to the fields of American and African American Studies and, through their passionate teaching, having a significant collective impact on my decision to become an academic, I thank Hazel Carby, George Creeger, Robert O'Meally, Richard Slotkin, and Clarence Walker. For playing important mentoring roles at crucial moments during the earliest phases of this project, I thank Catherine Clinton, Sarah Deutsch, David Herbert Donald, Frances Foster, the late Nathan Huggins, and Barbara Johnson. Finally, for taking a long walk on a very hot day in South Carolina, I thank Darlene Clark Hine, who expressed interest in my work and belief in my abilities at a time when such support was especially valuable, and has continued that endorsement ever since. I wish to thank Darlene for her assistance and to acknowledge my particular pleasure in publishing this book under the mantle of the Blacks in the Diaspora series, which is so ably piloted by Darlene and her co-editors, John McCluskey, Jr. and David Barry Gaspar.

For offering additional guidance and stimulating intellectual prodding, I thank my co-panelists at the 1993 American Studies Association Conference: Roy Bryce-Laporte, Selwyn Cudjoe, Peggy Leavitt, and Mary Waters. For their affirmation and encouragement, I thank Jamaica Kincaid and Michelle Cliff. I am also grateful to William and Barbara Graham, as well as to Gregory Nagy and Holly Davidson, heads of Currier House at Harvard University, who provided an employment and living situation that enabled me to focus on this project during graduate school. For financial support, I am especially indebted to the American Association of University Women for the assistance offered by a Dissertation

Fellowship, as well as to the Committee on Research at Marquette University for a Summer Faculty Fellowship.

A whole range of people at Indiana University Press have shepherded this project into being. Joan Catapano and her assistant, Grace Profatilov, must be credited and thanked for the crucial guidance and aid they provided at various stages of the process. Jane Lyle deserves recognition for her phenomenal punctuality and efficiency. Finally, Susan Barnett warrants high praise and gratitude for going well beyond copyediting to engaging in an exciting dialogue with me about several important issues in the text.

I would be remiss in not expressing gratitude to my colleagues in the English department at Marquette University for their interest in and enthusiasm for my scholarship. I owe particular thanks to John McCabe, Michael Gillespie, Tim Machan, and Milton Bates, each of whom has provided extremely good counsel on a number of different occasions during the final phases of this project. I must also gratefully recognize the punctual and knowledgeable assistance provided by the Interlibrary Loan Office at Marquette's Memorial Library.

Two friends deserve special recognition. I am very pleased to be able to thank Sean Keepers for his cover design. Although less directly involved in the project than some others mentioned here, his love of language and literature, friendship, and intellectual prodding have contributed in no small way to this final outcome. So, too, and more directly, has that offered by Anthony Peressini. To Tony, who patiently read multiple drafts of these chapters with his keen analytical eye and, perhaps more importantly, who provided vital moral support on a regular basis, I owe considerable thanks.

Finally, I come to that person for whom a "thank you" is wholly inadequate, Nigel Rothfels, who reads every word—again and again and again. For his intellectual camaraderie, emotional sustenance, and participation in every phase of this project from early grant proposal writing to final footnote editing, I am inexpressibly grateful.

A Note on Terminology

THROUGHOUT THIS STUDY, I use a variety of terms that warrant clarification. The terms "Caribbeaner" and "African Caribbeaner" are used to refer generally to black immigrants to the United States from any of the Caribbean islands. The term "African American" in this study refers to individuals of African descent who are born in the United States, as does the term "native-born black." "Foreign-born black" refers to blacks born outside the United States, including but not limited to those born in the Caribbean. "Black Americans" refers to all blacks, regardless of nativity, who live in the United States. Whenever possible, I describe the United States as the "United States" rather than "America," and the Caribbean region as the "Caribbean" rather than the "West Indies." When I do use the terms "America" or "American," I usually intend for them to connote the stereotypical and mythic immigrant conception of the United States as the "land of opportunity," the "golden land," etc. At times, for purposes of clarity, I must use these terms simply to refer to the United States; in such instances, however, I trust my meaning is clear from the context.

Caribbean Waves

Introduction

IN THE MID-THIRTIES, Ira de A. Reid collected the "life stories" of African Caribbean immigrants to the United States for his sociological study *The Negro Immigrant: His Background, Characteristics and Social Adjustment, 1899–1937* (1939). The following passage, excerpted from a "collective autobiography" of a Virgin Islander that was written in the voice of one individual but was intended to convey the experiences of many, suggests the tension black immigrants during the period felt between a pull toward the "new land" and a desire to remain in the "home land."

I am a Virgin Islander—a laborer, a master tradesman, a business-man, whatever I am, I can make one "heap of all my winnings" and risk it on foreign shores. I am an inveterate traveler. The size of the islands, their topography, limited natural resources and opportunities have made me so. Surrounded by water, I develop an adventurous and hardy spirit. I cannot expand the area of the island nor increase beyond a certain point its economic opportunities. I set sail on the Caribbean seeking greater economic and educational opportunities. New York City is my Mecca. . . . Those who have preceded me at times return. Their transformation seems miraculous to me. . . . [they] often-times seem to be persons who have been born again.

I am in New York. Dazzled by the bright lights? Yes. Bewildered by the fast ways? Most assuredly. I long for those I knew, for the familiar spots that meant so much to me. Frantically I write letters, a dozen, two dozens a week. Anxiously I await the weekly arrival of the mail. Through the letters I live vicariously the events of the homeland. I feel the longings, the hankerings; the petition is always there: hurry up and send me the steamer fare. . . .

I am a Virgin Islander. I usually return home. During my temporary stay, I enjoy many perfect days. I walk along the lanes and byways of my home. I roam through shrubbery and fields of grass. The ruins of buildings and lonely arches and columns grimly remind me of a civilization that hoped to be. I go to the crescent-shaped beach that runs along the roadstead. In this land that once furnished safe havens to buccaneers, where the torch razed magnificent buildings, where men keep up a constant fight for economic justice and political rights, I find solace. Over and above the turmoil there seems to soar a weirdness that soothes my soul and lures me into forgetfulness. But it is only a visit.[1]

As a group, these narratives, much like those of white immigrants serialized two decades earlier by Hamilton Holt in the reformist journal *The Independent*, highlighted many of the central issues that characterize the experience of immigration generally.[2] Like the above excerpt from the "life story" of a Virgin Islander, they conveyed how the risks of migration were balanced by an irrepressible optimism about the potential for success in the new country. They described the forces that drove immigrants from their homelands toward foreign cities, the immigrants' shock upon arriving in the "mecca," and the concomitant impulse to maintain ties to the islands in the face of unfamiliar and perhaps even hostile new environments. Finally, they recounted the fundamental transformation of the individual that often occurs upon the act of migration—a transformation that can leave one forever distanced and different from the land and people of one's origin, if also from the land of one's adoption.

This potential for displacement, particularly as it pertains to African Caribbean immigrants to the United States, provides the impetus for this study. While the sense of dislocation experienced by black immigrants is comparable on many levels to that experienced by white newcomers, it also differs importantly because of the ways in which "race" emerges as a dramatic factor affecting the reception and identification of blacks in U.S. society. Thus, an inquiry into the position of African Caribbean immigrants has significant implications for race, ethnic, and immigration theory. But it is important to note that the terms of this discussion pertain only to the United States, since the complexity of racial and ethnic classifications and their modes of operation differ radically from nation to nation. What holds true as an association between religion and "ethnicity" in Bosnia, for example, does not necessarily carry over to the United States. Linkages between "ethnicity" and class that may shape cultures more traditionally rooted in genealogically based aristocracies might be rendered moot by the dynamics of social mobility in the United States. Indeed, because of the sensitivity of issues concerning "ethnicity" to the specifics of a situation, combined with the general way in which "ethnicity" has traditionally been theorized, it is imperative to locate the terms of this discussion geographically, popularly, and theoretically in order to come to a clearer understanding of the concept itself and its relation to "race" in the United States.

On a popular level, due in large part to the black/white dichotomy that is deeply rooted in the history of the United States, conceptions of "ethnicity" and "race" have generally been formed according to a simplistic binary. As Maxine Hong Kingston's decidedly unhyphenated Chinese American protagonist, Wittman Ah Sing, explains in her novel *Tripmaster Monkey* (1990), when discussing "American" identity, the per-

against the binary of gradation

ception that generally governs in the United States is "that Americans are either white or black. I can't wear that civil-rights button with the black hand and the white hand shaking each other. . . . I have a nightmare— after duking it out, someday blacks and whites will shake their hands over my head. I'm the little yellow man beneath the bridge of their hands and overlooked," proclaims "Wit Man."[3] Moreover, "race" in the United States, at least in popular thinking and discourse, generally supercedes distinctions of "ethnicity," thus creating a hierarchical taxonomy in which the racial ascriptions of "white" and "black" stand as primary signifiers while the "ethnic" categories of, for example, "Irish," "Italian," and "German" or "Jamaican," "Haitian," and "Antiguan," etc. (if recognized at all) provide a secondary function of classification.

On a more theoretical level, the relationship between "race" and "ethnicity" in the United States has been the subject of considerable debate. While it is impossible to attend to the intricacies of this discussion here, it can be summarized briefly by assigning theorists to one of two camps. In one stand such figures as Nathan Glazer, Harold Abramson, and Milton Gordon, for example, who assert that it is most useful to conceive of "race" on a continuum with or in relation to "ethnicity," believing that the distinction between the two is a matter of degree rather than of kind. In the other camp are such scholars as Michael Omi, Howard Winant, M. G. Smith, Pierre van den Berghe, and David Theo Goldberg, among others, who believe that "race" must be conceptually distinguished as altogether different from "ethnicity" for a variety of social, political, and/or pragmatic reasons.[4] Moving away from these more sociologically- and ethnographically-based theorizations are a multitude of literary critics who inevitably and implicitly define themselves according to one of these two positions as they approach their work. Werner Sollors, for example, who has investigated the potentially "inventive" processes associated with ethnic identity construction, adopts the former, more universalist interpretation, while Edward Said, in contrast, although not focusing on the United States, tends to subscribe to the latter view, as he conceives the relationship between the "white" West and the "non-white" non-West in terms of an oppositional racial dyad. Nevertheless, as Rey Chow has pointed out, the field of literary studies, despite its immersion in the subject of "ethnicity," has not fully provided the tools with which to comprehend the concept as it relates both to culture and to writing. Accordingly, this study seeks to incorporate the insights of ethnic theory with the standard tools of literary analysis in an effort to come closer to understanding "ethnicity" in terms of its relation to the production of literature in the United States. Especially relevant to the theorization undertaken here of the position of African Caribbean writers in

U.S. society is the second view, which envisions a conceptual difference between "race" and "ethnicity," because it allows for a distinction among "ethnic" groups within the "black" race.

This distinction operates differently for first- and second-generation Caribbean immigrants in the United States. Most first-generation immigrants tend to view themselves as the Virgin Islander of the "life story" does: as a Virgin Islander who happens to have been "relocated" to the United States, not as someone who is "ethnically" Virgin Islander, "racially" black, and nationally "American." As he asserts, "I *am* a Virgin Islander"; the Virgin Islands is his "home," even if he can only travel there for "temporary stays"; the United States is and will always be a "foreign shore." For second-generation Caribbeaners who have been born and generally raised in the United States, however, the use of the term "ethnicity" to refer to Jamaican or Haitian or Antiguan ancestry is more practically applicable because of this group's socialization within U.S. systems of racial and ethnic classification. Indeed, most second-generation immigrants tend to consider themselves racially "black" and "ethnically" "Barbadian," for example, and U.S. nationals by virtue of birthplace, at least, if not necessarily "Americans" in the stereotypical sense of the term.[5] Nevertheless, because of the propensity toward binarism that dominates racial conceptions in the United States, both first- and second-generation African Caribbean immigrants have been routinely classified by popular, institutional, and even academic cultures as "African American" or simply as "black." But this categorization obviously overlooks key cultural and national differences that have profoundly shaped the interaction between African Americans and African Caribbeaners, and even more seriously risks reducing the plurality of black American identities to a monolithic entity based on skin color alone.

At the same time, different immigrant groups in the United States have negotiated the black/white dichotomy in a variety of ways, as Wittman/Wit Man/Whitman/Whit(e)man Ah Sing's efforts in *Tripmaster Monkey* suggest. Certain immigrant groups who fall into the troublingly vague "people of color" category have at times been "granted" or eventually "earned" a type of "honorary white" status that has socioculturally positioned them, to borrow Timothy Powell's phrase, somewhere "beyond the binary."[6] Think of Ralph Ellison's example of "a shoeshine boy who," during the early part of this century, "had encountered the best treatment in the South simply by wearing a white turban instead of his usual Dobbs or Stetson," for just one famous literary example.[7] While white racism in the United States clearly acts on black immigrants in ways that are comparable to the treatment received by African Americans, some black immigrants, by virtue of national origin, education, or class standing, are treated with a greater sense of privilege—and consequently possess a higher degree of "cultural capital"—than their native-born counterparts (not unlike the way that African American expatriate intellectuals and entertainers in the twenties and thirties were received by the French, even while North African colonials who had immigrated to their "mother" country for employment often faced severe discrimination).[8] Not until we understand the ways in which race, ethnicity, and immigration figure in questions of individual and group identity formation in and reaction to the United States can we come to a more thorough understanding of meanings of "Americanness."

This work contributes to that process by examining one understudied aspect of difference within racial sameness in the United States using as case studies the lives and writings of two of the most prominent African Caribbean immigrants and authors, first-generation Jamaican immigrant Claude McKay (1890–1948) and second-generation Barbadian immigrant Paule Marshall (b. 1929). As figurative bookends to this century (McKay's first collection of poems was published in 1912 and Marshall's most recent novel was published in 1992), the work of both authors, particularly when studied in tandem, helps us to understand the ways in which literature has probed and can be used to probe the complexities of displacement and identity that have accompanied migratory experiences over the past one hundred years. Close analysis of McKay's and Marshall's writings reveals how the forces of migration, racial and national affiliation, and "Americanization" can merge to produce uniquely hybridized, and at times profoundly homeless, black American immigrant identities. Ultimately, this inquiry is motivated by an interest in the rather elusive answers to the most basic questions that surround identity: what makes us who we are and why? The lives and writings of McKay and Marshall provide useful avenues along which to approach these questions because they offer a set of tangible and analyzable illustrations of how the multiple ways in which we cast ourselves and are cast by others—especially in terms of race, nationality, and gender—affect identity formation. By examining the ways in which these two especially prominent authors of African Caribbean descent explore and negotiate issues of cultural (dis)location in their artistic productions, this study seeks to complicate essentialized notions of "African American," "black," and "Caribbeaner." As important, by assessing select texts of two specific writers within the clearly delineated cultural contexts of their construction, this approach will help to historicize, and thereby ground in concrete examples, such prevailing litanies as "race, class, gender, ethnicity, nationality," that dominate contemporary literary discourse.

By positing "African American" and "African Caribbeaner" as provisionally discrete entities, however, this investigation admittedly risks establishing another dichotomy that is as troubling as the one that it seeks to dismantle. Indeed, despite the analytical value of such "strategic essentialism" (to use Gayatri Chakravorty Spivak's term in a different context), this inquiry must necessarily overlook important distinctions of both region and nationhood, not to mention class, that require similarly rigorous scrutiny in order to understand the details of both differentiation and division that characterize the larger black American community. When discussing the migration of multiple distinct national groups (i.e., Jamaican, Haitian, Dominican, Puerto Rican, Cuban, Antiguan, or Barbadian, etc.), for example, attention should be addressed not simply to the specificities of cultural frameworks, national identities, and historical contexts from which these migrations stem, but, perhaps even more importantly, to the fundamentally recreative process of nationhood that occurs upon arrival in new, and in most cases more modern, environments. The act of migration itself is obviously disruptive to geographic and sociocultural boundaries that engender a sense of national homogeneity. As Homi Bhabha argues in his analysis of the process of "DissemiNation," upon migration, issues of national identity shift from "the 'selfhood' of the nation as opposed to the otherness of other nations" toward "the nation split within itself, articulating the heterogeneity of its population." This "barred Nation *It/Self*," Bhabha asserts, "alienated from its external self-generation, becomes a liminal signifying space that is *internally* marked by the discourses of minorities, the heterogeneous histories of contending peoples, antagonistic authorities and tense locations of cultural difference."[9] Thus, given the disintegration of any type of "national homogeneity" upon migration, combined with the multiple national groups constituting the Caribbean itself, the category of "African Caribbeaner" can be considered as inappropriately monolithic and historically static as are those of "black," "white," and even "African American." Given this line of reasoning, nearly all attempts at classification by race or nation risk verging on futility.

This study seeks to avoid the pitfalls possible in such forms of cultural analysis by considering not the two communities at large but, rather, the lives and writings of two distinct African Caribbeaners. Indeed, by concentrating on individualized models of possible immigrant reaction to the United States, rather than on the more generalized entities of large cultural groups, as a basis for theorizing the notions of "African Caribbeaner" or even "African Caribbean cultural studies," this inquiry provides two sound test cases against which to problematize both terms: what, for example, constitutes the ethnic label itself in "African Caribbeaner" or "African Caribbean cultural studies"?[10] Such an understanding, of course, must be predicated upon additional "case studies" of other figures in the large and active African Caribbean population of politicians, intellectuals, and artists who have contributed to black thought and culture in the United States. While Harold Cruse began to delve into this area in his 1967 study, *The Crisis of the Negro Intellectual: The Historical Failure of Black Leadership*, when he asserted that African Caribbeaners clearly constituted a distinctive subculture within the United States, his claim for distinctiveness was based on his premise that "the West Indians," ranging from Marcus Garvey to Stokely Carmichael and including McKay and Marshall, were shaped by such a "peculiar" cultural history and psychology that their experience and influence was rendered irrelevant to African Americans. Cruse's vituperative assault, intending to achieve precisely the opposite effect, actually signified the profound impact of Caribbean immigration on African American and American political culture through the sixties—an impact whose legacy began with Harlem Renaissance–era notables Garvey and Richard B. Moore, carried on through Civil Rights activists Carmichael and Shirley Chisolm, and has resurfaced most recently in the figure of General Colin Powell.

Powell, in fact, presents an especially interesting illustration of how the forces of race, ethnicity, and nationality can variously frame the lives of contemporary African Caribbeaners in the United States. A second-generation Jamaican immigrant, Powell was routinely described by the media during the 1996 Presidential campaign as African American and as the first "black" leader in U.S. history to successfully "represent" both the black and white communities. Somewhat ironically, however, one of the pivotal features that contributed to Powell's cross-racial success was his background as an immigrant. Powell explicitly highlights these aspects of his experience in the opening pages of his autobiography, tellingly titled *My American Journey*, as he makes valuable use of the long tradition of the rags-to-riches motif in immigrant writing in the United States to appeal both within and across racial lines:

> Mine is the story of black kid of no early promise from an immigrant family of limited means who was raised in the South Bronx and somehow rose to become the National Security Advisor to the President of the United States and then Chairman of the Joint Chiefs of Staff. It is a story of hard work and good luck, of occasional rough times, but mostly good times. It is a story of service and soldiering. It is a story about the people who helped make me what I am. It is a story of my benefitting from opportunities created by the sacrifice of those who went before me and maybe my benefitting those who will follow. It is

a story of faith—faith in myself, and faith in America. Above all, it's a love story: love of family, of friends, of the Army, and of my country. It is a story that could only have happened in America.[11]

Despite the patriotism professed here, the opening scene of the book calls into some question exactly which country Powell wishes us to understand as "his country." The narrative begins not with the familiar "I was born . . . " story of Powell's birth in the Bronx (which is both an autobiographical convention as well as a particular trope within African American autobiographical narratives), but rather with a description of his return trip to Jamaica—a trip made during fevered discussions of his possible presidential bid and with the benefit of accompanying television cameras. Then–Prime Minister Michael Manley had, according to Powell, "been after" him "ever since the Gulf War: 'Get some rest, dear boy,' he had said in that compelling lilt the last time he had called. 'Come home, if only for a few days. Stay at our government guesthouse.'"[12] Indeed, Powell's invitation to occupy the "government guesthouse" was warranted not by his position as the prodigal son, but rather by his prominence in American military and political circles. Despite the emphasis Powell gives his immigrant past here, he had not returned "home" since his childhood. Powell's description of his relationship to his Jamaican ancestry at most points in the narrative, in fact, most closely resembles what theorist Herbert Gans has described, in reference to third-generation immigrants, as "symbolic ethnicity": "a nostalgic allegiance to the culture of the immigrant generation, or that of the old country; a love for and pride in a tradition that can be felt without having to be incorporated in everyday behavior." Symbolic ethnicity can be characterized by the celebration of ceremonial holidays, the partaking of ethnic foodways, or an affinity with the "old world"—all of which Powell recounts—in a way that does not "take much time nor upset the everyday routine." Indeed, "old countries are particularly useful," according to Gans, "as identity symbols because they are far away and cannot make arduous demands on American ethnics."[13] "My country," says Powell—is it Jamaica, where he chooses to begin his life story, the United States, where he has lived nearly all of his days, both, neither? Apparently, for this particular contemporary African Caribbean immigrant, affiliations to nation, "race," and "ethnicity" are transmutable.

Clearly, as this brief discussion of the example of Colin Powell suggests, the area of "African Caribbean cultural studies," both in the present and the past, is ripe for research. While important models exist in the pioneering work begun by Stuart Hall and Paul Gilroy on the black diaspora in the United Kingdom, a notable gap remains in research on black Atlantic cultures in the United States. Somewhat surprisingly, Ira de A. Reid's 1939 study still stands as a definitive resource for scholars in the field. More recently, a number of important sociological analyses by Delores Mortimer, Roy Bryce-Laporte, Elsa Chaney, Constance Sutton, Philip Kasinitz, and Mary Waters have documented patterns of political, economic, and cultural adaptation by Caribbean immigrants in New York in particular, and historian Irma Watkins-Owens has valuably chronicled the early period (1900–1930) of African American–African Caribbean [*contribution*] interaction in Harlem.[14] No study, however, has sought to reconsider the plurality of black American culture through its manifestations in literature and literary history.[15]

Here I hope to do just that by focusing, from a cross-cultural angle, on the work of McKay and Marshall—two African Caribbean writers in the United States whose work has too often been mono-dimensionally read within the canon of either African American or Caribbean letters. McKay is most frequently associated with the Harlem Renaissance, and literary and cultural analyses of his work tend to center on his "American" poetry (that which was written during the particularly productive period following his migration to the United States), on his novels, or on his political activities and ideologies. Nearly all anthologies, despite the growing acknowledgment of his "outsider" status in relation to the African American elite in the twenties and thirties, continue to present him as a pivotal player in black American arts during this era. Another set of criticism is constituted by a handful of studies that concentrate on the dialect poetry McKay produced during his early years in Jamaica, and these tend to highlight his position as one of that nation's foremost authors and native sons.[16] Marshall criticism tends to fall into a similar predicament. Most early studies address her relationship to African American writers and consist of critics seeking to claim for Marshall, at a time when women writers in general were being overlooked, her rightful place in African American literary history by virtue of themes and concerns that her works share with prominent male African American authors.[17] The second phase of Marshall criticism seems to have emerged from the developing womanist philosophies of Alice Walker and the burgeoning of black women's writing in the late 1970s and early 1980s. This body of analysis emphasizes the feminist elements of Marshall's writings in an effort to stress her relation to what was then being construed as an African American women's literary "tradition."[18] The third phase is comprised of more recent critics who seek to feature and celebrate Marshall's international connections to Africa and the Caribbean, but, again, many of these critics tend to posit the process of "black unification" articulated in Marshall's works in reference to her relationship to African American authors.[19]

While all of these approaches have valuably illuminated our understanding of the writings of McKay and Marshall, it is now time for a more pointed cross-cultural consideration of both authors that moves beyond these restrictive paradigms toward a more specific appreciation of how the work of McKay and Marshall, when read in light of their perspectives as members of two cultures, provides unique insight into each culture as well as demands a relocation of the two writers within the realm of black diasporic letters more generally.

By focusing on the processes of exchange, interchange, and also rejection that surround the act of immigration, this study will reveal how each author, for a variety of complex reasons, depicts in dramatically different ways the experience and reverberations of the migratory condition. On one hand, McKay, as a first-generation migrant who was himself literally on the move throughout his entire life, fathers a series of fictional characters who are fundamentally and irrevocably alienated from both their home and host societies. On the other, Marshall, as a second-generation immigrant who identifies equally with U.S. and Caribbean culture, creates characters who feel intimately linked to and move freely between both worlds. These contrasting portrayals of dislocation and dual location raise important questions about the role that differences in generation and gender might play in shaping black immigrant reaction to the United States. As important, however, this grounding will also provide the foundation necessary for understanding patterns of association and dissociation that mark the work of both earlier and more recent African Caribbean authors in the United States. It will enhance our knowledge of the web of forces acting on the many first- and second-generation Caribbean immigrant authors—consider, for example, June Jordan, Michelle Cliff, Jamaica Kincaid, Derek Walcott, and the late Audre Lorde—who have played or are playing central roles in shaping American literary history, curricula, and criticism. [20] In addition to McKay and Marshall (both to some extent "canonized" at this point), numerous more recent African Caribbean authors are appearing with increasing frequency on American and African American Studies course syllabi across the country. Derek Walcott's receipt of the 1992 Nobel Prize for Literature, for example, testifies to the growing, if overdue, recognition of the significance both of his work in particular and of Caribbean and Caribbean American writing more generally. This present circumstance, however, can only be understood by retracing its origins. Given the unique nexus of two momentous issues in American history—the "Caribbeanization" of many areas of the United States due to the increasing presence and influence of high numbers of African Caribbean immigrants, combined with the related attention to issues of canon formation and "multiculturalism"—it seems vital to place the subject of Caribbean immigrant writing in literary and cultural context.

Before examining the work of McKay and Marshall in detail, however, it is necessary to understand the historical period which framed each author's aesthetic production, that surrounding the "first wave" of Caribbean immigration to the United States which took place roughly between 1900 and 1930. While McKay's literary career loosely spanned this period (his first piece after migrating to the United States was published in 1919, and his last in 1937), Marshall too, especially in her early work and particularly in her first novel, *Brown Girl, Brownstones* (1959), was influenced by the legacy of "first wave" interaction as a second-generation immigrant born in 1929 whose attitudes were shaped by the early history of African American/African Caribbean relations. Accordingly, the first chapter of this study considers the place and historical moment when African Americans and African Caribbeaners first began to interact on a large scale in the United States—Harlem in the 1920s and 1930s.

1

"A Special Issue"

Blacks in Harlem during the First Wave of Caribbean Immigration

IN NOVEMBER 1926, *Opportunity: A Journal of Negro Life*, the literary organ of the National Urban League, published a "Special Caribbean Issue." According to the opening editorial, the purpose of this "Special Issue" was to provide *Opportunity*'s predominantly African American readers with a "wider and deeper acquaintance . . . with the large group of Negroes who have come to these shores, as millions of others have come, seeking a new economic and cultural freedom."[1] In so doing, however, the magazine also sought to address an issue of even greater urgency—the growing hostility between African Caribbean immigrants and native-born African Americans in Harlem that emerged as a result of high levels of immigration during the early decades of the twentieth century. As *Opportunity* editor Charles Johnson stated, the unique edition of the magazine was expressly designed to cultivate "an essential friendship" between foreign- and native-born blacks based on the "conviction that friendships usually follow the knowing of one's neighbors" (334). The works of Claude McKay and Paule Marshall provide two important case studies of how this larger cultural quest for "essential friendship" played out in the actual lives—and influenced the literary productions—of two distinct African Caribbean immigrant authors. But in order to appreciate how McKay's and Marshall's individual experiences as black immigrants call for a reconsideration of their writing, we must first understand the larger collective struggles and triumphs of the African Caribbean immigrant community that framed McKay's and Marshall's artistic endeavors. To that end, this chapter turns our attention to the historical context that formed the backdrop for their works—New York City during the "first wave" of African Caribbean immigration to the United States.

Although Caribbean–U.S. immigration has been nearly constant throughout the twentieth century, immigration scholars commonly classify it according to three distinct phases or "waves." The first took place between 1900 and 1930 and reached its peak in the 1920s. The second fell between the Depression and 1965 and was much smaller than the first, encompassing an average of no more than three thousand Caribbeaners per year. Movement during this wave ebbed and flowed primarily according to economic factors and immigration laws in the United States, so that at the height of the Depression, for example, it was reduced to a virtual standstill. Immigration then slowly grew again after World War II until the passage of the McCarran–Walter Act in 1952 reduced the flow by restricting the number of colonial subjects who could enter under the quotas of their "mother" country. The third and current wave, the largest to date, resulted from changes in immigration laws in both England and the United States that shifted the focus of nearly all Caribbean immigration from the islanders' previous "mother" countries to what might rightfully be considered the region's new "mother" country, the United States. First, in 1962, anticipating and accompanying the attainment of independence of many Caribbean nations, Britain severely restricted inter-Commonwealth migration. Second, in 1965, the United States passed the Hart-Cellar Immigration Reform Act, which replaced the national quota system that was first initiated in 1924 and then reinforced by the McCarran–Walter Act in 1952 with a hemispheric quota policy that allowed for a maximum of 120,000 immigrants per year from the western hemisphere, but that did not place quotas upon individual countries.

The impact of Caribbeaners on black life in Harlem during the first wave of immigration was profound.[2] While by 1930 the total number of first- and second-generation black immigrants living in the city constituted only 1.5 percent of the total black population, a review of the numbers arriving during such a short span of time suggests in part why the presence of the new arrivals appeared so momentous.[3] In 1899, 412 black immigrants entered the United States. In 1902 the number of newcomers doubled to 832; in 1903 that number rose to 2,174 and by 1907 doubled again to reach 5,633. From 1908 to 1924 between 5,000 and 8,000 African Caribbeaners immigrated to the United States annually, and by 1924 the numbers peaked at 12,243 arrivants entering during a twelve-month period.[4] By 1930, 177,981 foreign-born blacks and their children lived in the United States. Nearly all of these immigrants came from the "West Indies," the "non-Hispanic" Caribbean, and the majority settled in New York City.[5]

A variety of "push" and "pull" factors drove immigrants out of the Caribbean and toward the United States between roughly 1890 and the stock market crash of 1929.[6] A considerable amount of regional migration occurred as people sought work on banana and sugar plantations in Cuba and the Dominican Republic, on the railroad in Costa Rica, and on dry docks in Bermuda. As historian Irma Watkins-Owens has argued in her important study, *Blood Relations: Caribbean Immigrants and the Harlem Community, 1900–1930* (1996), however, the creation of the Panama Canal between 1906 and 1914 presented a large impetus for Caribbean migration toward the United States. By working on the Canal, many Caribbeaners were able to finance eventual moves to "the States." Paule Marshall, whose parents immigrated to Brooklyn during this period, describes the cultural significance of "Panama Money": "This was the name given to the remittances sent home by fathers and sons who had gone off to work building the Panama Canal. My Mother, for example, came to the 'States' on money inherited from an older brother who had died working on the Isthmus. 'Panama Money'—it was always spoken of with great reverence when I was a little girl."[7] More significantly, the transnational exchange of cultural products and commodities that occurred between the two regions as a result of a large U.S. presence in Panama, offered Canal workers glimpses of at least the material, if not necessarily the social, possibilities presented by life under U.S. governance. All of these factors combined to result in the Canal serving as a temporary layover for many U.S.-bound immigrants.[8]

But the Canal also introduced workers to the limitations of life in the United States—namely, those imposed by the strict codes of American racism. Black canal workers were discriminated against in terms of job assignments and wages, and between 1906 and 1923 more than 20,000 of these 'pick and shovel' men died as a result of poor working and living conditions.[9] While employment with the Canal project did offer valuable earnings, it also meant long hours, hard, dangerous labor, and perhaps most importantly, since it was supervised by U.S. officials and Marines, a rather startling introduction to the strict forms of segregation practiced in the United States. As Watkins-Owens has stated, Jim Crow ruled the Canal Zone just as it ruled the American South. But in an ironic reflection of the economic motivations underlying the Canal's construction, the designations "colored" and "white" at all public facilities were replaced by those of "silver" and "gold." Black workers were labeled "unskilled" regardless of their actual abilities and paid in Panamanian silver; white workers were routinely considered "skilled" and paid in gold.[10]

This classification system resulted, in part, from Panamanian discomfort with racial designations, as well as from an importation of U.S. modes of social organization. Categorizing workers by race was uncommon in the Republic of Panama and Colombia, and immigrant laborers, used to social hierarchies based more on class than on color distinctions, were unaccustomed to such stratifications; thus "silver" and "gold" standards were established by U.S. officials.[11] But these labels, if superficially different from "colored" and "white," accomplished the same purpose of entrenching a racial caste system. One observer during the period noted that "very often a West Indian doing clerical work with a long and good record is discharged to make room for some white ne'er-do-well. When he complains to authorities he is often told: 'Well, we'll give you a job as foreman over a gang in the shops. No matter what class of work you're doing you can't make any more than seventy-five dollars per month.'" Additionally, American officials deliberately encouraged intraracial hostility in order to prevent the formation of labor unions. The same observer described "a spirit of hatred" as being "kindled among the islanders. . . . The Jamaican [is told] that because some Caucasian blood flows through his veins he is better than the Trinidadian. The Barbadian has been taught that because he is more nearly of pure Negro blood he is better than the mixed people of Jamaica. . . . Thus they go, ever fighting, ever hating each other. The Barbadian hates the Jamaican, the Trinidadian hates the Barbadian and the Jamaican hates them all."[12]

Many of these tensions were captured in the fiction of Eric Walrond, an important but understudied figure in Harlem during the first wave of Caribbean immigration. Walrond was born in British Guiana in 1898 to a Barbadian mother and a Guianese father, but when he was eight years old his father abandoned the family and Walrond moved with his mother to Barbados. Several years later, Walrond sought out his father in the Canal Zone, eventually settling in Colón until his immigration to the United States in 1918. Much of what he observed in Panama provided the foundation for his writing. His 1926 collection of stories, *Tropic Death*—to which, notably, Waldo Frank's review in "The Special Caribbean Issue" of *Opportunity* called attention—considers the roles played by racial prejudice, alienation, and imperialism in shaping the social milieu of the Canal Zone. Walrond's story, "The Yellow One," for example, provides a fictional illustration of the type of intraracial hostility described above as it probes the complexity of color and class codes in the Zone, using the metaphor of a boat traveling between the islands as a microcosm of the region itself. Walrond's most widely anthologized tale, "The Wharf Rats"—whose title itself deliberately connotes the dehumanizing impact on black workers of life in the Canal Zone—explores the exploitation of those housed in "Silver City," the "Silver Quarters" which, he explains, "harbor the inky ones." The story "Panama Gold" ironizes the "riches" obtained from laboring on the Canal as it posits physical and emotional scars as the reward for one worker who is forced to return to Barbados as a result of a work-related injury. "Subjection" tells the tale of a murder by a white Marine of a black worker who has objected to the beating of one of his peers, while "Tropic Death" and

"The Black Pin" consider themes of forced migration and cultural dislocation. At the time of his death in London in 1966, Walrond was working on another book-length manuscript about the Canal Zone, but it as yet remains unpublished.

Despite the rather harsh introduction to the "American way" presented by conditions surrounding the building of the Panama Canal, however, Walrond, as well as many Canal workers themselves, still sought the promise of prosperity offered by the "land of opportunity."[13] Underscoring scholar Peter Linebaugh's suggestion that "the ship remained perhaps the most important conduit of Pan-African communication before the appearance of the long-playing record," Caribbean immigrants began the gradual and evolving process of transplanting island cultures to U.S. soil as they took to the sea.[14] Some took advantage of the newly established mail and shipping routes running between New York and the Isthmus by booking passage on these vessels; others traveled via United Fruit Company ships which were carrying on a lucrative export business to major cities along the eastern seaboard.[15] All, like the members of the "Great Migration" of African Americans from the southern United States, were drawn to urban centers in the north in search of the jobs and wealth resulting from the wartime economic boom.[16]

This massive black migration resulted in a dramatic convergence of peoples in New York City, in particular, the consequences of which manifested themselves in singularly "American" ways. On one hand, as reflected in Jamaican immigrant writer W. A. Domingo's description of New York in 1925, the United States did indeed appear to be a new type of "melting pot" for the dark-skinned peoples left out of Crèvecoeur's original conceptualization of the term:

> Almost unobserved, America plays her usual role in the meeting, mixing, and welding of the colored peoples of the earth. A dusky tribe of destiny seekers, these brown and black and yellow folk, eyes filled with visions of an alien heritage—palm-fringed seashores, murmuring streams, luxuriant hills and vales—have made an epical march from far corners of the earth to the Port of New York and America. They bring the gift of the black tropics to America and to their kinsmen. With them come vestiges of a quaint folk life, other social traditions, and as for the first time in their lives, colored people of Spanish, French, Dutch, Arabian, Danish, Portuguese, British and native African ancestry meet and move together, there comes into Negro life the stir and leavening that is uniquely American.[17]

Like so many white immigrant groups who had preceded them, foreign-born blacks contributed an internationalism to U.S. soil that made it, paradoxically enough, quintessentially "American." On the other hand, in an equally "American" manner, the presence of these immigrants also provoked hostility, nativism, and fear. As both newcomers from the South and the islands competed with black New Yorkers for the same jobs, housing, and monetary rewards, considerable tensions arose.

These tensions infused all aspects of African American–African Caribbean interaction. Differences between the two groups in terms of educational background, employment status, class standing, and political affiliations, for examples, became grounds for potential discord. Under all lay the central fault line between racial similarity and ethnic and/or national differences. As Charles Johnson lamented, "Of the same blood and, in the United States of the same status with American born Negroes, [black immigrants] represent vastly different social and political backgrounds, even among themselves. It is inevitable that [native- and foreign-born blacks] should fail either to know or understand each other or to profit fully by the virtues of each other. And all the while, the single, inexorable pressure of race,—with a characteristic indifference to the disaffection between elements of minorities of the same class, proceeds on the assumption that being alike, they are the same" (334). But in nearly all ways but one, African Americans and African Caribbean immigrants were not "the same." In terms of educational background, for instance, immigration records show that 98.6 percent of black immigrants admitted in 1923 could read and write; a decade later the statistics held firm at 99.0 percent.[18] The educational structure on each island was modeled upon that of the local colonial power and was generally perceived by Caribbeaners to be superior to that offered in the United States; some immigrants, in fact, including the parents of politician Shirley Chisolm and singer-activist Harry Belafonte, sent their children back to the Caribbean to be educated. In her autobiography, *Unbought and Unbossed* (1970), Chisolm reflects that "years later I would know what an important gift my parents had given me by seeing to it that I had my early education in the strict, traditional, British-styled schools of Barbados. If I speak and write easily now, that early education is the main reason."[19] Following elementary and secondary education, African Caribbeaners who could afford to do so often sent their children for additional schooling in England or France. In contrast, the strict enforcement of separate and unequal public educational facilities for blacks in the United States created multiple barriers to the attainment of higher degrees for African Americans—and, perhaps more importantly, to the skilled and professional positions which these degrees helped secure.

Indeed, related to differences in educational background between the two communities were differences in work experience and skill levels. Ira de A. Reid noted in 1939 that, "distinctly out of proportion to the prevalence of such classes in the occupational schemes of the native-born Negro are the high proportions of [immigrant] workers who had been employed as skilled artisans, as bankers, agents, merchants, clerical workers in commerce and finance, and as professional persons."[20] Upon arriving in the United States, many of these immigrants either relied upon money earned in the islands to set up small businesses, practiced their previous work in such skilled trades as carpentry, shoe-making, baking, or tailoring, or continued in the professions of medicine, dentistry, or law. Furthermore, immigrants who had become accustomed to social standings based on class in their homelands resisted being demoted upon immigration to less skilled positions simply by virtue of their race. Unaware that certain jobs were theoretically "unavailable" to them as blacks, Caribbean immigrants more frequently sought and obtained positions for which African Americans did not even apply, often using their British or French citizenship and the consulate of the "mother country" as arsenals against discrimination. (Nella Larsen, another prominent author in Harlem during the twenties, who was the daughter of a Danish mother and African Caribbean father, steadfastly maintained her Danish citizenship in an effort to assert her ties to her ethnic background—a background which, according to scholar George Hutchinson, few of her peers were willing to accept, with the exception of Carl Van Vechten, himself a white Scandinavian.)[21] While this pattern of adjustment to the United States often resulted in the provision of important services and the breaking down of certain employment barriers to the African American community, it also created a xenophobic competition for the scarce opportunities and compensation resources that were available to blacks in general.

A combination of financial standing and cultural institutions that facilitated immigrant prosperity in the "new world" also proved to be a source of intraracial tension. African Caribbean groups, and British "West Indians" in particular, developed associations of rotating credit in which individuals contributed a certain portion of their monthly incomes to a central fund, which was then distributed to the members of the group on a rotating basis. This system of collective financing, rooted in African traditions carried first to the Caribbean and then to the United States, both enabled members to obtain interest-free loans that fostered entrepreneurial activity within the community and also allowed black immigrants to remain independent of white lending institutions. For a variety of reasons related to the peculiarities of the institution of slavery in the United States as well as to the economic conditions with which African Americans were confronted upon emancipation, however, these community-based economic collectives and fraternal organizations which have often arisen among newly-arrived immigrant groups did not develop in the native-born black community.[22] Thus African Americans were not only at the mercy of white bankers and financiers whose lending decisions were often racially based, but the native-born community felt that the newly arrived immigrant group was usurping commercial territory rightfully belonging to the local population.

A different type of territory was at issue between African Americans and African Caribbeaners in the realm of politics. Caribbean immigrants were active in the Harlem political scene in disproportionate numbers, generally exhibiting a higher degree of radicalism than their native-born counterparts (as is reflected by the prominence of Caribbean immigrants in such organizations as the African Blood Brotherhood, the Socialist Speakers Bureau, and the Peoples Educational Forum). The key roles that Caribbean natives Cyril Briggs, Richard B. Moore, Hubert Harrison, Frank Crosswaith, W. A. Domingo—and most significantly Marcus Garvey, leader of one of the most powerful forces during this period, the Universal Negro Improvement Association (UNIA)—played in local politics, as well as Garvey's role in solidifying lines of ethnic difference within the black American community, are beyond the scope of this essay.[23] But it is important to recognize here that, as minorities within a minority in the United States, these activists did not necessarily have access to traditional political forums which were controlled either by white Tammany bosses or, to a limited degree, by the African American elite. In response, beginning around 1917 and continuing through the 1930s, Caribbean radicals developed a new means of educating their peers about political issues through streetcorner speaking or the "stepladder forum."

Throughout the period, Caribbeaners could be heard delivering political commentaries and intellectual presentations to listeners from atop stepladders perched on Harlem street corners. Watkins-Owens cites a *New York News* reporter's description of one forum led by one of the most famous of these speakers, St. Croix native Hubert Harrison, which suggests the cultural significance of these informal symposia:

The Age of Pericles and Socrates in ancient Athens had nothing on the present age of Harlem in New York. Coming out of the "movies" between 137th Street and 138th Street on Seventh Avenue, we saw one of the biggest street corner audiences that we have ever met in this block, which is famous for street corner lectures, and the subject was "Evolution." This was not a selected audience but the "run of the street," and their faces were fixed on a black man who stood on a ladder platform, with his back to the avenue and the passing buses and his face to the audience who blocked the spacious sidewalk. . . . And what was he talking about? . . . The theory of evolution, and its illustration in different lines of material and biological development—the Darwinian science of the evolution of life, and the Marxian philosophy of the evolution of capitalism—and a possible development from capitalism to a state of communism.[24]

As is perhaps best illustrated by Ralph Ellison's fictional depiction of Ras the Exhorter in his monumental novel, *Invisible Man* (1952), these speakers often skillfully integrated intellectual issues with radical politics in an effort to move listeners toward a more committed activism in the quest for racial equality. But the popularity of these African Caribbean orators, combined with the factors of foreign birth and a socialist-grounded distance from the political mainstream, led many African American leaders to perceive these immigrant counterparts as threats. Claude McKay, himself affiliated with both groups, described a "sharp struggle for place and elbow room" as having been waged between the educated classes of immigrant and native-born blacks during the period. Indeed, members of W. E. B. Du Bois's "Talented Tenth" were struggling to assert their own authority to "represent the race" to the larger white populace and, according to McKay, "resent[ed] the aggressiveness of the foreign-born Negroes, especially in politics."[25] In this venue in particular, the ethnic and national differences between African Americans and African Caribbeaners became vital issues for the black American community overall as intraracial tensions led at times to the fragmentation of united black efforts toward obtaining equal rights for the race as a whole.

The tensions between the two communities, stemming from key differences in educational practices, employment opportunities, class status, and political views, not to mention additional strains surrounding religion, language, and citizenship, amply illustrate that the two black groups in the United States were indeed *not* "the same," despite the perception of outsiders to the contrary. Not surprisingly, in fact, the very merging of the two groups within the clearly defined and relatively closed boundaries of Harlem resulted in the common pattern of each group identifying itself based on its opposition to the "other." Ethnic theorist George Devereux has explained how the process of ethnic identity construction involves "two symmetrical specifications": the determination that "(1) A is an X" (for our purposes, so-and-so is a Caribbeaner), is necessarily predicated upon the knowledge that "(2) A is not a non-X" (so-and-so is not, in this instance, an African American). The identification of self is fundamentally linked to one's awareness of one's difference from an other. Devereux continues, stating that "specifications as to what constitutes ethnic identity develop only after an ethnic group recognizes the existence of others who do not belong to the group. At the start, these specifications may conceivably include only certain real (racial, cultural, personality) traits of the group. But it is almost inevitable that these distinguishing traits will eventually acquire also evaluative connotations."[26] The experience of African Americans and African Caribbeaners in Harlem provides a valuable case study of this process in action. The act of migration forced the two groups to interact within a closed space; each group, in an effort to distinguish itself from the other, defined itself in relative opposition to the other; soon, the "real" differences that loomed large between African Americans and Caribbeaners acquired "evaluative connotations" as they became codified into rigid sets of reciprocal stereotypes.

Ira de A. Reid interviewed members of both communities and catalogued the most common stereotypes held about Caribbeaners during the period. Foreign-born blacks were regularly taunted with the slurs of "monkey-chaser," "ring-tail," "king Mon," and "cockney." One of the most popular street songs during the twenties began: "When a monkey-chaser dies / Don't need no undertaker / Just throw him in de Harlem River / He'll float back to Jamaica."[27] Desires among Caribbeaners to save money, acquire property, or engage in entrepreneurial activities fostered the popular stereotype that Caribbeaners were stingy, "craftier than the Jew, and not to be trusted in financial matters."[28] Indeed, it was commonly stated during that period that "when a West Indian got ten cents above a beggar, he opened a business."[29] Previous education in the islands or the pursuit of higher education in the U.S. contributed to the belief that immigrants were "intellectual prigs" and perceived themselves to be "smarter" than native-born blacks.[30] Distinguishing oneself by accent or nationality before race led to charges that Caribbeaners felt "superior to the native-born Negro" as well as to the criticism that they were "so British . . . that [they didn't] have time to be [themselves]." An emphasis on class rather than race as an index of status, inherited from the social structures on many Caribbean islands, perpetuated the belief that the newcomers "lacked race-pride." At the same time, however, high levels of political radicalism led to charges of "trouble-making" with whites and paradoxical perceptions that African Caribbeaners were "too race conscious." Involvement with other immigrants in the form of fraternal and community organizations provoked resentment about the "clannishness" of Caribbeaners. Finally, expressing the same blindness that was directed toward their own community by whites, African Americans during the period tended to believe that "all the foreigners were just alike."[31]

Caribbeaners held comparable and converse stereotypes about African Americans as well. Paule Marshall recalls being aware of these biases in her parents: "It seems to me from what I observed as a child that the West Indian woman considered herself both different [from] and somehow superior [to the African American woman]. From the talk which circulated around our kitchen it was clear, for example, that my mother and her friends perceived of themselves as being more ambitious than black Americans, more hard working and in terms of the racial question, more militant and unafraid in their dealings with white people."[32] Caribbeaners during the period generally viewed African Americans as less educated, less industrious, and less willing to challenge their designation as second-class citizens in their own country. At the same time, however, revealing again the paradoxes of such biases, Caribbeaners believed African Americans to be overly preoccupied with racial slights and barriers.[33] Because of the perception that African Americans were a "keep-back" to immigrant advancement, intermarriage among members of the second generation was strongly discouraged. Adam Clayton Powell, Jr. recalled that, in the 1930s, "the same feeling the average white bigot had when a Catholic married a Jew was the experience of Harlem Town when a West Indian married an American black."[34]

By the mid-twenties, relations within the race had become so strained that the leaders of the National Urban League, a non-profit organization founded in 1910 to promote better relations between the races, felt compelled to publish the "Special Caribbean Issue" of *Opportunity* in an effort to intervene. An analysis of the issue, however, suggests that even within the context of this deliberate effort to unify blacks, classifications based on binary constructions of "foreign" and "native," of "self" and "other" were extremely difficult for the contributors—African Caribbean and African American alike—to overcome.

Charles Johnson's opening editorial explains the purpose of the edition and provides a microcosm of the concerns that framed its inception. First Johnson establishes that the goal of the "Special Issue" is to discuss "questions dealing with the Caribbean countries and their sons now living in the United States" in order to familiarize *Opportunity*'s largely African American readership with the newcomers. To that end, the "Special Issue" consists of a series of articles, the majority of which are written by prominent Caribbean immigrants, that provide factual information about Caribbean history, geography, and arts.[35] Upon identifying this objective, however, Johnson emphasizes that underlying this goal is a desire to improve relations between the two groups whose association has been hindered by misunderstanding: "This well selected group [of Caribbeaners] posited in the midst of a large and varied Negro population has brought its questions and difficulties. The situation has encouraged snobbishness and jealousies, resentment and group selfishness. The American Negro who dislikes West Indians and applies to them offensive names, can be matched by the West Indian who can outlaw a fellow countryman for associating too much with American Negroes." Johnson praises the immigrant group which, "however small in number, has made itself felt" by "provid[ing] business and professional men and a substantial group of workers," and he asserts that African Caribbeaners have much to contribute not simply to intraracial culture but to interracial interactions as well. "The present foreign Negro population is closely selected," he states. "Their interests are keen, as their preponderance at most of Harlem's forums and the libraries indicate. And among the more intellectual ones, the play of their minds against the peculiar angles of North American race situations, offers, for the American born Negro an invaluable stimulation." But most importantly, Johnson claims, although significant "social and political" differences divide African Caribbeaners even from one another, it is imperative that they and African Americans forge an "essential friendship" precisely because of the "inexorable pressure" of race that binds the two groups indelibly to one another in the United States.

Perhaps nowhere else are the tensions surrounding these differences more apparent than in the subtext and context of the article contributed by Jamaican immigrant and journalist W. A. Domingo—an article whose interest lies less in what it says than in what it does not say. As the first item following Johnson's editorial and titled simply "The West Indies," this flagship essay was clearly intended to offer that "wider and deeper acquaintance" with the Caribbean about which Johnson spoke in his opening comments. To this end, Domingo sketches a brief history of the Caribbean from the colonial period to the present. He describes the conquest and development of slavery, reports on geographic and demographic characteristics of the region, outlines the islands' political, economic, and educational structures, and comments briefly upon race relations. He also discusses Caribbean relationships with both Great Britain and the United States. Throughout this overview Domingo is careful to emphasize the significant differences among the nations that make up the region, seeking implicitly to break down the simplistic conception of "the West Indies"—or more recently "the Caribbean"—that gripped U.S. thinking and discourse about the area.

What is unusual about Domingo's contribution to the "Special Issue," however, is the absence of more explicit references to the specific topic at hand—African Caribbean–African American relations. Domingo's only nod in this direction is found in the closing two sentences of his essay, in which he states that, "by virtue of the presence of thousands of West Indians in the United States, a bond is being forged between them and American Negroes. Gradually they are realizing that their problems are in the main similar, and that their ultimate successful

solution will depend on the intelligent cooperation of the two branches
of Anglo-Saxonized Negroes" (342). Domingo's relative silence on the
matter is most surprising because of comments he made in "The Gift of
the Black Tropics," the piece he had contributed just one year earlier to
Alain Locke's hallmark 1925 anthology, *The New Negro*: in this essay, he
had confronted head-on the topic of the "Special Issue" by discussing not
"The West Indies" but rather "West Indians" (and African Americans) in
the United States.

Early in the 1925 essay, Domingo draws attention to how reductive
and essentialist conceptions of race in this country pose unique problems for black immigrants: "Divided by tradition, culture, historical background and group perspective, these diverse peoples are gradually ham-
mered into a loose unit by the impersonal force of congested residential
segregation. Unlike others of the foreign-born, black immigrants find it
impossible to segregate themselves into colonies; . . . they are inevitably
swallowed up in black Harlem" (341–42). While differences in ethnic
or national origins, language, or religious practices are perceived by the
native-born white community as features that distinguish white immigrants both from one another and from themselves, racial similarity alone
serves as the criterion for a blind association of African Caribbeaners with
African Americans upon the black immigrant's arrival. But, Domingo
continues, the native-born black community subsequently falls victim to
similarly simplistic classifications: "To the average American Negro, all
English-speaking black foreigners are West Indians, and by that is usually
meant British subjects. There is a general assumption that there is everything in common among West Indians, though nothing can be further
from the truth. West Indians regard themselves as Antiguans or Jamaicans
as the case might be, and a glance at the map will quickly reveal the physical obstacles that militate against homogeneity of population; separation
of many sorts, geographical, political, and cultural tend everywhere to
make and crystallize local characteristics" (343). Even from within the
veil of race, Domingo claims, blindness persists: the presence of one false
dichotomy—that of black and white—facilitates the development of another—that of "West Indian" and African American.

But these gulfs between self and other prove impossible for even
Domingo to bridge. While this is perhaps neither surprising nor, on the
surface at least, terribly ominous, the history of hostility between African
Caribbeaners and African Americans, combined with the pattern of ethnic identity construction based on opposition that seems to be at play
in this historical instance, makes the rhetoric of "Gift" implicitly con-
demnatory and confrontational. As Werner Sollors has argued, ethnicity

is not a thing-in-itself but is rather a relation based on contrast.[36] This sense of ethnicity as rooted in contrast is illustrated throughout "Gift" as Domingo repeatedly attributes positive characteristics to African Caribbeaners that stand in juxtaposition to his notable silences about African Americans. In this particular context, Domingo's ascription of certain qualities to African Caribbeaners implies the contrary about African Americans.

Describing African Caribbean employment circumstances in the United States, for example, Domingo states in "Gift" that, "coming from countries in which they had experienced no legalized social or occupational disabilities, West Indians very naturally have found it difficult to adapt themselves to the tasks that are, by custom, reserved for Negroes in the North." Continuing, Domingo makes increasingly problematic inferences about levels of ambition and industry between African Caribbeaners and African Americans: "Skilled at various trades and having a contempt for body service and menial work, many of the immigrants apply for positions that the average American Negro has been schooled to regard as restricted to white men only, with the result that through their persistence and doggedness in fighting white labor, West Indians have in many cases been pioneers and shock troops to open a way for Negroes into new fields of employment" (345). This statement implies strongly that Domingo believes African Americans are unskilled at trades, have little contempt for body service and menial work, are resigned to white-constructed barriers of segregation, and are neither "persistent" nor "dogged" in confronting white labor.

Domingo continues, referring to the behavior of Caribbean immigrants as evincing a "freedom from spiritual inertia," and goes on to say that this quality allows Caribbeaners to be especially enterprising. Becoming more explicit, Domingo claims that "while American Negroes predominate in forms of business like barber shops and pool rooms *in which there is no competition from white men,* West Indians turn their efforts almost invariably to fields like grocery stores, tailor shops, jewelry stores and fruit vending *in which they meet the fiercest kind of competition.* In some of these fields they are the pioneers or the only surviving competitors of white business concerns" ("Gift" 345; my emphasis). In terms of worship, Domingo describes African Americans as being "inclined to indulge in displays of emotionalism that border on hysteria" while African Caribbeaners, "in their Wesleyan Methodist and Baptist churches maintain . . . all the punctilious emotional restraint characteristic of their English background" ("Gift" 347). He concludes the essay with a statement that can be considered at best a firm pronouncement of patriotism and at worst as bordering on vainglory: "The outstanding contribution of West Indians to American Negro life is the insistent assertion of their manhood in an environment that demands too much servility and unprotesting acquiescence from men of African blood. This unwillingness to conform and be standardized, to accept tamely an inferior status and abdicate their humanity, finds an open expression in the activities of the foreign-born Negro in America" whose "dominant characteristic" is that of "blazing new paths, breaking the bonds that would fetter the feet of a virile people" (349). In the heated political and cultural moment in which Domingo writes, to argue that African Caribbeaners are "insistent[ly] assert[ing] . . . their manhood" is to more than suggest that African Americans are not; to praise African Caribbeaners for refusing "to accept tamely an inferior status and abdicate their humanity" is to intimate that African Americans do not; to assert that the "dominant characteristic [of African Caribbeaners] is that of . . . breaking the bonds that would fetter the feet of a virile people" is to insinuate that African Americans cannot do this for themselves.

Granted, the objective of "Gift" was to highlight for readers of *The New Negro* the contributions African Caribbeaners were making to black American culture. Indeed, it is not insignificant that Locke, in his effort to redefine the image of the black for the twentieth century, chose to include not only the essay by Domingo but also additional pieces by Puerto Rican Arthur Schomburg, British Guianan Eric Walrond, and Jamaican Claude McKay, suggesting that in Locke's mind, at least, foreign-born blacks were vital elements in the development of the "New Negro" as a cultural force. But the very different goals of the *Opportunity* edition, combined with the inflammatory rhetoric of "Gift of the Black Tropics," do suggest why Domingo's contribution to the "Special Issue" could not echo his earlier work.

Although Domingo's informative but more benign article in *Opportunity* sets an optimistic tone by ending on a note of resigned if not hopeful conciliation for African Caribbeaners and African Americans, the piece that concludes the "Special Issue" suggests that relations between the two groups still had a long way to go. The final word on the topic, contained in a "Symposium on West Indian–American Relations," consists of a dialogue between Jamaican immigrant Ethelred Brown, a prominent religious leader in Harlem, and African American Eugene Kinckle Jones, Executive Secretary of the National Urban League. Brown begins by attributing "responsibility for the unsatisfactory relations of the past . . . in almost equal measure" to "both parties in the conflict," but concludes with the assertion that the prospect of eradicating these tensions rests firmly on the shoulders of African Americans: "If the Americans will but remove the last lingering remains of misunderstanding, suspicion and jealousy, forget as much as possible the accident of geographical origin, and show more of the spirit of the kindly host, I am strongly of the opinion that in a few years the relations . . . will have become . . . genuinely cordial and . . . mutually helpful" (356). Jones's response is less imputative but no more promising in its vision of the potential for collaboration over important political, social, and cultural issues: indeed, he cites the cooperation of the two groups only in a recreational realm—in the development of the American Tennis Association—as providing "the best example of the possibility" of "good fellowship" between African Americans and African Caribbeaners (356). Placing perhaps too much faith in symbols of conciliation as providing actual tools for healing, he expresses his firm belief that the "Special Issue" itself will be "most effective in cementing the good will between Negroes of whatever place of birth" (356). A full decade after the publication of the "Special Issue," however, the National Negro Congress felt obligated to "go on record as condemning any form of discrimination practiced against foreign-born Negroes in the United States, . . . as opposing any attempt at deporting . . . or dropping them from relief; . . . as seeking to bring about a better relationship between the foreign-born and native Negroes; . . . [and] as supporting foreign-born Negroes in their struggle for economic and political freedom in their respective homes." [37] Clearly the tensions of the previous years had not fully abated.

The "essential friendship" which the "Special Issue" was intended to foster was indeed difficult to forge during the "first wave" of Caribbean immigration to the United States. Due to an overriding racial essentialism that pervaded both popular and institutional cultures during the period, African Americans and African Caribbeaners were uniformly lumped together in housing, employment, economic, and sociocultural arenas. But significant differences, stemming largely from disparate national origins, caused friction between the two communities. These differences became more pronounced and acquired value connotations within the closed geographic and social space that the groups were forced to share, leading each to define itself in binary opposition to the other.

But binaries are not inherently oppositional, and it would be historically inaccurate to present the two communities investigated here as always standing in antagonistic relation to one another. As subsequent newcomers have arrived on U.S. shores, the relations between African Americans and African Caribbeaners have developed, shifted, and, at times, improved, possibly validating the *Opportunity* staff's conviction that familiarity breeds friendship. Indeed, as sociologist Mary Waters' studies have shown, contemporary African Caribbean immigrants exhibit a range of responses to a racial system in the United States which, although showing slow signs of change, continues to regard "blacks" and "whites" as monolithic entities. Some black newcomers identify themselves most prominently as Americans; others continue to see themselves as ethnic Americans in a way that establishes a distance between themselves and African Americans; still others conceive of themselves first and foremost as immigrants in a way that does not engage American racial and ethnic categories at all.[38] Similarly, changes in the political dynamics of black/white relations have also affected allegiances between African Americans and African Caribbeaners. When a twenty-year-old Trinidadian man was murdered by a mob of white teenagers in the Howard Beach section of Queens in 1986, for example, African Americans and African Caribbeaners rallied together to challenge systems of racism and oppression. Jesse Jackson's 1988 presidential bid provided another occasion for intraracial unity as blacks of a variety of ethnic and national backgrounds joined other members of the "Rainbow Coalition" to place the concerns of people of color in the national political spotlight. These examples illustrate that, as Paul Gilroy has noted, "homogeneity can signify unity but unity need not require homogeneity."[39]

Clearly, African American and African Caribbean cultures, like all cultures, modified and will continue to modify one another, particularly in the hybridizing space of the city in which the two communities are still concentrated. With each new wave of immigration, the dramas of association and dissociation that began during the first stage of contact will continue to shape and be shaped by the historically specific complexities of racial, ethnic, and national identity formation in the United States. The one constant of which we can be certain, however, is that "black foreigners," and African Caribbeaners in particular, will continue, as Domingo stated in 1925, to remain "considerable factor[s] and figure[s]" in the changing nature of the American social fabric. Two of the most influential of these figures are first-generation Jamaican immigrant Claude McKay and second-generation Barbadian immigrant Paule Marshall.

2

"A Thing Apart" and "Out of Time"

The Poetry of Claude McKay

INTO THE VOLATILE climate of pre-Renaissance Harlem entered Claude McKay, one of the most mercurial figures in American literary history. Described at various points in his life as a nationalist, a Communist, a radical, a proletarian, a rebel, a Catholic, an aesthete, a humanist and even a fascist, few have considered McKay in terms of the characteristic that consistently and most profoundly affected all other aspects of his identity—his status as a migrant. McKay migrated to the United States from Jamaica in 1912 with the intention of studying agriculture at Booker T. Washington's Tuskegee Institute but, by 1914, had made his way to Harlem, initiating a pattern of nearly constant movement that would dominate his life. I purposely distinguish McKay as a migrant (one who moves from place to place) from an immigrant (one who moves to another region to settle) because his very inability to settle, his very need to "keep going"—as he would have liked to title his autobiography—provides the key to understanding how this complex man could embody any or all of the above sobriquets during his lifetime.[1] Indeed, an assessment of McKay's poetic writings against the backdrop of his identity as a migrant reveals the roots of the author's pervasive sense of being "a thing apart" or one "out of time," as he suggests in his poem "Outcast," and demonstrates how this constant *dis*placement shapes every element of his poetic expression.

The themes of movement (if not yet migration) and difference (if not yet displacement) are traceable to McKay's early childhood. In the memoir of his youth written during the last decade of his life and published posthumously in 1979, *My Green Hills of Jamaica*, McKay describes how, because of his parents' stature in the community, he and his siblings were held apart from the peasants he later glorified in his dialect poetry. Born on September 15, 1890, he was the last of eleven children (eight lived to adulthood) of Thomas Francis and Hannah Ann McKay, both of whom were community leaders in McKay's hometown of Sunny Ville.[2] Although classified as peasants within the social structure of late-nineteenth-century Jamaica, McKay's parents were more secure financially than most members of the community.[3] McKay states that his father, in contrast to the majority of villagers, who worked small leased plots, "did not believe in renting" and instead worked "grimly hard, buying a piece of land wherever it was for sale until he owned over a hundred acres." On this land McKay's father built not an ordinary thatched house like those occupied by most of Sunny Ville's inhabitants, but rather "a spacious five-roomed place with cedar floors and broadleaf shingles, mahogany chairs and a porch." He was "one of the few . . . who possessed enough worldly goods to establish himself as a voter," according to McKay and as such, exerted considerable "influence over the rest of the peasants." Indeed, the elder McKay's strong sense of justice, combined with his relative wealth and position as church deacon, earned him the role of a "village leader, as they have in Africa," a "patriarch of the mountain country."[4] McKay describes his mother, née Hannah Ann Elizabeth Edwards, as equally well-respected in the village and as even better liked than her often foreboding husband: she "didn't care very much about what people did and why and how they did it. She only wanted to help them if they were in trouble. She wanted to help those who were outcast, poor and miserable."[5]

McKay's parents apparently demanded from their offspring adherence to the same standards of character and behavior that they set for themselves. According to McKay, this expectation resulted in his relative dissociation from his peers. He remembers, for example, that he and his brothers were forbidden from dating peasant girls; his father, according to McKay, stated firmly that he was "'not educating [his] boys for any of these village girls no matter how pretty they may be.'" Similarly, McKay's only sister, Rachel, after having been sent away to study with her older brother U'Theo, who taught school in a small town on the outskirts of Montego Bay, was considered upon her return to Sunny Ville to be "too 'highly educated' for a village man."[6] McKay recalls that he and his brothers were not allowed "to carry loads [of cane] on [their] heads like other peasant boys" but instead were expected to hoist burlap knapsacks over their shoulders, like their father did, when they went into the fields. None of the McKays were expected by the family to remain peasants; indeed, three of McKay's brothers became teachers, one became an Episcopalian missionary, and his oldest sibling, U'Theo, became a local celebrity for his leadership in education and politics. While the subtle sense of superiority that accompanied their family's elevated status must have, on some levels, instilled pride and confidence in the McKay children, McKay notes that it also inhibited their full participation as equals in the peasant community. This feeling of being somehow different from those around him was only reinforced for McKay when he, too, at age six, was sent to U'Theo's to study.[7]

At U'Theo's, in the shadow of the more metropolitan world of Montego Bay, McKay claims that he experienced a more "refined" life. He describes his brother's house as filled with "things that we did not have in the hills," and recalls having to wear there his first pair of shoes. He tells of his sister-in-law's determination "to make a little gentleman" out of him by teaching him to ride using a saddle, and of her efforts to associate him with the children of the more elite "mulatto families who owned property" in the area. According to McKay, he "received so many little privileges" because of his status as U'Theo's younger sibling and charge: "I was made a member of all the important school clubs even though I was not of age. In the school I was put into much higher classes than the kids of my own age. Very often I had to depend on other classmates to work out my problems for me. They were all willing to do it."[8] In addition to growing socially distant from his peasant peers while living with U'Theo, McKay embarked on an enterprise that further divided him intellectually from most of his schoolmates as well: he became immersed in his brother's extensive library. He recalls reading "Matthew Arnold's *Literature and Dogma*, [Haeckel's] *The Riddle of the Universe*, Draper's *The Conflict between Religion and Science*, and a number of Herbert Spencer's books. My interest was also awakened in the great philosophers such as Spinoza, Schopenhauer, Kant and Berkeley."[9] U'Theo encouraged his brother to read widely and, breaking from the strict Calvinism of their father, started to school him in the ideas of "free-thinkers" from a variety of disciplines who did not consider life to be dictated strictly by religious principles. Under U'Theo's guidance McKay began to read "freethinking books with greater interest" and to see and think "of life solely from the free thought angle."[10] As his education progressed, however, his association with his peer group diminished, and McKay became increasingly independent—as well as more isolated.

When McKay was fourteen, U'Theo decided to take a break from teaching in order to lease and farm a large estate near Sunny Ville. McKay returned to the village of his youth, but the place was no longer his home and his family was no longer his own:

I had been entirely cut off from my associations in Sunny Ville because I had never written to my father, mother, or any of my brothers. When

my brother received a letter from home he would sometimes say that my
father or mother had said 'hello' to me. . . . I had scarcely known my
father and mother when I had left with my brother about seven years
previous. Now I had to become reacquainted with my own family.[11]

This was not an easy process. When McKay discovered that he would have
to share a room with two of his brothers, he remembers that "somehow, someway, I . . . wangled out of [the double] bed to have my own
little cot." Significantly, he claims that "all through life, wherever I have
travelled, I have always managed to preserve some form of personal aloofness even if I were living in the poorest neighborhood."[12] His relationship
with his parents was no more intimate. McKay never achieved a comfortable rapport with his father, and his mother, suffering from congestive
heart failure and dropsy, was permanently bed-ridden upon McKay's
return.

The distance McKay felt from his family during this period extended
to his relationships with the larger Sunny Ville community, as well. Describing a Great Revival that swept the village, he recalls how both he and
U'Theo, as freethinkers among a crowd of Baptists, were seen as "children of Satan" whose learning was considered by the worshipers to resemble "more of a compact with the devil than real education." Importantly, he remembers that "the villagers now looked at me strangely as
one who was among but not really of them. . . . "[13] This feeling of difference, of being "a thing apart," provoked McKay to leave Sunny Ville,
beginning a series of migrations that would eventually lead him out of
Jamaica altogether.

By 1906, McKay had decided to attend trade school and left home
for Kingston. Shortly after his arrival, however, an earthquake decimated
the city and forced him to return to Sunny Ville, but he remained there
only a few months. By the end of 1907 he had found a position as an
apprentice to a cabinet maker and wheelwright in Brown's Town, a small
community in neighboring St. Ann's Parish. He remained there until
1909, by which time his mother's illness had progressed to the degree
that he was forced to return again to Sunny Ville to care for her until
her death in December. Upon his mother's death, McKay again left for
Kingston, where he worked odd jobs until he joined the constabulary in
1911. He received initial training in Spanish Town but was eventually
transferred to Half-Way Tree, an area north of Kingston. The one constant during this period of physical and emotional flux was provided by
McKay's friendship with Walter Jekyll, a white Englishman who would
have a profound influence on McKay's early dialect poetry.

McKay met Jekyll in 1907 during his apprenticeship in Brown's
Town. The owner of the shop, knowing that Jekyll was a writer and folk-

lorist, introduced the two and Jekyll asked to read some of McKay's work.[14] McKay had been writing poetry since he was a child, having begun when he lived with U'Theo. Partly in response to the expectations of his family and partly because life as a peasant-poet seemed neither lucrative nor even possible in Clarendon Hills, he had resigned himself to more "practical" forms of employment. Jekyll was the first to show a serious interest in McKay's writing, and a correspondence quickly developed between the two men. McKay began to visit Jekyll at his home in the Blue Mountains northeast of Kingston to discuss philosophy, languages, and poetry, and by early 1910, shortly following his mother's death, the young poet had "packed up a few things in a battered old suitcase and [gone] off to Kingston," feeling—but not wanting to tell Jekyll—that he "had run away from home to be near him."[15]

Some critics have speculated about a homosexual attraction between McKay and Jekyll. Wayne Cooper, in his groundbreaking biography of McKay, claims that evidence does exist to suggest that Jekyll was homosexual, although the material Cooper is able to cite is necessarily speculative and circumstantial. He notes, in contrast, that McKay's sexual relations with both women and men are well documented. According to Cooper, however, "evidence indicates [McKay's] primary orientation was toward the homosexual on the spectrum of human sexual inclinations." He argues that "a homoerotic component most likely underlay the relationship" between Jekyll and McKay, and that McKay "did once indirectly suggest that Jekyll introduced him to the reality and the moral legitimacy of homosexual love." If indeed McKay was homosexual, one might argue that a sexual orientation that was socially unacceptable in turn-of-the-century Jamaica may have been further cause for his alienation from the culture.[16]

Regardless of the nature of their relationship, Jekyll, because of his own interest in Jamaican folk culture, was especially fond of McKay's dialect poems and encouraged his pupil/friend to pursue this type of writing. "He . . . told me that he did not like my poems in straight English—they were repetitive," McKay recalls. "'But this,'" Jekyll stated of a dialect piece, "'this is the real thing. The Jamaican dialect has never been put into literary form except in my Annancy stories. Now is your chance as a native boy [to] put the Jamaica dialect into literary language.'" This statement suggests much about the developing relationship between the two men. Not only did Jekyll appropriate the Annancy tales of Jamaican folklore, but he also projected onto McKay the role of a "native" mouthpiece for—or "representative" voice of—the Jamaican peasantry. McKay himself "was not very enthusiastic" about the idea of writing in vernacular, however, because, as he explains in *My Green Hills*, "to us who were getting an education in the English schools the Jamaican dialect was considered a vulgar tongue." Reflecting his own adherence, as a product of a colonial education, to British standards of language, McKay believed that "all cultivated people spoke English, straight English." The "Negro dialect," he claims, "was regarded as the mark of an inferior person."[17]

To some degree, as P. S. Chauhan has noted in his important recasting of McKay as a quintessentially colonial writer, McKay internalized the teachings of Jamaica's colonizer by learning to discredit the expression of the Jamaican folk.[18] In response to Jekyll's claim that each new dialect poem was "more beautiful than the last," McKay himself concedes that "a short while before I never thought that any beauty could be found in the Jamaican dialect." He admits that he continued to write in the vernacular, however, mainly because Jekyll, an Englishman whose knowledge and authority he admired, deemed these verses superior to those he composed in standard English. "Now this Englishman had discovered beauty and I too could see where my poems were beautiful."[19]

But to attribute McKay's attitudes about literary language and form solely to a tendency to identify with the linguistic legacy of his colonizer is to underestimate the complexity of the forces acting upon the author's early aesthetic development. On one hand, the relationship between McKay and Jekyll clearly seems paradigmatic of those existing between many "colonials" and metropolitan elite "patrons" in which the financial sponsor desires that the writer create " 'authentic' " or " 'native' " art that differs from metropolitan codes.[20] Charlotte Osgood Mason's admonitions to both Langston Hughes and Zora Neale Hurston to depict the "folk" offers merely one of the most well-known examples. (Mason describes her lifelong fascination with such topics in a 1929 letter to McKay himself, in fact: "I cannot remember the day when I was not interested in primitive peoples, their fine living and their art, and spring will make me seventy four!"[21]) Jekyll's initial investment in McKay as "the real thing" (to use Jekyll's words in a different context), combined with his role as McKay's primary financial sponsor, provide some insight into the possible roots of McKay's consistent impulse throughout his career to attempt to capture the voices of both African American and Jamaican "folk" in his fiction.

McKay's educational sponsorship by Jekyll—his tutelage under this expatriate patron from the metropole whose training as a folklorist enabled him to revere (if also relish) Jamaican vernacular—may also have provoked a need on McKay's part to negotiate between his own (admittedly colonial) desire to be what he perceived as a "real poet"—one who writes in traditional British forms—and the desire to fulfill the expectations of his (admittedly colonizing) teacher that he would be an "authentic" Jamaican poet—one who writes in the "native" or peasant vernacular. These competing impulses placed the young writer in an ironic bind in that they forced him literally to perform the primitive if he wanted to be taken seriously as a poet by the friend and critic he most admired. McKay attempted to comply, but the result was a collection of dialect poems, *Songs of Jamaica* (1912), that is, on some levels, an act of mediation. Indeed, a close reading of this collection reveals that these songs seem neither to be *of* Jamaica nor *of* the poet himself but rather *about* Jamaica— songs that read more like transcriptions, comparable to his mentor's recordings of the Annancy tales, of a world that McKay admired and observed, but to which he did not fully belong.[22]

The linguistic legacy of McKay's complicated relationship to the speech of the peasantry pervades not only "Whe' Fe Do?," the subject of Chauhan's valuable rereading, but nearly every work in the author's first two volumes of poetry. While the social protest and generally more political themes of the poems in his first book seem to come straight from the soul of this poet well-schooled in social theory and experienced in imperial oppression, the actual language through which these themes are expressed does not ring true. Frequently, what appears to be McKay's voice, that of one who speaks in the "cultivated" tongue of "straight English," interrupts the mood and tone of the dialect that is intended to characterize the peasant speaker. Lloyd W. Brown, in his excellent chapter on McKay in his more general study of West Indian poetry, argues that McKay deliberately mixes standard English and African Caribbean language and form to "enforce the poet's perception of the duality that is inherent in his literary heritage . . . and in his cultural milieu; and this kind of objective conforms very well with McKay's preoccupation with a sense of aptness on choosing the diverse forms and cultural structures which were available to him." Brown acknowledges, however, that "such intermingling merely creates a sense of jarring incongruity," and attributes these flaws to "the insecurity of an inexperienced poetic imagination."[23] While McKay's early work does reveal poetic inexperience, the limitations of his dialect verse seem to result less from a conscious effort to wrestle into one form the two arms of his literary heritage and more from an inability to suppress his self-chosen "native" tongue—standard British English—for the tongue imposed on him as a "native"—Jamaican dialect.

McKay's struggle to mediate between these two voices is illustrated, for example, in "The Hermit." In this poem, McKay's reverence for the pastoral themes of the British romantics undermines his efforts to create a believable peasant speaker. In the very first stanza, words of dialect and formal English clash against one another:

> Far in de country let me hide myself
> From life's sad pleasures an' de greed of pelf,
> Dwellin' wid Nature primitive an' rude,
> Livin' a peaceful life of solitude.

The first line uses only standard English except for the unlikely insertion of "de" in place of "the," which leaves the reader uncertain about the form the poem will take. The second line is plagued by similar irregularity: the dialect "an'" and "de" contrast sharply with the nearly archaic "pelf," as well as with the remainder of the line. As the poem progresses, these discrepancies continue both in language and in structure. "Dere by de woodland let me build my home," the first line of stanza two, seems wholly out of place when followed by, "Where tropic roses ever are in bloom." The inversion of "ever are" appears artificial in the context of the surrounding dialect. This same unnatural pattern is expressed in lines three and four of this stanza, as the subject of line four, "de waterfall," is placed stiffly at the end of the sentence: "An' t'rough de wild cane growin' thick and tall / Rushes in gleeful mood de waterfall." Stanza three is effectively bisected by formal English and Jamaican dialect: the first and second halves of the verse seem to be spoken by two different voices entirely.

> Roof strong enough to keep out season rain,
> Under whose eaves loved swallows will be fain
> To build deir nests, an' deir young birdlings rear
> Widouten have de least lee t'ought of fear.

McKay's attempt to maintain a formal rhyme scheme and meter hinders his ability to portray convincingly the dialect voice of the hermit. Indeed, the romance of living with "tropic roses," "young birdlings," and "woodland creatures" is subverted by the last line, which describes our hermit as "sad" and lonely in his isolated retreat.

The intrusion of formal style and language into dialect verse occurs throughout *Songs of Jamaica*. At times, a full stanza interrupts the flow of the dialect (see stanza eleven of "Ribber Come-Do'n"), while at others, just a few words or phrases disclose McKay's poetic ambivalence about Jamaica's common tongue. In "Nellie White," for example, the standard "love" and "loved" surprisingly replace the more colloquial and equally comprehensible "lub" and "lubbed," even though the speaker is a laborer whose voice is dominated by the vernacular. The disparity between such couplets as "Cry not, except 'tis for joy; / Can't you trus' dis big-heart boy?" undermine McKay's poetic intention. In "Whe' Fe Do?," as Chauhan has demonstrated, McKay repeatedly juxtaposes words that are pronounced in standard English using a soft "th" with similar words that he records as being pronounced with a hard "d."[24] For example, in a line that reads, "Fe t'ings *th*at bring more loss *d*an gain," we are left questioning why the formal "that" is used alongside the colloquial "dan" when the words are linguistically comparable and consistent use of the dialect term would not hinder the reader's comprehension. Similar doubt surrounds the lines, "And *th*ough *d*e wul' is full o' wrong," or "We happy *th*ough *d*e baby bawl," especially when McKay goes so far as to define, in an editorial note, "da's" as "that's" in the line, "An' da's de way we ought to live." Jekyll, who edited the volume, attempts to explain these inconsistencies in his preface. While he states that "generally" the soft "th" is spoken as a "d," he notes that "in these poems *the, they, there, with,* etc., are not always written *de, dey, dere, wid,* etc; and the reader is at liberty to turn any soft *th* into *d,* and any *d* into soft *th.* . . . for fear of confusion with well-known words, *though, those* are always written thus, although generally pronounced, *dough, dose.*"[25] Granted, dialect poetry can only sustain a given number of alterations from standard English per line in order for its meaning to remain clear to the reader. Nevertheless, McKay's linguistic irregularities, which do not occur in an identifiable system or pattern, combined with the structural inconsistencies which characterize much of the verse in *Songs of Jamaica,* force us to question whether he or Jekyll, as his guide, fully trust dialect to convey accurately the meaning the author hopes to express.[26] This subtle invalidation of the vernacular, combined with the intrusion of McKay's more formal voice, results in an inconsistent and, in many respects, unconvincing volume of poetry.

If McKay's dialect songs of nature and romance are somewhat uneven in form and content, however, his work in the vernacular becomes decidedly more impressive when it is underscored by his strong political beliefs. Indeed, this is the key factor that distinguishes McKay's dialect work from that of Paul Laurence Dunbar, to whom McKay is often compared. As Jean Wagner explains in *Black Poets of the United States,* Dunbar's poetry lost some of its efficacy as a mechanism for social commentary because he wrote in a dialect tradition that had been overtaken and misused by Plantation School white writers to ridicule or demean blacks.[27] McKay, on the other hand, was the first Jamaican poet to use the local dialect as a vehicle of social protest. When he writes about the poverty of the peasants, the frustration of toiling in the hot sun for the benefit of a white landowner, the evils of tourism, alcoholism, or the brutal effect of urban life on prostitutes and constables alike, his poetry gains a potency that is absent from the love poems or pastorals. "Two-An'-Six," for example, makes clear the economic defenselessness of the peasants as it describes the tragedies that strike when, as in the poem, "Sugar sell fe two-an'-six."[28] "Quashie to

Buccra" and "Hard Times" focus on the rage of laborers who must work for a lazy, aristocratic landowner who knows nothing of the crops, their cultivation, or the exertion that was put into their production—and yet who benefits from their harvest while the peasants themselves gain nothing. "Fetchin' Water" castigates white tourists who, like "Buccra," find the daily chores of peasant children in the hot sun to be quaint and "sweet" while they themselves, by their very presence, reinforce the imperialism that keeps these children chained to lives of poverty and oppression. "Dat Dirty Rum" reveals the debilitating effects of liquor on those who give in to the temporary escape it offers from the trials of impoverishment. Most powerfully, "A Midnight Woman to the Bobby" captures the tension that emerges between peasant-turned-prostitute and peasant-turned-constable under the corrupting influence of the city. In all of these poems, McKay's dialect, despite its linguistic limitations, is powered by a social consciousness and anger that dramatically increase its impact.

At the same time, however, many of the poems that comment upon the poverty of the peasants end in a conciliatory manner. In almost all cases, McKay adopts a noble martyr motif that enables the peasant to feel the "hardship melt away," to "try an' live as any man, / An' fight de wul' de best we can," or to "trust on in me Gahd" (see "Quashie to Buccra," Whe' Fe Do?" and "Hard Times"). "Whe' Fe Do?" epitomizes this tendency and also foreshadows McKay's increasingly romantic vision of the peasants themselves, a vision which, as he moves further from Jamaica literally and figuratively, will appear more frequently in his work and will culminate in his final novel, *Banana Bottom*. The abnegation voiced by his peasant speakers stands in marked contrast to his later American poetry (consider "If We Must Die" as just one example) as well as to the most arresting poems in *Songs of Jamaica*—those that are written in standard English.

Indeed, the poems in which McKay offers social commentary in his own tongue—"straight English"—are unquestionably the most persuasive in the collection. Only three poems in *Songs of Jamaica* are written in standard English, and the most political of these, "Strokes of the Tamarind Switch," poignantly reveals McKay's difference from the peasants who surround him.[29] The poem tells the story of the beating of a young man by the police and is based on an experience McKay had as a constable. As he explains in the "Note by the Author," the subject of the poem

> was a lad of fifteen. No doubt he deserved the flogging administered by order of the Court: still, I could not bear to see him—my own flesh—stretched out over the bench, so I went away to the Post Office near by. When I returned, all was over. I saw his naked bleeding form,

and through the terrible ordeal—so they told me—he never cried. But when I spoke to him he broke down, told me between his bursts of tears how he had been led astray by bad companions, and that his mother intended sending him over-sea. He could scarcely walk, so I gave him tickets for the tram. He had a trustful face. A few minutes after, my bitterness of spirit at the miserable necessity of such punishment came forth in song, which I leave rugged and unpolished as I wrote it at the moment.[30]

According to McKay, part of the pain of this incident involved his iden-tification with the victim: "I could not bear to see him—my own flesh—stretched out over the bench." The reference to his "own flesh" suggests that McKay could not bear witnessing a child of a race and class back-ground comparable to his own beaten at the hands of the colored con-stables. This affiliation is further reinforced in the final stanza of the poem when McKay links himself to the lad through a memory of being beaten as a youth himself: "I too was very rude: / They beat me too, though not the same, / And has it done me good?"[31] McKay even implies that the similarities between the boy and himself prompt the child to become tearful not because of the flogging but because of the gesture of intimacy extended by one of his own "people."

In "Strokes," with a power and intensity that is generally absent from the dialect pieces in *Songs of Jamaica*, McKay explores the complex dimensions of the speaker's emotions. McKay writes that his "spirit" is "filled with hate" at the "depravity" of men who can whip a young boy until his legs look like "boiling bark." The speaker's eyes, McKay tells us, become "dim" with "tears" when thinking of the "monstrous wrong" that society "bring[s] upon" itself by perpetuating a system that drives impoverished children to crime. The impact of "Strokes"—particularly in contrast to the dialect pieces spoken by fictional peasant personas—re-sults, of course, from the deep affinity that McKay feels with the actual speaker—clearly himself. Indeed, the poem stands out from the others in the collection precisely because it is written in McKay's own voice. His rage and compassion—as well as his confusion about his relation to the abuser and the abused—burn more heatedly because of the abrupt inser-tion of his own intense emotion.

But ironically, this very sincerity also highlights McKay's difference from the youth and all he represents. As Lloyd Brown has argued, the lan-guage that McKay employs in "Strokes"—"straight English"—actually signals his affiliation not with the young man being whipped, but with the white and mulatto establishment represented by the constabulary.[32] His use of the "cultivated tongue" of the British binds McKay linguis-tically and symbolically more closely to the ruling systems that subjected this lad to such abuse rather than to the lad himself. Certainly McKay's donning of the constable's uniform links him to the barbarity that he detests and exposes through the poem, but so too do his literary voice, his education, and his position. Contrary to McKay's assertion, he is not the peasant boy on trial, but rather the man who holds the switch.

Nevertheless, McKay's attitude toward the constabulary—and the cultural capital that his affiliation with it earns him—is far from unambiguous. Indeed, his dissatisfaction with this role becomes increasingly apparent in his second volume of dialect verse, *Constab Ballads* (1912). As he readily "confess[es]" in the book's Preface, "I had not in me the stuff that goes to the making of a good constable; for I am so constituted that imagination outruns discretion, and it is my misfortune to have a most improper sympathy with wrongdoers." The majority of poems in the volume, therefore, critique the constabulary using both dialect and "straight English" and express McKay's "fierce hatred of injustice," which he attributes largely to the police system itself. His tendency to "make peace" instead of "cases," combined with his self-proclaimed "unadaptive temperament," prevented McKay from performing his work as a law enforcer, and in 1911 he resigned.[33] Although he refused to become an agent of police tyranny, however, he could no longer simply return to the people of Sunny Ville as a peasant and peer. Feeling out of place in both the city and back at home, especially following the death of his mother, McKay's ties to Jamaica began quickly to dissolve.

Like many Caribbean authors who have followed his path since, McKay began to feel that he could not continue to develop as a poet if he stayed in Jamaica; he sought "fuller expression" and a "bigger audience," and he hoped to find these in the United States. Reflecting the general supposition among islanders about the virulence of racism in the United States, however, many of McKay's friends (most notably Walter Jekyll and Thomas H. MacDermot, the prominent editor of the *Jamaica Times*) worried that McKay would "be changed, terribly changed" by America's harsh and segregating social structure. As McKay recalls, "many of the people thought I would have been better off if I had gone to Europe," but, he claims, indicating the force of the factors pushing talented people out of the islands during the first two decades of this century, "everybody wanted me to go someplace." Echoing the optimism about the United States that is routinely expressed in immigration narratives and illustrated in the life story of the Virgin Islander with which this study begins, McKay recollects his own conviction that

> going to America was the greatest event in the history of our hills; America was the land of education and opportunity. Even though Miss

[Henrietta Vinton] Davis had told us that it was not a good place for coloured people—we all believed in it. We thought of England, France, Germany and the rest of Europe . . . but we thought of America in a different sense. It was the new land to which all people who had youth and a youthful mind turned. Surely there would be opportunity in this land even for a Negro.[34]

McKay left Jamaica in 1912 for Booker T. Washington's Tuskegee Institute, avowedly to study agriculture, but upon arriving in Alabama he found the school's regimented routine and paramilitary structure as stultifying as he had found similar aspects of the constabulary.[35] He withdrew and moved on to Kansas State College to continue his studies in a more open setting, but he was never fully devoted to his subject. After all, McKay had come to the United States only on the pretense of learning improved farming techniques to take back to his island; in reality, he had come to develop his skills as a poet. As he states in his autobiography, *A Long Way from Home* (1937),

. . . after a few years of study at the Kansas State College I was gripped by the lust to wander and wonder. The spirit of the vagabond, the daemon of some poets, had got hold of me. I quit college. I had no desire to return home. What I had previously done was done. But I still cherished the urge to creative expression. I desired to achieve something new, something in the spirit and accent of America. Against its mighty throbbing force, its grand energy and power and bigness, its bitterness burning in my black body, I would raise my voice to make a canticle of my reaction.

And so I became a vagabond—but a vagabond with a purpose. I was determined to find expression in writing.[36]

Not surprisingly, after a brief time in Kansas, McKay turned his sights on New York and in 1914 traveled to Harlem, the emerging cultural mecca for blacks from all over the globe.

In New York, McKay's aesthetic and personal philosophies began to change and develop. Inherent in this evolution seems to have been his growing awareness, shared by many immigrants from the Caribbean, where class was as important a determinant of social status as color, of the definitive impact that race alone had on every aspect of his life in the United States. Under the realities of American segregation, in a world where he was now a member of the minority rather than the majority, McKay became critically aware—as MacDermot and Jekyll predicted he would—of what it meant to be black in his new culture. Whereas the social criticism of his Jamaican poetry revolved almost exclusively around class oppression, the focus of McKay's American verse shifted to address the barbarities of racism. Through these poems he did indeed "make a canticle of [his] reaction" to the United States and in the process, he achieved something very "new," something uniquely in "the spirit and accent" of this immigrant nation: he expressed the rage felt by black new-comers, in particular, who came to America hoping to be welcomed into its melting pot, but who found themselves ostracized on the basis of skin color alone.

In New York, free from Jekyll's influence, McKay abandoned dialect verse and fully adopted—but also radically transformed—the form of his colonizer, the traditional sonnet, to express the plight of a differently colonized people—African Americans and black Caribbeaners in the United States. Some critics have argued that McKay's message was too furiously intense to be contained in the form of the sonnet. Nathan Huggins, for example, asserts that McKay's adherence to this restrictive tradition reduced the poet's "defiance" and "militancy" into merely "hol-low rhetoric."[37] McKay himself, moreover, suggests in "O Word I Love To Sing" that he had found formal poetic diction to be at times "too tender," "too slender" to express fully his "hatred for the foe of me and mine."[38] But this very coupling of the formally confining sonnet with an explosive voice of rebellion against American racism is what makes McKay's early American poetry so distinctive. Indeed, it is precisely the tension between these two contrasting components of form and content that hallmarks McKay's sonnets as remarkably innovative pieces which reflect his own complex heritage as a British colonial, a black, and a mi-grant.[39] Through these poems, McKay captured the attention of Ameri-can literary circles and the allegiance of his African American peers.

McKay's most famous poem, for example, "If We Must Die," was written in response to the increasing racial violence of the Red Summer of 1919 and became virtually a national anthem for American blacks dur-ing the twenties. Despite McKay's own claims later in life that he had no intention of encouraging unified action—"I myself was amazed at the general sentiment for the poem. For I am so intensely subjective as a poet that I was not aware, at the moment of writing, that I was trans-formed into a medium to express a mass sentiment"—"If We Must Die" has been put to many different uses over the years.[40] Senator Henry Cabot Lodge submitted it in the *Congressional Record* as evidence of the dangers of black radicalism. During World War II, despite McKay's own feelings about colonialism, the poem was requested by an English anthologist for a collection intended to boost morale; later, it was found on the body of a white American soldier who had been killed in battle.[41] More recently, inmates in the Attica Prison rebellion of 1971 reportedly circulated it among themselves as a means of sustaining support for the uprising, although *Time* magazine, upon discovering it in the prison following the riots, did not recognize its rightful author and attributed it instead to the pen of a prisoner.[42] McKay's rigorously formulaic Shakespearean sonnet, which captured the defiance and determination of people fighting for their lives during a period of race riots, lynchings, and escalating violence by the Ku Klux Klan, clearly has had universal appeal.

Many other poems from this period also ally McKay with his fellow blacks as they explicitly record the frustration and sorrow, as well as the determination and resilience, with which many African Americans responded to the denial of civil and human rights (see, for example, "The Lynching," "Exhortation: Summer, 1919," or "A Roman Holiday"). "Enslaved," for example, emphasizes McKay's affiliation on a grand scale with his "long-suffering race" as it expresses his apocalyptic desire to destroy "the white man's world of wonders utterly" in order to "liberate [his] people from its yoke."[43] Similarly, "In Bondage" acknowledges, if somewhat disdainfully, a forced unity—due to racism—of blacks all over the world.

A traditional English sonnet, "In Bondage" is composed of three quatrains and a closing couplet. The first quatrain and opening couplet of the second quatrain depict a world free of racial distinctions where "man," "bird," and "beast" live "leisurely." "Life is fairer" here, it is "less demanding," and children "have time and space for play." In short, the world he describes resembles strongly the nostalgic depictions of Jamaica that characterize many of the poems in *Spring in New Hampshire* (1920), McKay's third volume of poetry. But at line seven, McKay manipulates his form by introducing a slight turn that signals an actual turning point in the lives of the poem's children and in that of the speaker himself: it marks the moment when they, having "come to years of understanding"—perhaps like McKay after having lived for a few years in the United States—realize the world is ruled by men and women motivated by "lust," by people who will wage "wars" to ensure their place over others. Line seven's position at the center of the first stanza and its closing punctuation of a hyphen suggest a hesitancy and sense of continuing realization, as well as dread, about what those "years of understanding" imply. The remaining quatrain, however, then reverts back to describing the speaker's ability to transcend earthly greed by remembering that "life is greater than the thousand wars" and that it will "remain like the eternal stars / When all that shines to-day is drift and dust."[44]

The closing couplet of "In Bondage," however, abruptly undermines the transcendent tone characterizing the first twelve lines of the poem. In keeping with the traditional form of the Shakespearean sonnet, McKay crafts the volta to fall between lines twelve and thirteen. Whereas the closing couplet of a traditional sonnet usually provides some type of resolution for the conflicts or issues described by the poem's first three quatrains, however, the "resolution" offered by "In Bondage" is one of utter despair as the speaker acknowledges, "But I am bound with you in your mean graves / O black men, simple slaves of ruthless slaves." This final couplet and its separation from the first part of the poem force both the speaker and reader toward the realization that racelessness is impossible in their world. Reluctantly, the speaker admits that, despite his origins in a land that he conceives to be "fairer, lighter, less demanding," he is irrevocably bound with all black men and women who must toil under the demands of "ruthless slaves" to white bigotry. (Not surprisingly, the sentiments expressed in many of these early American poems made McKay an inspirational model for black nationalist movements both in the 1920s and 1960s in the United States, as well as for the founders of the Négritude literary movement in France in the 1930s.[45])

But one cannot simply dismiss McKay's own statements regarding the individualist impulses behind his writing. How might we make sense of his repeated and insistent pleas that he intended to speak for no one but himself? Once again, in revisiting these poems, McKay's history as a migrant becomes especially relevant and illuminating. While his poetry has been read most commonly against the backdrop of the Harlem Renaissance, reconsideration of it within the context of his Jamaican birth and eventual expatriation gives rise to alternative interpretations that valuably reconcile some of this poetry's most troubling ambiguities. Indeed, several works produced during this period clearly highlight McKay's sense of distance and difference from those around him, including other blacks. Many of the most powerful are written in the acutely personal voice of "Strokes of the Tamarind Switch," and reveal that he considers the battle against discrimination in the United States to be primarily his own (e.g., "To the White Fiends," "The White House," "The Barrier," or "The White City"). His frequent use of personal pronouns in these poems, in fact, emphasizes themes of isolation and independence, and reinforces a distinct separation between speaker and reader, between individual and group struggle. Consider "Baptism," for example, which powerfully conveys McKay's sensation of alien(ation) from both blacks and whites in his adopted land. Dominated by the personal pronouns "I," "me," and "my," "Baptism" metaphorically suggests McKay's own confrontation with the racism of the United States. The first quatrain describes the speaker's individual journey into the hell of ignorance and blind hate. The opening line of this Petrarchan sonnet beseeches us, "Into the furnace let me go alone," while our remoteness is firmly established by our position outside, standing back, "in terror of the heat." The speaker's vulnerability as well as his strength are symbolized by his "naked"[ness] as he prepares to enter "the weird depths of the hottest zone." The second quatrain depicts his brave resistance to the hell-fire as he stands boldly and silently before it, awaiting his "fate."[46]

"Baptism" then turns at line nine, when the tense shifts from future to present, and the speaker actually enters the flames. Surrounded by "aspish tongues" and "fiery spears," his sheer determination to withstand the heat "destroys" and "consumes" whatever "mortal fears" he may have harbored, and "transform"[s] him "into a shape of flame" that is both one with, and yet able to resist consumption by, the other flames seeking to envelop him. The final couplet completes the journey resiliently as the speaker returns to our "world of tears / A stronger soul within a finer frame."[47] But despite this victorious conclusion for the individual subject of the poem, nowhere in "Baptism" does the speaker invoke the strength of his black peers for assistance; nowhere does he suggest that the peril of the fire can be better faced as a group.

The tensions between individual and group, between man and "race," are perhaps the most distinguishing features of McKay's writing during the first period of his residency in the United States. On one hand, it is clear that McKay, as an artist, wished first and foremost to be seen as a poet—independent of racial classification. But he could not escape the barrier that race created for him in the United States. While he migrated to "find fuller expression," McKay found that most American editors, upon discovering that he was black, would publish only those poems involving "race" material. Despite his criticism of William Stanley Braithwaite in *A Long Way from Home* in 1937 for not writing enough about race, McKay, during the first years of his tenure in the United States, was strongly sympathetic with Braithwaite's call for a universalist writing that transcended artificial categories of "black" and "white."[48] In a letter written to Braithwaite on January 11, 1916, for example, McKay complained to the African American editor about being pigeon-holed as a black writer: "This has set me wondering whether Fine Art is not beyond nation or race—if one's mind can be limited to one's race and its problems when Art is as sublime as He who gave it to man."[49] Braithwaite, as George Hutchinson has described, actually praised McKay's early sonnets for their ability to use "'racial material' in ways that expressed the 'fundamental passions and primary instincts of humanity.'"[50] In another letter to Braithwaite written about a month later, McKay implies that race issues generally do not serve as the inspiration for his creative energies.[51] Yet as we have seen, McKay's confrontation with the brutality of prejudice in the United States clearly did incite him to produce some of his best-known work.

This apparent incongruity can be better understood if we recognize that McKay's personal aesthetic code discouraged him from exploiting race for either artistic or propagandistic purposes. Referring to his heated debate with Michael Gold, with whom McKay shared editorial responsibilities for a time at Max Eastman's radical journal, the *Liberator*, McKay explains his belief about the distinction between art and propaganda: "there were bad and mediocre, and good and great, literature and art, and . . . the class labels were incidental. I cannot be convinced of a proletarian, or a bourgeois, or any special literature or art. I thought and still think that it is possible to have a proletarian *period* of literature, with labor coming into its heritage as the dominating social factor, exactly as we have had a Christian period, a Renaissance period, and the various pagan periods. But I believe that whenever literature and art are good and great they leap over narrow group barriers and periods to make a universal appeal."[52] Similarly, given this line of reasoning, McKay resists any categorically determined form of *black* art as well. Rather, he explains that the reason why much of his poetry revolves around blackness is because his work, like any writer's, is inherently at some level a reflection of himself. He could not submerge his racial identity in his poetry because "my poetic expression was too subjective, personal, and tell-tale. Reading a selection of it, a discerning person would become immediately aware that I came from a tropical country and that I was not, either by the grace of God or the desire of man, born white."[53] But at the same time, McKay wished not to be forced to write solely about race and resisted presumed obligations to serve as a mouthpiece for all black Americans, especially given the ethnic and cultural differences not only within the black community but also those that divided him from African Americans specifically.

Although McKay was adopted as a literary spokesman by large segments of the African American public, especially following the publication of "If We Must Die," he was never fully welcomed by, nor did he allow himself to become an insider of, African American literary and intellectual circles. In fact, though he is occasionally named as a precursor or father figure of the movement, McKay predated the rise of the New Negro philosophy undergirding the Harlem Renaissance and was actually in Europe during most of the era. He himself admits in *A Long Way from Home* to having "learned very little about the ways of the Harlem elite during the years I lived there. When I left the railroad and the companionship of the common blacks, my intellectual contacts were limited mainly to white radicals and bohemians."[54] Beyond this, however, McKay had substantial aesthetic disagreements with Alain Locke, the movement's "midwife," as he has been called, and later with W. E. B. Du Bois, one of the leading African American intellectuals of the period and editor of the influential *Crisis*. In addition to the significant hostility between McKay and Locke that resulted from Locke's renaming, without permission, McKay's poem "The White House" to "White Houses" in all editions of *The New Negro* (1925) in order to avoid political conflict, McKay disdained Locke's "effete European academic quality" and believed his aesthetic sense to be "reactionary" and "rococo."[55] Du Bois and McKay would clash years later over the publication of McKay's first novel, *Home to Harlem* (1928), but even in the early twenties the two possessed distinctly different ideas about racial uplift and the role of art in that effort.[56] Like his character Ray in *Home to Harlem* (1928), as well as like many Caribbean intellectuals and activists during the Harlem Renaissance period, McKay's foreign background, colonial education, and leftist political interests pushed him away from alliances based solely on race and toward those based on shared political sympathies—namely, to white radicals like Sylvia Pankhurst in England and Max Eastman in the United States.

Between 1919 and 1921 McKay lived in England and, while there, worked for a time as a writer for British radical Sylvia Pankhurst's *Worker's Dreadnought*. Initially he came to the attention of the Pankhurst group because of a letter he had written in response to a propaganda campaign launched by the *Daily Herald*, London's only socialist daily, against French occupation of the Ruhr Valley in Germany. The campaign, motivated by the *Herald's* fear that the occupation might destabilize the Weimar government and thus open the door for more extreme factions, sought to arouse public support against the French by playing upon racial fears about the "Black Scourge in Europe: Sexual Horror Let Loose by France on [the] Rhine." Accusing the French African troops of an unbridled hypersexuality that posed a threat to white women in the region, the article also cast broader aspersions on blacks in general. McKay's retort pointed out the falsehoods of these allegations and challenged the racist assumptions of the article, but the *Herald's* editor refused to print McKay's response. The *Worker's Dreadnought* picked it up instead, and it proved to be the only meaningful reply to the absurdities published in the British radical press.[57]

McKay continued to write articles for the *Dreadnought* for the next few years and addressed a wide range of political concerns of interest to the socialists. As part of an international cosmopolitan intelligentsia, for example, he was as interested in the occupation of Ireland as he was in West Indian colonialism. But his primary focus remained on race. Following a series of frustrations regarding issues of racial significance ranging from the Rhine story to discrimination by British dockworkers against their black and Asian "brothers," McKay came to believe that the prejudice that permeated England's postwar conservativism also infected leftist circles. In 1921, he sailed for the United States once again.[58]

As is suggested by McKay's debate with Michael Gold about whether art should be categorized according to the creator's race, class, or gender, however, the poet's involvement with Max Eastman's *Liberator* was no more "race-free" than any of his previous experiences in the United States or in England. Particularly revealing of this are the comments of Eastman, whom, not incidentally if somewhat surprisingly, McKay considered to be one of his closest friends. Eastman refers to McKay in the introduction to *Harlem Shadows* (1922) as a member of a "*most alien* race among us" (my emphasis).[59] In the "Biographical Note" that precedes the 1953 edition of *Selected Poems*, Eastman describes McKay's laughter as "that high, half-wailing falsetto laugh of the recklessly delighted Darky— [that] was the center of my joy in him throughout our friendship of more than thirty years," suggesting that he viewed McKay more as a source of minstrel-like entertainment than as a friend and intellectual equal.[60] Eastman goes so far as to lament to his wife, upon hearing of McKay's death, that "perhaps we should have kept him as a cook or a maid."[61] Regardless of the intimacy of their friendship as it is described by both men, throughout his years on the *Liberator* staff McKay was never invited to the Eastman summer home on Martha's Vineyard because, as Eastman admitted to historian Nathan Huggins, something about McKay's "very blackness" and "the fact that 'we always swam in the nude'" prevented him from thinking it appropriate for McKay to be present.[62]

The most revealing incident illustrating McKay's status as outsider among the white radicals on the *Liberator*, however, involved his assignment to provide a theatrical review of Leonid Andreyev's play, "He Who Gets Slapped," in 1922. After being ushered to his orchestra seat with *Liberator* artist William Gropper, McKay was suddenly removed by the manager and reassigned a seat in the balcony because of a supposed mistake concerning the dates on his ticket. The real reason for his banishment from the press seats—despite his title as drama critic for a major paper— was, of course, because McKay was black.[63] As he wrote in his review of "He Who Gets Slapped": "I had come here as a dramatic critic, a lover of the theater, and a free soul. But—I was abruptly reminded—those things did not matter. The important fact, with which I was suddenly slapped in the face, was my color. I am a Negro."[64] More appalling to McKay than the public humiliation of his segregation, however, was his *Liberator* comrades' betrayal in not responding to the incident. Neither Max or Crystal Eastman, nor Michael Gold or Eugene Debs, did more, according to McKay, than merely express sympathy and supposed outrage at their colleague's degradation. These friends, who preached integration, cooperation among black and white laborers, and racial equality under socialism, did far too little, in McKay's mind, to protest the discrimination he faced. Tyrone Tillery, in *Claude McKay: A Black Poet's Struggle for Identity*, argues that this revelation of McKay's peers' disloyalty drove McKay not only to reevaluate the theoretical premises of socialism regarding blacks, but it also drove him to leave the *Liberator* staff—and even the country—altogether.[65] In 1922, he signed on as a stoker on a ship bound for Russia.

From the moment of his arrival in the United States in 1912 to the beginning of his twelve-year excursion abroad in 1922, McKay struggled to find a place for himself.[66] Not surprisingly, his profound and distressing alienation from his adopted culture is reflected in many of the poems that he wrote during this period. His well-known poem "Outcast" perhaps most trenchantly alludes to the multitude of allegiances McKay sought, only to find himself in the end alone, "far from [his] native clime," out of place and "out of time." The first quatrain of this English sonnet expresses the speaker's desire to be a part of a rather mystical conception of Africa, "the dim regions whence [his] fathers came," where his "soul would sing forgotten jungle songs." Here, he would live in "darkness" and in "peace." But lines six through eight acknowledge that he is inescapably a product of the "western world" and will forever "bend [his] knee" to the "alien gods" that control it. The third quatrain explains, however, that this homage exacts a heavy toll:

> Something in me is lost, forever lost,
> Some vital thing has gone out of my heart,
> And I must walk the way of life a ghost
> Among the sons of earth, a thing apart.[67]

According to McKay, in succumbing to the "alien gods," the poem's speaker has lost his connection both to Africa and its diaspora. The ultimate tragedy comes when, realizing this loss, he also recognizes the massive gulf that separates black from white in the "western world" generally and in the United States in particular, and thus confronts his suspension in a racial no-man's land, untethered to all but himself. While McKay's poem "Mulatto" laments a comparable, though more literal, suspension between white and black worlds, "Outcast" suggests the poet's own perception of himself as a cultural mulatto. It romanticizes Africa and reveals McKay's self-determined inability to possess fully the "vital thing"—evidently, in his mind, some form of essential(ized) blackness or Jamaican-centered feeling of "home"—due to his ineluctable attraction to and contact with the "white" aspects of Western culture. As he comments in *A*

Long Way from Home, "My damned white education has robbed me of much of the primitive vitality, the pure stamina, the simple unswaggering strength of the Jakes [the urban vagabond of his 1928 novel, *Home to Harlem*] of the Negro race."[68]

Another of McKay's poems, "My House," illustrates equally well his feelings of isolation in the United States.[69] "My House" was published in the very same November 1926 "Special Caribbean Issue" of the *Opportunity* which, somewhat ironically, given the thrust of the poem, was intended to increase community sentiment among African Americans and Caribbean immigrants. In the first quatrain McKay describes his "house" as painted with a "peculiar tint," "peculiar in an alien atmosphere," reflecting his strong sense of his own distinctiveness and dislocation in the United States. "Where other houses wear a kindred hue," McKay claims to experience "a stirring always very rare" that denies him the kinship of those around him. Seemingly encapsulating the pain he felt as a brilliant child in Jamaica and a black migrant in the United States, the second stanza explains that he

> . . . know[s] the dark delight of being strange,
> The penalty of difference in the crowd,
> The loneliness of wisdom among fools,
> Yet never have I felt but very proud,
> Though I have suffered agonies of hell,
> Of living in my own peculiar cell.

McKay's intense pride provides some salvation from his "loneliness," yet as the closing couplet states, he continues to suffer "agonies of hell" for the very "strangeness" and "difference" that he embodies. Verse four reassures us that his suffering is not all in vain because it leads him to a more intimate understanding of himself and his place in the universe:

> Oh each man's mind contains an unknown realm
> Walled in from other men however near,
> And unimagined in their highest flights
> Of comprehension or of vision clear;
> A realm where he withdraws to contemplate
> Infinity and his own finite state.

The second line, of course, reiterates a theme that recurs throughout McKay's fiction and autobiography—the notion that no matter how close two individuals may be, a fundamental "wall" forever separates them.[70] McKay himself cultivated the privacy that this figurative "wall" allowed, for, as he explains in the fifth stanza of "My House," his distance even from those closest to him allowed him to "catch a god-like glimpse / Of mysteries that seem beyond life's bar," and to "drink" in and "echo" through his poetry "accents of the laugh divine."[71] The seclusion of his "house" grants McKay a Whitmanesque god-like vision, and as a poet, this vision is worth its isolating price. But in many ways, McKay has become "The Hermit" he described years earlier in dialect, "peaceful" and yet "sad" in his lonely retreat.

"My House" then ends, as so many of McKay's poems do, with an affirmation of the personal strength that results from social struggle. Like many of his sonnets that conclude with the speaker's emergence from a period of trial stronger and more resolute in his convictions, the speaker of "My House" wakes from his celestial dream, still in his "same house painted blue / Or white or green or red or brown or black," but now possessed of knowledge that is inaccessible to "average [people] since he has dreamt his dream!" But this vision is less exhilarating than McKay claims in his poem; indeed, this poetic insight proves insufficient to fulfill McKay's need for communion with others, to satisfy those sides of himself that yearn to feel, as he himself describes it, "the strength and distinction of a group and the assurance of belonging to it."[72]

As much as McKay continually sought community, the very distinctiveness of his vision kept him "walled in"—and necessarily walled out—from the many different groups with which he attempted affiliation. He repeatedly arrived on the shores of various places only to retreat when he found that for one reason or another, he did not "belong" there. In some places he did not belong because he was too educated or intellectual or "unadaptive." In other places, he did not belong because he was too "black." In still others, he did not belong because he was not "black" enough. In all cases, McKay paradoxically seemed to seek connection and yet resist it at the same time. He seemed to beckon others toward him with one hand, and push them away with the other. First growing beyond the camaraderie of his peasant family and friends in Jamaica, he retreated to the companionship of his books, his poetry, and his friend Walter Jekyll. Eventually growing beyond the limitations imposed by his native land altogether, he sailed to the United States. But there, this migrant was neither fully African American nor fully white radical. Finally, feeling as though he clearly had no "home in Harlem" or anywhere else in the United States in 1922, McKay left for Russia, seeking under Communism a fellowship that transcended America's racial barriers. During the next twelve years, between 1922 and 1934, McKay continued both his peregrinations and his pursuit of community, creating fictional models of both in his three novels, *Home to Harlem, Banjo,* and *Banana Bottom.*

3

Searching for That "Strange, Elusive Something"
The Novels of Claude McKay

DURING THE TWELVE years between Claude McKay's departure from the United States in 1922 and his return in 1934, he continued the pattern of restless movement that had characterized the first period of his life. Engaging in a series of migrations that carried him across Europe and into Africa, first McKay traveled to Russia with the intention of attending the Fourth Congress of the Third Comintern, not as "a member of the Communist Party," according to McKay, but rather as "a social-minded being and poet" who—characteristically for this vagabond—claims to have been possessed simply by "the dominant urge to go."[1] As an unofficial delegate to the convention, McKay was unable to participate fully in the proceedings, but he became tremendously popular with the Russian public—by his own definition, a "black ikon in the flesh"—and toured widely speaking about art, race, and politics. After approximately six months, McKay moved on again, journeying first to Germany and then to France. For a while, he associated with white American expatriates in Paris, but he felt divided from these peers due to "the problem of color." As he explains in his autobiography, *A Long Way from Home*, "color-consciousness was the fundamental of my restlessness. And it was something with which my white fellow-expatriates could sympathize but which they could not altogether understand." Invoking the very language of exoticism for which he criticizes his peers, however, he goes on to state that "for all their knowledge and sophistication, they couldn't understand the instinctive and animal and purely physical pride of a black person resolute in being himself and yet living a simple civilized life like themselves. Because their education in their white world had trained them to see a person of color either as an inferior or as an exotic." Partly in response to this limited vision, McKay abandoned the eclectic salons of Paris for the more proletarian docks of Marseilles where, in contrast to the earlier sense of alienation, he felt "relief . . . to live among a great gang of black and brown humanity. Negroids from the United States, the West Indies, North Africa and West Africa, all herded together in a warm group. Negroid features and complexions, not exotic, creating curiosity and hostility, but unique and natural to a group." Although McKay recalls relishing "the strength and distinction of [this] group and the assurance of belonging to it," after a few years he again sought new moorings, first in Barcelona and then in Morocco. Reminiscent of experiences in Jamaica, however, he describes himself in Africa as living "on the edge of native life, among them, but not one of them." By 1934 he had returned to the United States, where he would remain until his death in 1948.[2]

During these peripatetics in Europe and Africa, McKay authored three novels, *Home to Harlem* (1928), *Banjo* (1929), and *Banana Bottom* (1933).[3] Since their publication, scholars have frequently analyzed these works in terms of their relation to the Harlem Renaissance, even though McKay was neither in Harlem during the movement's peak years nor did he feel particular affinity with its goals and aspirations.[4] Reexamining McKay's fiction in light of his experiences as a migrant, as a black (im)migrant, and as a British Caribbeaner, however, illuminates facets of his writings that have been previously misinterpreted or misunderstood due to the tradition of locating McKay within the restrictive categories of "African American" or "West Indian" literature. Indeed, reconsidering McKay's fiction from this new perspective reveals a political philosophy that transcends narrowly defined conceptions of socialism, communism, or any other form of codified political association, and an aesthetic philosophy that escapes artificially constructed categories of Harlem Renaissance writing, African American letters, or Caribbean or post-colonial literature. In the end, McKay's three novels demonstrate his frustrations with divisions and limitations that are imposed by categorical assumptions based on race, ethnicity, nationality, or political conviction, as well as illustrate his attempt to reconcile his role as a black writer—and the concomitant expectation by many that he "represent" the "race" through his work—with his goals as an intensely individual artist.

Home to Harlem

Immediately upon its release in 1928, Claude McKay's first novel, *Home to Harlem*, enjoyed rocketing sales and equally explosive criticism. W. E. B. Du Bois claimed that its descriptions of Harlem cabarets, brothels, and black working classes "nauseated" him and made him feel "distinctly" in need of "a bath," while Dewey Jones, writing for the Chicago *Defender*, argued that McKay's novel only perpetuated stereotypes of blacks as "buffoons, thugs, and rotters." Numerous other critics accused McKay of merely capitalizing upon the current white appetite for "the lowdown on Harlem, the dope from the inside."[5] Benjamin Brawley, for example, in keeping with his general critique of the Harlem Renaissance as overly focused on unusual and exotic aspects of black culture, claimed that McKay wrote *Home to Harlem* merely to ride the financial wave initiated by Carl Van Vechten's *Nigger Heaven*, another "Harlem novel" that had been a commercial success upon its publication two years earlier.[6] "After the success of Mr. Van Vechten's *Nigger Heaven*," Brawley asserted, McKay "and some other authors seemed to realize that it was not the poem or story of fine touch that the public desired, but metal of a baser hue; and he decided to give what was wanted. The result was a novel, *Home to Harlem*, that sold thousands of copies but that with its emphasis on certain degraded aspects of life hardly did justice to the gifts of the writer."[7] But McKay's first published novel is far more than a voyeuristic foray into Harlem "low life" or an attempt to make a fast buck. Indeed, this purportedly apolitical text reveals the early stages of McKay's efforts to express his intense political convictions through the medium of modernist fiction.

This effort is revealed immediately in the terse opening chapter of *Home to Harlem*, in which McKay cloaks under scene-setting description and dialect speech a clear picture of ethnic and national hierarchies in England and the United States in the early 1920s. Nearly every paragraph of this chapter comments on how differences of race, ethnicity, or nationality can be used as divisive mechanisms through which to alienate people from one another, and the chapter's position as the introduction to the main tale suggests that these issues will continue to be among the novel's primary concerns. McKay based the early chapters of *Home to Harlem* on his own experiences as a stoker on the ship which secured his passage to Russia in 1922, but in the novel, the ship is returning to the United States carrying the novel's A.W.O.L. hero, Jake Brown. In the first pages, McKay informs us of the racial and ethnic echelon of life on the freighter. He describes the ship's top deck—and its top tier—as comprised of "white sailors who washed the ship" but who "would not wash the stokers' water closet"—not surprisingly in the ship's bowels—"because they despised" the Arab crew who shared Jake's job.[8] The cooks, too, also "hat[ed] the Arabs because they did not eat pork" and thus required special meals on various occasions (1). Although Jake initially attempts to get along with his co-workers, under the influence of the others he eventually "also began to despise the Arabs" and, revealing a distinctly American brand of ethnocentrism, grows disgusted with the personal habits and cleanliness standards of his non-American peers (2).

Despite these feelings, however, Jake is well aware of his kindred status with the Middle Easterners in this closed microcosm of the larger world. He dismisses the affected congeniality that the white sailors offer him when they claim that he's "the same" as them and not "like them dirty jabbering coolies" because he knows that if that were truly the case, "he might have signed on as a deckhand and not as a stoker" (2–3). Exposing the frustration of black soldiers during the First World War, McKay portrays Jake as having signed on to the freighter while on leave from his position as a soldier stationed at Brest because he had discovered that black recruits, despite their "daydreams of going over the top" (4), were enlisted primarily to tote lumber "for the hundreds of huts that were built . . . to house the United States soldiers" (4). In the War, according to McKay, white folks were soldiers and black folks were laborers, regardless of their common military garb: skin color proved to be the definitive uniform.

In portraying Jake's attempts to get along with people from a variety of different national and ethnic origins—his Irish boss, his Arab and "white" shipmates, and the British dockworkers in Limehouse who "gave him their friendly paws and called him 'darky'"—McKay considers, in this first chapter, how English and American racism compare. With deliberate irony McKay notes that the arrival of large numbers of blacks into London's East End—and the consequent racial battles this arrival provokes—infuse Jake "with the awful fever of lonesomeness" for the United States (7). Under this influence Jake's English mistress, despite her efforts "to get down into his thoughts and share them with him," suddenly becomes utterly alien to him—"now only a creature of another race—of another world" (8). Suggesting that the only true happiness for this African American protagonist can be found in the all-black world of Harlem, McKay sends his protagonist "home."

What appears to be simply a stage-setting chapter providing the impetus for Jake's return to Harlem, then, actually proves to be a politically laced depiction of both the national and international scene following the First World War. McKay's decision to set the novel in Harlem, and to suggest Harlem as a possible place of comfort for a dislocated black veteran, allows him to explore the potential of the city to serve as a unifying and empowering force for displaced blacks during the height of the Great Migration more generally. He does so through the voices of the novel's two protagonists—Ray, a deracinated Haitian intellectual, and Jake, the returning African American soldier/vagabond. While critics have argued that Jake and Ray embody McKay's conception of universal human conflict between oppositions variously labeled as "instinct and reason," "realism and idealism," "order and disorder," or "essential Negroness" and "white civilization," it is more helpful to consider these two characters as, like Toni Morrison's Nel and Sula, complementary halves of the same whole.[9] That same whole is McKay himself. Realistically or not, McKay envisioned himself, as biographer Wayne Cooper has shown, as both a "rebel sojourner" moving from one place to the next with no clear plan to his life *and* as a deracinated/de-race-inated Caribbean intellectual working with the proletariat while attempting to write poetry. Certainly, after nearly ten years of moving from one country to the next, McKay considered himself on some levels as very much like Jake, "one blackamoor that nourished a perfect contempt for place" (42). The same "strange, elusive something that [Jake] felt in himself, sometimes here, sometimes there, roaming away from him, going back to London, to Brest, Le Havre, wandering to some unknown new port, caught a moment by some romantic rhythm, color, face, passing through cabarets, saloons, speakeasies, and returning to him. . . . " parallels closely McKay's responses to his own "vagabondage."[10] But McKay also embodies elements of Ray. Numerous incidents in McKay's life reveal similarities between himself and his character, and most critics have assumed that McKay intended Ray to be his mouthpiece in *Home to Harlem*. Ray's recollections of Haiti, for example, his commentaries on colonialism, his feelings of being burdened by knowledge, and his general critiques of civilization (conveyed most explicitly in the chapter "Snowstorm in Pittsburgh") clearly reflect McKay's own opinions on these subjects.[11] The literary mentors that McKay ascribes to Ray in "Relapse," moreover, are those he appropriates for himself, and the character's contemplations of art powerfully evoke the struggle in which McKay himself was enmeshed:[12]

> Dreams of making something with words. What could he make . . . and fashion? Could he ever create Art? Art, around which vague, incomprehensible words and phrases stormed? What was art, anyway? Was it more than a clear-cut presentation of a vivid impression of life? . . . he still felt more than ever the utter blinding nakedness and violent coloring of life. But what of it? Could he create out of the fertile reality around him? (228)

By portraying Jake and Ray as two extremes, and by investing them both with the authority to express his own political and ethical convictions, McKay is able, using the fictional space of the city as a backdrop, to explore the ability of Harlem to serve as "home" not simply for the wide range of black immigrants pouring into the city during the era, but also for himself.

McKay does this through a number of expressly political scenes in the novel. Early in *Home to Harlem*, the issues of unions, scabbing, and racism among workers are raised, matters with which McKay himself was quite involved during his tenures on both Sylvia Pankhurst's *Workers' Dreadnought* and Max Eastman's *Liberator*. Indeed, in *A Long Way from Home*, McKay himself petitions for the "class-consciousness" of *Home to Harlem* based on these very subjects. "When Jake in *Home to Harlem* refused to scab, wasn't that class-conscious? And when he refused to pimp, didn't he demonstrate a high sense of social propriety? Perhaps a higher sense than many of us critical scribblers."[13] The scene about scabbing to which McKay refers involves a portrayal of Jake working as a laborer unloading spoiling fruit from a docked tanker. Soon after starting the job, Jake discovers that he has been hired as a scab. Realizing that "the union leaders were against the strike, and had connived with the police to beat up and jail the pickets," Jake immediately quits, forsaking the high pay for a good conscience instead (44). When a white man asks him to join his union, claiming that it is "the only one in the country for a red-blooded worker, no matter what race or nation he belongs to" (45), Jake declines:

> "Nope, I won't scab, but I ain't a joiner kind of fellah, . . . I ain't no white folks' nigger and I ain't no poah white's fool. When I longshored in Philly I was a good union man. But when I made New York I done finds out that they gived the colored mens the worser piers and holds the bes'n a' them foh the Irishmen. No, pardner, keep you' card. I take the best I k'n get as I goes mah way. But I tells you, things ain't none at all lovely between white and black in this heah Gawd's own country." (45–46)

Jake's response, alluding to racial and ethnic antagonism within unions, reflects McKay's conviction that no labor organizations in the United States, with the exception of the International Workers of the World, had accepted blacks as true equals by 1928. In the chapter on "Labor Leaders and Negroes" contained in his 1923 study, *The Negroes in America*, McKay had condemned the corporate use of black strikebreakers to defeat unionization drives throughout the United States in the late teens, particularly prior to the Red Summer of 1919, and had attributed a large degree of racial tension between workers to such ethnic scapegoating.[14] Urging greater class-consciousness among workers across racial lines, McKay depicts Jake, who has discovered two white men beating a fellow black worker, scaring off the assailants and counseling his friend not to return to the job where workers are pitted against one another: "Let the boss-men stick them jobs up. They are a bunch of rotten aigs. Just using us to do their dirty work" (46). Jake recognizes his role as a pawn in a battle not his own, and avoids further conflict by quietly removing himself from the scene of trouble and "haul[ing] bottom away" (47).

In another important scene, McKay directs our attention to the ways

in which economic pressures imposed by urban living tempt the op-
pressed to exploit those even further down on the socioeconomic ladder.
Upon realizing that many more of his friends have been beaten at the
work site, Jake asks his buddy, Zeddy, who arranged for the jobs, why he
told no one that they would be strikebreakers. Zeddy responds: " 'What
was I going to let on about anything for? The boss-man done paid me to
git him mens, and I got them. Ain't I working there mahself? I'll take
any job in this heah Gawd's country that the white boss make worf mah
while to work at' " (48). When Jake objects that " 'it ain't decent to scab,' "
Zeddy thunders forth that decency is not the issue when racism is the
question:

> "I'll scab through hell to make mah living. Scab job or open shop or
> union am all the same jobs to me. White mens don't want niggers in
> them unions, nohow. Ain't you a good carpenter? And ain't I a good
> blacksmith? But kain we get a look-in on our trade heah in this white
> man's city? Ain't white mens done scabbed niggers outa all the jobs
> they useter hold down heah in this city? . . . One thing I know is nig-
> gers am made foh life. And I want to live, boh, and feel plenty o' the
> juice o' life in mah blood. I wanta live and I wanta love. And niggers
> am got to work hard for that. Buddy, I'll tell you this and I'll tell it to
> the wo'l'—all the crackers, all them poah white trash, all the nigger-
> hitting and nigger-breaking white folks—I loves life and I got to live
> and I'll scab through hell to live." (48–49)

Both Jake and Zeddy recognize that the racism of the unions holds them
back from regular employment and thus forces them to scab if they want
to earn a living. While Zeddy does indeed earn some money by scabbing,
however, his income is soon outpaced by his debt to a Harlem money-
lender: thus, *zed* finishes last literally, financially, and ethically in McKay's
tale. On the other hand, Jake realizes that his complicity with the white
bosses for the sake of short-term wealth will only lead to more trouble between black and white workers in the long run, and finds it simply against
his "socialistic" moral code to scab on a fellow worker.[15]

Jake's diplomacy is intimately linked to a more general form of humanitarian ethics advocated by McKay through his depictions of both
protagonists in *Home to Harlem*. Jake and Ray continually work to dismantle the other's misperceptions, as well as those of their peers. At one
point, for example, McKay describes Ray's attempts to dispel Jake's prejudices about lesbians as "bulldykers" and "all ugly womens" (129). McKay
also writes of Ray's efforts to combat intraracial discrimination through
the character's support of an African American physician who "was struggling to overcome the prejudice of the black populace against Negro doc-
tors" (219). In another instance, McKay depicts Ray as refuting Jake's

charge that he must hate "waiting on them ofays" in the railroad car by stating that, "it isn't so bad. Most of them are pretty nice" (138). Throughout the novel, McKay creates Ray as a model who privileges the uniqueness of each individual over all else. Similarly, he describes Jake as comparably equanimous, if also less intellectual about his actions, as he mixes freely with people of all creeds and colors in the cabarets—places which McKay significantly described as "free-zones" in a racist country, as those "strange un-American world[s] where colored meets and mingles freely and naturally with white" (106). Being well aware of the prejudices of African Americans against "foreign" blacks during the period, McKay captures this hostility in Jake whom he describes as "very American in spirit" and thus "shar[ing] a little of that comfortable Yankee contempt for poor foreigners. As an American Negro he looked askew at foreign niggers. Africa was jungle, and Africans bush niggers, cannibals. And West Indians were monkey-chasers." But McKay also invests Jake with the ability, after meeting Ray and learning about the achievements of blacks from all nations, to appreciate the complexity of the world around him: he stood "like a boy . . . with the map of the world in colors before him, and [felt] the wonder of [that] world" (134). When Zeddy pulls a knife on a man, Jake convinces his friend not to commit murder, and thereby saves the life of the victim as well as "save[s] [his buddy] from Sing Sing" (53). After witnessing a battle over money in a gambling house, Jake befriends the stunned and beaten victim by offering him cabfare, buying him a drink, and escorting him home (73). When all Jake's mates on the railroad launch a steady war against the chef, Jake, although he "found himself on the side of the waiters," could "not hate the chef ([he] could not hate anybody)." Rather, McKay characterizes him as standing quietly "in his corner in the coffin, doing his bit in diplomatic silence" (163). As many critics have acknowledged, McKay does align Ray and Jake along loose lines of "reason" and "instinct," but these traits are not set in opposition to one another, as is so frequently assumed. Rather, McKay capitalizes upon the radically different backgrounds and educations of each of these characters to illustrate that a personal philosophy that promotes cooperation rather than division is not dependent upon schooling, "cultivation," or social status.

Despite the humanitarianism to which Jake and Ray aspire, however, McKay does not intend for *Home to Harlem* to portray a world where racial antagonisms are irrelevant or easily overcome. Indeed, neither Ray nor Jake denies the pervasive racism they encounter daily, nor do they dismiss the formidable barriers it creates in their own lives. Throughout the novel, McKay uses Ray, often through the discursive strategy of a form of free indirect thought, as in the passage below, to condemn the global oppression of blacks by what he views as the forces of white "civilization":

> What a unique feeling of confidence about life the typical white youth of his age must have! Knowing that his skin-color was a passport to glory, making him one with ten thousands like himself. All perfect Occidentals and investors in that grand business called civilization. That grand business in whose pits sweated and snored . . . all the black and brown hybrids and mongrels, simple earth-loving animals, without aspirations toward national unity and racial arrogance. (154–55)

In this passage, "civilization" is depicted as the sum of racism, capitalism, and ethnocentrism. Through Ray, who resents the expectation that he "have and love a race"—who believes instead that "races and nations" are "things like skunks, whose smells poisoned the air of life"—McKay expresses disdain for the grouping and systematic abuse of people according to any monolithic category (153–54). Like many writers, black and white alike, during the period who evoked a return to the "primitive" as an antidote to the increasing mechanization and alienation of the modern world, McKay suggests in all three of his novels—and particularly in *Banana Bottom*, as will be discussed later in this chapter—that the solution to the ills of modernity can only be found within the "primitive vitality" and "simple unswaggering strengths of the Jakes of the Negro race."[16]

What we might call an "ethics of inclusion" in *Home to Harlem* does not, however, apply to women. Indeed, throughout this decidedly homosocial novel, women are generally portrayed as irrational beasts or as one of the halves of the virgin/vamp dualism. Consider Lavinia Curdy, whom McKay describes as "a putty-skinned mulatress with purple streaks on her face," for example: "two of her upper front teeth had been knocked out and her lower lip slanted pathetically leftward. She was skinny and when she laughed she resembled an old braying jenny" (60). In another scene Curdy, whose name itself seems intended to repulse, is portrayed with another female character, "Gin-head Susy," as lions circling in on prey:

> Gin went round . . . and round . . . and round . . . Desultory dancing. . . . Dice. . . . Blackjack. . . . Poker. . . . The room became a close, live, intense place. Tight-faced, the men seemed interested only in drinking and gaming, while Susy and Miss Curdy, guzzling hard, grew uglier. A jungle atmosphere pervaded the room, and, like shameless wild animals hungry for raw meat, the females savagely searched the eyes of the males. (68)

Repeatedly McKay describes women as passion-driven, untamable animals willing to fight to the death over men. Early on in *Home to Harlem*, he depicts another "putty-skinned mulattress" charging a cabaret singer during her performance, knocking her down, stamping on her ribs, and spitting in her face over a supposed affair with their apparently mutual lover (33). Later, two "monkey-chasing" women are portrayed as "boxing" each other "up ovah a dutty-black 'Merican coon" in the midst of a crowd of bemused onlookers (97). Most absurdly, McKay renders two more "West Indian" women engaging in naked wrestling and head-butting before an entire apartment house of viewers (306–10). This reduction of women in the novel to beasts is not even escaped by *Home to Harlem*'s one "virgin," Agatha, the upstanding, educated lover of Ray, to whom McKay assigns the role of sow when describing Ray as likening the prospect of raising children with Agatha to that of "litter[ing] little black piggies" (263).[17]

Clearly, despite the general humanitarian code that McKay ascribes to Jake and Ray, some of the author's most powerful biases converge in his depictions of women. Importantly, all of the women in the above passages are either mulattoes or "West Indians."[18] According to McKay scholar Jean Wagner, as well as to the recollections of McKay's friend, Ellen Tarry, McKay detested mulattoes. Wagner claims that McKay believed that "moral degradation" was "the price [mulattoes should] pay for denying their black ancestry," and that their "lack of racial pride placed them . . . irredeemably beyond the pale."[19] McKay's depiction of mulattoes in other works bears further investigation. In his poem "Mulatto," for example, McKay follows a plot line running from Charles Chesnutt's short story, "The Sheriff's Children" to Langston Hughes's several meditations on the same theme when he describes an enraged child seeking murderous vengeance upon his white father.[20] In McKay's own short story, "Near-White" (contained in *Gingertown* [1932]), he depicts, perhaps significantly in light of the foregoing discussion, a female mulatto who attempts to pass, but is rejected by her unsuspecting white lover with the explanation that he would sooner love "a toad" than a person of mixed blood. Finally, another of McKay's short stories, "The Mulatto Girl" (originally published in Russia in 1925), again focuses on relationships between white men and mulatto women, and again it depicts social ostracism directed against the mulatto woman as the inevitable result of her "tainted" blood. Moreover, McKay's depictions of Caribbean women as barbaric beasts from the islands conform frighteningly to standard 1920s stereotypes of Caribbeaners and African Americans alike as bestial and/or comical "coons." On one hand, McKay's prejudices, at least as they seem to be reflected in the scenes cited above, add weight to the argument outlined earlier that he, to some degree, internalized the stereotypes with which he was confronted daily and suggest that, while physically fleeing the colonial forces of Jamaica and the United States, he was perhaps less successful at escaping colonial mentalities.

On the other hand, it is important to note that McKay's relegation of women to the status of animals in *Home to Harlem* as a means of establishing male authority is neither unusual during the period nor terribly surprising: it reflects the common "dissociative" practice of defining one's "other" as the antithesis of oneself. McKay's women are not simply the opposite of men but the antithesis of *hu*man. While this form of misogyny is not difficult to discern in the novel, more interesting is McKay's investment of female sexuality, particularly in the space of the city, with the capacity to render men irrational and to corrupt their ethics. Throughout the novel, McKay presents women as using their sexuality to control situations to their own advantage:

> a woman could always go farther than a man in coarseness, depravity, and sheer cupidity. Men were ugly and brutal. But beside women they were merely vicious children. Ignorant about the aim and meaning and fulfillment of life; uncertain and indeterminate; weak. Rude children who loved excelling in spectacular acts to win the applause of women. . . . *They* were the real controlling force of life. . . . Men fought, hurt, wounded, killed each other. Women, like blazing torches, egged them on or denounced them. Victims of sex, the men seemed foolish, ape-like blunderers in their pools of blood.[21] (70)

The demonization of women that pervades *Home to Harlem* reflects the widespread conception during the twenties—graphically depicted, for example, in the character of "Maria" in Fritz Lang's film "Metropolis" (1927)—of women's sexuality, and especially urban women's sexuality, as representing a pervasive threat to male authority. The vamp who wrought the complete destruction of "Metropolis" parallels McKay's Harlem women in that both come to represent the alluring, intimidating, humiliating qualities of the urban landscape itself, qualities which seek to divide "good" men from each other. As will be discussed later, this portrayal is particularly noteworthy because of the shift in the depiction of women that occurs in McKay's two subsequent novels, one set in the liminal space of the international beachfront and the other in a rural Jamaican village.

Far from writing *Home to Harlem* simply to cash in on the voguish appetite for Harlem primitivism, then, McKay set forth in his first novel a thoughtful critique of post-war urban life generally, and of the sociocultural climate of Harlem more specifically. Through the dual mouthpieces of Jake and Ray, he explores the possibilities Harlem offers as a "city of refuge" (to borrow the title of Rudolph Fisher's 1925 short story) for black urban vagabonds and deracinated intellectuals. In both cases Harlem is paradoxically both a land of opportunity and a land of limitation. The glorification of Harlem life that McKay presents through Jake's hedonism is undermined by Ray's resentment toward the restrictions that an essentially segregated city poses, especially for blacks who, by virtue of national, ethnic, or political affiliation, do not envision themselves as part of a community formed on the basis of race alone. Not surprisingly, at the novel's close Ray is left to "wander and wonder" in a seemingly perpetual condition of existential distress while Jake moves on to Chicago to explore his next temporary resting place. For neither of these characters, as for McKay himself, did Harlem prove to be "home."

To emphasize the political aspects of *Home to Harlem*, however, is not to deny its artistic innovation: indeed, McKay's first novel marks the earliest stages of his efforts to experiment aesthetically with the parameters of modernist fiction. While the content of the novel obviously explores to some degree the sense of post-war malaise and quest for meaning common to modernist writing, the form of the text also bears some of the signal traits of modernist literary technique. McKay mimics jazz structure by organizing the novel episodically through a series of non-linear chapters that actually embody the non-linear, and necessarily improvisational, patterns of his fictional vagabonds. In so doing, he challenges traditional conceptions of character and plot. Following Ezra Pound's dictum to "make it new," McKay employs the traditional picaresque to glorify an unprecedented hero, the African American urban drifter, and—as he did in his sonnets—thus transforms a traditionally "white" form into a distinctly "black" literary achievement. Finally, describing himself as wishing to do "in prose for Harlem . . . what I had done for Jamaica in verse," McKay attempts to "recapture the spirit" of African American urban drifters through the use of colloquialisms and slang, thereby exalting African American vernacular as a mode of literary discourse and reinvesting it with an authority that had been stripped from it by white Plantation School authors.[22] McKay develops these strategies and motifs on an international scale in his second novel, *Banjo*.

Banjo

Banjo: A Story Without a Plot (1929) is so similar in structure and style to *Home to Harlem* that it might profitably be considered the sequel to—or even a rewriting of—McKay's first attempt at fiction. Through a series of episodic chapters, *Banjo* recounts the escapades of an African American drifter, Lincoln Agrippa Daily—familiarly known as Banjo—and his crew of friends, among whom is Ray, the Caribbean intellectual first introduced in *Home to Harlem*. Again these two characters embody complementary, if also contrasting, impulses toward life; again, through these figures McKay explores art, politics, and the relationship between the two. But *Banjo* is importantly distinguished from *Home to Harlem* by its setting. While the brilliance of McKay's first novel is, in part, as Carolyn Cooper has stated, "a function of its cultural hybridity—its attempt to interrogate both 'blackness' and the meaning of 'home' in the riotous meeting of ethnically diverse African cultures in Harlem," *Banjo* is set in an even more culturally hybridized space—the international port of Marseilles.[23] This change in geography enables McKay to shift his focus from American forms of racism, the corrupting potential of urban life, and the feasibility of New York City to provide a "home" for blacks during a period of cultural flux, to more global issues including jingoism, the liberating potential of the waterfront as a new frontier (as opposed to the confinement of the city), and the possibility for diasporic allegiances among blacks. Thus, *Banjo* provides McKay the opportunity to explore, express, and extend the discussion of his political convictions in a worldwide context.

Located on the edge of the Mediterranean, Marseilles represents the world's door as it symbolically creates passage between what McKay defines as the realms of European "civilization" and African "primitivism." "All shades of Negroes came together there," McKay writes. "All the British West African blacks, Portuguese blacks, American blacks, all who had drifted into this port that the world goes through."[24] Through *Banjo*'s cast of itinerant black seamen hailing from Africa, the Caribbean, and the United States, McKay uses multiple mouthpieces to offer a layered critique of chauvinistic nationalism based on his own experience as a migrant. Indeed, he describes himself in *A Long Way from Home* (1937) as having been born in Jamaica, as having lived in the United States, and as existing as a British subject on paper—but as "prefer[ring] to think of [him]self as an internationalist." When pushed for a more precise definition of that term, he laughingly responded that "an internationalist is a bad nationalist," so it is not surprising that nationalism in all its manifestations is the central issue receiving harsh scrutiny by the characters in McKay's second novel.[25]

Banjo opens with the introduction of the protagonist, Lincoln Agrippa Daily—who, as his name implies, "seizes each day" as it comes. Both the character's given name and his nickname, Banjo, are significant, however: Lincoln calls to mind the American popularly deemed as responsible for the emancipation of the slaves, while the banjo, a classic African American folk instrument, visually marks the character's designation as the prototypical American in the group. Through Banjo, McKay presents and critiques American culture, values, and politics. Acting as supporting cast are a variety of characters from all over the globe. All are career vaga-

bonds with no real home. Malty, Ginger, and Bugsy are Caribbeaners who, not unlike McKay, left the islands early in life and have not returned since. Dengel is Senegalese; Goosey is a self-proclaimed American "race man"; Taloufa is a Nigerian-born, London-bred Garveyite; and Ray reappears as the unmoored Haitian artist. In addition to these male characters there is Latnah, an Indo-African woman whose depiction, as will be discussed later in the chapter, marks an important departure from McKay's portrayal of female characters in *Home to Harlem*.

> They were all on the beach, and there were many others besides them—white men, brown men, black men. Finns, Poles, Italians, Slavs, Maltese, Indians, Negroids, African Negroes, West Indian Negroes—deportées from America for violation of the United States immigration laws—afraid and ashamed to go back to their own lands, all dumped down in the great Provençal port, bumming a day's work, a meal, a drink, existing from hand to mouth, anyhow any way, between box car, tramp, ship, bistro, and bordel." (6)

Through these characters and their interaction, McKay expresses his views on subjects ranging from America's black bourgeoisie to British imperialism, frequently employing a specific character or chapter in *Banjo* to probe a single issue.

Goosey, for example, becomes the center of several discussions involving black leadership strategies in the United States. A northern-educated, French-speaking mulatto, Goosey is a firm believer in W. E. B. Du Bois' theory of the "talented tenth," which proposed that the top 10 percent of the African American community should be responsible for the "uplifting" of the lower classes. As McKay's appellation of the character suggests, "Goosey" accepts uncritically the philosophies of the northern "Negro intelligentsia" led by Du Bois, and is used by McKay to critique the ideas of the prominent African American leader. McKay disagreed with Du Bois on a number of issues, but the two debated most strongly about the role that art should play in programs of racial advancement.[26] As Du Bois argued in his 1926 essay, "Criteria of Negro Art," he believed that black writers were obligated, as part of the battle to end segregation and discrimination, to depict images of the black community rooted in "truth" and "goodness," and that these portrayals should revolve primarily around educated "race men and women" who were leaders in business, cultural, or political arenas. According to Du Bois, "Thus all art is propaganda and ever must be, . . . I stand in utter shamelessness and say that whatever art I have for writing has been used always for propaganda for gaining the right of black folk to love and enjoy. I do not care a damn for any art that is not used for propaganda. But I do care when propaganda is confined to one side while the other is stripped and silent."[27]

McKay, implicitly in *Home to Harlem* and *Banjo* and more directly in his 1932 essay, "A Negro Writer to His Critics," challenged Du Bois by arguing that the lives of the common man and the "lowly things that go to the formation of the Aframerican soil" should be "artistically exploited," since it is the "real experience" of the black underclass that constitutes "the fundamental rhythm of Aframerican life." In fact, according to McKay, in this "the best, the most pretentious of Aframerican society still has its roots." To "write faithfully about the people [one] knows from real experience and impartial observation," McKay argues, to heed the calls of one's own "esthetic values" and "artistic conscientiousness," is the mandate of any writer.[28]

Despite McKay's strong resistance to and even resentment toward the idea that art should be used for "propagandistic" ends, however, *Banjo* consists almost solely of the loosely-fictionalized articulation of its author's political beliefs. For example, McKay goes so far as to continue his own argument with Du Bois in fiction through a debate between Goosey and Ray concerning the very issue of censoring black life and art for white eyes. When Goosey questions Ray's intentions to "write about how these race boys live in the Ditch here and publish it" because he fears that "the crackers will use what [he] write[s] against the race," Ray's response, paralleling strongly the oft-quoted passage by Langston Hughes in his 1926 essay, "The Negro Artist and the Racial Mountain," clearly expresses McKay's own well-known beliefs:[29]

> Let the crackers go fiddle themselves, and you, too. I think about my race as much as you. I hate to see it kicked around and spat on by the whites, because it is a good earth-loving race. I'll fight with it if there's a fight on, but if I am writing a story—well, it's like all of us in this place here, black and brown and white, and I telling a story for the love of it. Some of you will listen, and some won't. If I am a real story-teller, I won't worry about the difference in complexion of those who listen and those who don't, I'll just identify myself with those who are really listening and tell my story. (115)

Throughout the text, McKay reinforces his belief that "the best Negroes are *not* the society Negroes." Using Ray as his spokesperson, he protests that "I am not writing for them, nor" (almost forecasting the famous diner scene in Ralph Ellison's *Invisible Man*) "the poke-chop-abstaining Negroes, nor the Puritan Friends of Color, nor the Negrophobes nor the Negrophiles. I am writing for people who can stand a real story no matter where it comes from" (117). In a 1926 letter to Hughes, McKay urged his fellow writer not to "be bothered about the whims and prejudices of the Negro intelligentsia. They are death to any would be Negro artist. A plague on them and however hard hit and down I am they won't get their claws on me."[30] In his creation of Banjo, his version of the prototypical African American folk protagonist, McKay ardently asserts that to deny the existence of the folk—in art or in reality—is to deny a crucial element of oneself. Most importantly, it is to exhibit the same kind of chauvinism that Du Bois so ardently fought against. In the end, the text of *Banjo* embodies its author's own "propagandistic" position on the depiction of African Americans in art specifically, and on the use of "words as weapons" (to anticipate Richard Wright's revelation in *Black Boy* [1945]) more generally.

This type of political/cultural commentary pervades the novel. Through Goosey's shipmate, the Nigerian Taloufa, McKay critiques the theories of Marcus Garvey, the Jamaican immigrant and popular leader during the teens and twenties who promoted a highly nationalist program of racial improvement most popularly known by its sentiment and slogan, "back to Africa" for people of African descent.[31] Taloufa firmly believes the fictionalized Garvey's pronouncement that "colored people scattered all over the world should come together" and return to their native land (91). Taloufa's complicated history of national affiliation sheds light on the possible motivations for his commitment to a Garvey-like cause. McKay writes that Taloufa "came from the Nigerian bush" and attended a mission school until the age of thirteen, when he was taken to England by a minor British official to serve as his "boy" (101). Taloufa served this "master" for three years until he finally "got tired of it, full fed up of seeing white faces only," and ran away to Cardiff, "where he found more contentment among the hundreds of colored seamen who live in that port" (101). Later, he moved to America, where he remained until "the passing of the new quota immigration laws" caused his deportation.[32] While in the United States, Taloufa joined Garvey's crusade as a "faithful believer" in "the great dream" intended "to link Negroes of the New World with those of Africa" (101). Nigerian natally, British colonially, black racially, and pan-African politically, Taloufa is a colonial subject who was removed from his predominantly black birthplace to a "white" "new world." Having lived the majority of his life in the ideologically Western cultures of England and the United States, Taloufa is portrayed by McKay as possessing a complex desire to blend his African heritage with his Occidental upbringing. Marcus Garvey's professed goal to reunite the African diaspora in its original homeland, however ill-fated, thus provides Taloufa with a seemingly perfect solution for the reconciliation of his own disjointed self.

But McKay himself was not an uncritical proponent of Garveyism in his life or his fiction, and he uses Taloufa's story to assess Garvey and his movement. Recognizing the importance of Garvey's appeals for racial pride, greater self-sufficiency, and group unity, McKay initially supported Garvey's United Negro Improvement Association and published in its international newspaper, the *Negro World*.[33] At that point in his career, McKay believed that nationalist liberation movements in colonial regions could open the door for the spread of Communist ideals and would thus promote the eradication of colonial systems worldwide. In his 1922 article titled "Garvey as a Negro Moses," McKay credits Garvey, albeit somewhat facetiously, with being the "universal advertising manager" and "biggest popularizer of the Negro problem" worldwide.[34] As Taloufa maintains in *Banjo*, "the Back-to-Africa propaganda had worked wonders among the African natives." Taloufa tells Ray "that all throughout West Africa the natives were meeting to discuss their future, and in the ports they were no longer docile, but restive, forming groups, and waiting for the Black Deliverer, so that, becoming aroused, the colonial governments had acted to keep out all propaganda, especially the *Negro World*, the chief organ of the Back to Africa movement" (102). As Garvey became increasingly monarchical, however, McKay dissociated himself from the U.N.I.A. and by 1922 had withdrawn all support.[35] As McKay makes clear in *Banjo*, while he believes that Garvey importantly stimulated a sense of racial cohesion and rebellion among certain segments of the African and African American populations, he also believes that Garvey exploited his followers by collecting their contributions and then squandering the money in risky and even deceptive business ventures like the Black Star Line, the shipping firm Garvey attempted to establish in order to transport blacks "back to Africa." Thus, while McKay lauds Garvey's promotion of black empowerment, he condemns the leader's greed which resulted in his own destruction as well as that of the financial savings and hopes of many black Americans and Jamaicans. In the end, Garvey's "stupendous vaudeville," according to McKay, succeeded only in reducing the "Negro problem" to the level of "Negro minstrelsy" and in betraying the very "folk" on whom McKay believes the future of the race rested.[36]

The critique initiated in McKay's assessment of Garvey's failings extends to groups and institutions far more powerful than the lone black nationalist. Indeed, chapter eleven of *Banjo*, significantly titled "Everybody Doing It," condemns the role that nearly all Western countries, and England and the United States in particular, play in the economic exploitation of less powerful nations. The chapter opens with multiple symbols of capitalism, the most prominent being an enormous "Dollar Line boat, and a British ship from the Far East," both loaded with wealthy tourists (133). A "brazen white dollar sign" emblazoned high on the boat's funnel signals haughtily to all that the United States has arrived (152). Representing the powerlessness of those whom the dollar overruns in the name of "improvement" or "development" are the gigolos and prostitutes who offer the disembarking passengers tours of the city or tours of themselves, all for negotiable fees. Commenting on his "motherland's" colonial hunger, McKay captures post-war French hostility toward the English by describing an incident where an "Englishwoman and her escort were nearly lynched" because she "tried to push her way too hastily through the crowd *while talking English*" (McKay's emphasis, 135). He describes the local papers as blaming the crowd's violence on "the post-war policy of the Anglo-Saxons . . . [that] treat[ed] France as if she were a colony" (135). The franc was falling while the pound and dollar were on the rise, and tourists from England and the U.S. flocked to the land of *egalité*, *fraternité*, and *liberté* to take advantage of economic misfortune.

Recalling his own self-designation as an "internationalist" (a.k.a. "a bad nationalist"), McKay casts Ray as an "internationalist" who is therefore, according to the author, a supposedly non-partisan observer of the unloading ship. Through him, McKay elaborates upon the critique of "civilization" begun in *Home to Harlem* by illustrating in more depth what he perceives to be the links between patriotism, capitalism, and racism. According to McKay, Ray is uniquely positioned to present this relationship because, as "a wandering black without patriotic or family ties," Ray cannot embrace "the sentiment of patriotism." As a British colonial, McKay writes, Ray "was a child of deracinated ancestry" for whom patriotism "was a poisonous seed that had, of course, been planted in his child's mind, but happily, not having any traditional soil to nourish it, it had died out with other weeds" of his colonial education. Through Ray, McKay argues that capitalism all too regularly leads to exploitation, and that exploitation in many instances bursts national geographic boundaries to result in colonization. Among both colonizers and many colonized rises a spirit of "patriotism," but it is a spirit based on the presumption of the superiority of one group or way of life over another, rather than on a sincere love of the ideals represented by any given country: "a patriot," we learn from Ray, "loves not his nation, but the spiritual meannesses of his life of which he had created a frontier wall to hide the beauty of other horizons" (137).

More specifically, McKay uses *Banjo* to suggest that capitalism, particularly as practiced by "Brutish America" and the "You-whited Snakes," is steadfastly bound to racism. In chapter fifteen, for example, the group of vagabonds are unable to enjoy themselves in a number of different bars due to the "White Terror"—the temporary presence of shiploads of white sailors from England and the United States. After being made sufficiently uncomfortable as blacks in the British-American bar, the group goes on to another, where the headwaiter is Ray's friend. Here too, however, they are asked to leave, because "there had been [trouble] before when there were colored men in the bar and English and American customers—especially Americans. Once [the] bar had been ordered closed for six months because of a colored–white incident" (193). Throughout *Banjo*, McKay laments the connection between

> Prejudice and business. In Europe, Asia, Australia, Africa, America, those were the two united terrors confronting the colored man. He was the butt of the white man's indecent public prejudices. Prejudices insensate and petty, bloody, vicious, vile, brutal, *raffiné*, hypocritical, Christian. Prejudices. Prejudices like the stock market—curtailed, diminishing, increasing, changing chameleon-like, according to place and time, like the color of the white man's soul, controlled by the exigencies of the white man's business. (193)

McKay firmly establishes the association of racism and capitalism in *Banjo*, and prophesies that as "long as the pound is lord and the dollar is king" the white man will exalt "business above humanity" (194).

But the United States and England are not designated as the sole proponents of exploitation in *Banjo*. Locating the novel in France affords McKay the opportunity to extend his analysis to the French, whom he depicts throughout the novel as proudly and constantly touting the virtues of French liberalism.[37] McKay claims that "the average Frenchman . . . takes it without question that a black man under French civilization is better off than he would be under any other social order in the world" (135–36). "'We will treat you right over here!'" the French say to Ray. "'It's not like America'" (136). But McKay exposes the hypocrisy of this liberalism by depicting the French in the novel as repeatedly discriminating against blacks. At one point, for example, Ray is assaulted and jailed overnight for no reason other than, according to the inspector, "all the Negroes in Marseilles [are] criminals." McKay implies that racism is virtually a cultural universal among Western nations. When a French student charges that Ray does not "appreciate the benefits of French civilization," that he does not recognize that France is "especially tolerant to colored people," and that, as "the most civilized nation in the world" France "treat[s] [blacks] better than the Anglo-Saxon nations," Ray responds:

> You use the same language that a hundred-per-cent American would use to me, with a little difference in words and emphasis, . . . Let me say that for me there is no such animal as a civilized nation. I believe there are a few decent minds in every nation, more or less, yet I wouldn't put them all through the test of Sodom and Gomorrah to find out. It's better to believe! You're right when you say you're more tolerant toward colored people in your country than the Anglo-Saxons in theirs. But

from what I have seen of the attitude of this town toward Negroes and Arabs, I don't know how it would be if you Europeans had a large colored population to handle in Europe. I hope to God you won't ever have to face that. (274–75)

Shifting from the more romantic and almost dream-like musings expressed by the character of Ray in *Home to Harlem*, McKay argues more directly in this novel that European racism, even if expressed less blatantly in the form of "an unveiled condescension," is nevertheless a "gall to a Negro who wanted to live his life free of the demoralizing effect of being pitied and patronized." McKay believes that throughout Europe and in France in particular, "like anywhere, . . . one black villain made all black villains as one black tout made all black touts, one black nigger made all black niggers, and one black failure made all black failures. . . . Exceptions were not considered" (275).

As defense against these incessant assaults, however, McKay fortifies his characters with that "primitive vitality" he perceives as being unique to blacks. Although discussions of "primitivism" permeate the text, McKay is characteristically vague when it comes to offering a more specific definition of the concept. The "primitive" in this text is clearly intimately linked to "instinct," and the "instinctive gifts" of black folks, according to McKay, are not quite the song, story, sweat, and spirit identified by Du Bois in *Souls of Black Folk*, but rather "laughter and melody and simple sensuous feelings and responses" (323). These qualities, McKay posits, grant their bearers a great "potential power for racial salvation"; indeed, Ray is described as being gifted with a "primitive sense of comparative values" and an "instinct" that allow him "to see through superficial appearances to the strange and profound variations of human life" (323, 276). As in *Home to Harlem*, McKay generally contrasts "primitivism" with "civilization" in *Banjo*, but given the international context of the tale, he broadens these themes to encompass oppositions between black and white, Eastern and Western, European and African. Ridiculing the pretension of morality maintained by all "civilized" peoples under the guises of Christianity, democracy, and liberalism, McKay describes Ray as "hating civilization because its general attitude toward the colored man was such as to rob him of his warm human instincts and make him inhuman" (163).

Banjo, too, is armed against civilization's atrocities not simply by his embodiment of the "irrepressible exuberance and legendary vitality of the black race" but also by his socialistic perception of his place in the world (324). He refuses, for example, to solicit money for playing his music because "he did not want to collect sous from a crowd of fellows just like himself" (46). He repeatedly shares his own food with other vagabonds or tells them where they can get some (61, 162, 186). Whenever he earns money, Banjo divides it among his buddies because "dividing up was a beach boys' rite. It didn't matter what share of the spoils the lucky beggar kept for himself, so long as he fortified the spirit of solidarity by sharing it with the gang" (158). Importantly, however, McKay describes Banjo's generosity as not dictated by race. On one occasion, after giving the boys some of his earnings and then buying them all dinner as well, Banjo, at the protest of some of his peers, also gives five francs to a poor and hungry white beggar (161–62). Demonstrating the "primitive" black's ability to resist the corrupting influence of "civilization," and echoing his own assertion that he chooses his friends based on the color of their minds and not on the color of their skin, McKay describes Banjo, like Jake in *Home to Harlem*, as unable to "see life in divisions of sharp primary colors. The colors were always getting him mixed up, shading off, fading out, running into one another so that it was difficult to perceive which was which" (170). "So much messy fuss" is made "about skin color," Banjo claims; "what's the difference!" (233).

As Banjo's comments suggest, McKay seeks to present in his second novel a type of international utopia in which chauvinisms of all sorts are rejected. In contrast to the dystopic aspects of the urban landscape in *Home to Harlem*, the panorama of the waterfront, opening to an expansive sea over which no nation can claim dominion, fosters a more harmonious relationship between the many characters that occupy this text. While each of the vagabonds serves as a mouthpiece through which to critique a specific political or cultural issue, and thus might be considered oppositional in this respect, as individual characters they rarely engage in serious conflict with one another (in comparison to interactions framed by the urban "pigpen of Harlem.") Indeed, within this utopian environment, even gender relations operate with more equanimity. While women in *Home to Harlem* were linked to the corrupting force of the city and seen as antagonists to men, the main female character in *Banjo*, Latnah—herself a multilingual and "international" melange of "Arabian" and "Persian" and "Indian"—is considered not simply equal to but a comrade of the men on the beach.

> Latnah was following precisely the same line of living as they. She came as a pal. She was made one of them. Whatever personal art she might use as a woman to increase her chance was her own affair. Their luck also depended primarily on personality. . . . It did not matter if Latnah was not inclined to be amorous with any of them. Perhaps it was better so. She was more useful to them as a pal. Love was cheap in the Ditch. . . . The boys were rather flattered that she stayed with them. . . . (32)

McKay describes Latnah as readily accepted by the beach boys who, "with their wide experience and passive philosophy of life," were "adept at meeting, understanding, and accepting everything" (31–32), but he also makes clear that she serves an important role in maintaining the group. She acquires food for the boys when they are hungry, cares for Banjo when he is injured, provides the men with "English and American cigarettes and a little change when she got 'em," and protects both them and herself in the face of danger, being willing in one instance, for example, to fend off an attacker with a dagger hidden in her clothing (10, 29–30). Because of her autonomy, Latnah serves as a stabilizing symbol; she remains a constant in the Ditch when the men move on at the novel's close, providing a welcoming base should they return.

McKay's depiction of Latnah warrants particular consideration because her very presence as a sustained female character contradicts the more general objectification of women that characterizes this, as well as McKay's previous, novel. When portraying "women" as a group or as objects of a male gaze in *Banjo*, McKay repeats the pattern first seen in *Home to Harlem*: nearly all of the female characters in *Banjo* make cameo appearances, remain unidentified, and are depicted as submissive, sexually needy, and generally pathetic. At one point McKay does attempt to parse out more specifically the ways in which women are commodified by the system of capitalism: both black and white women alike, he claims, "give themselves" to men because men "stand for power and property," and "property controls sex." But in the end, seemingly anticipating the implied conclusion of Zora Neale Hurston's "muck" scene in *Their Eyes Were Watching God* (1937) in which Teacake beats Janie, McKay leaves us with the essentialist conclusion that "it was just [a] woman's instinct to be under the protection of a man," for "woman is woman all over the world, no matter what her color is. She is cast in a passive role and she worships the active success of man and rewards it with her body" (206). McKay's actual presentation of Latnah as a specific individual contrasts markedly with these sweeping pronouncements about the general "nature" of women. In this novel intended to combat chauvinism, McKay's own artistic enterprise of creating a credible female character actually undermines the more general sexist assumptions into which he occasionally lapses. More importantly, McKay's depiction of Latnah's ability to contribute as an equal in his idealistic and "international" society, contrasting as it does with his negative association of women with urban America in *Home to Harlem*, suggests a belief that perhaps only in a non-nationalist, non-capitalist, utopian realm like the beach can individuals live by and be recognized for their merits. The alliance of McKay's characters against the outer world of "isms" in *Banjo*, however, is necessarily tenuous. In the end, structures built on the sand of a beach will eventually wash away, leaving the characters in *Banjo*—and McKay himself—to move on.

Banana Bottom

McKay's final novel, *Banana Bottom*, differs markedly from his first two works in a number of important respects. Whereas *Home to Harlem* and *Banjo* are innovative recastings of the picaresque narrative in their episodic structure, realistic tone, and satirical aim, *Banana Bottom* is modeled more along the lines of a classic romance. Whereas McKay first used dual and then multiple male mouthpieces through which to express his views in his first two books, his third novel pits a single protagonist against a single antagonist, both female, and substitutes political didacticism for plot development. Like conventional prose romances in which heroes and villains contrast dramatically, Bita Plant, the black Jamaican protagonist of *Banana Bottom*, is depicted in sharp literal and figurative contrast to Priscilla Craig, the white British antagonist. McKay's personification of colonialism in the character of Priscilla Craig allows him to stage a more direct conflict between hero and villain than in either of the two previous novels, where a variety of adversaries were represented by less tangible concepts like "civilization," "racism," or "imperialism." While the call of "primitive instincts" and the demands of "modern civilization" remain at odds in the first two novels, McKay attempts to reconcile them in *Banana Bottom* by orchestrating a literal marriage of the symbolic representatives of each force in the novel. Finally, while both *Home to Harlem* and *Banjo* are modernist fictions set in distinctly modern, post-war environs, *Banana Bottom* follows the typical romantic pattern of being set in the historical past—in this case, in a turn-of-the-century rural Jamaican village.

The more formulaic structure of McKay's final novel appears to signal a shift in his aesthetic agenda. The text's Jamaican setting—especially when McKay's fiction is considered within the context of his history of migrancy—seems to signal a metaphorical return to the land of his origin.[38] Wayne Cooper summarizes this view, held by numerous critics, when he argues that "with the creation of *Banana Bottom*, McKay's picaresque search for psychic unity and stability, begun with *Home to Harlem*, came full circle to rest again in the lost paradise of his pastoral childhood."[39] This interpretation is not unreasonable. Prior to writing *Banana Bottom*, McKay produced *Gingertown*, a collection of short stories that can be considered a transitional text between his first two and final novels in that it alternates in setting between urban geographies and rural Caribbean vistas. Additionally, the geographic context in which McKay wrote *Banana Bottom*—northern Africa—apparently stimulated his reflection upon and nostalgia for his youth. McKay writes in his autobiography that, upon arriving in Casablanca, "the first shock [he] registered was the realization that" the "Guinea sorcerers" whom he was observing "looked and acted exactly like certain peasants of Jamaica who give themselves up to the celebrating of a religious sing-dance orgy" (296). The detailed description of this scene which follows McKay's statement parallels directly a comparable religious exorcism in *Banana Bottom*. In another recollection in *A Long Way from Home*, McKay states that Marrakesh "was like a big West Indian picnic, with flags waving and a multitude of barefoot black children dancing to the flourish of drum, fiddle, and fife" (304). Finally, he claims that, while in Africa, he had "gravitated instinctively to the native element because physically and psychically I felt more affinity with it" (301).

While *Banana Bottom* does indeed, on the surface at least, seem to signal "the return of a native"—the return of McKay to his youth—a close reading of the novel shows that, in fact, it illustrates much more dramatically that one "can't go home again." Granted, the story is set in a village closely resembling Sunny Ville. Squire Gensir, who is described by McKay in an "Author's Note" as being the only character who is not wholly fictional, clearly represents McKay's close ally and mentor, Walter Jekyll. Malcolm Craig distinctly resembles William Hathaway, the first English missionary in Sunny Ville, whom McKay's father befriended and who became a close acquaintance of the family during McKay's youth. The peasant community is similar to that described in some of McKay's early poetry and in his memoir, *My Green Hills of Jamaica*. Finally, Bita Plant's struggle with the dualistic nature of her familial origins and educational influences parallels that experienced by McKay himself. But an analysis of the structure and content of *Banana Bottom* reveals just the opposite of a "return": rather than representing McKay's journey "home," his final novel reinforces just how distant from Jamaica he had become.

Banana Bottom tells the story of Bita Plant, a peasant child who is adopted by the local white missionaries, Malcolm and Priscilla Craig, and sent by them to England for a formal education. The catalyst for Bita's adoption is significant, for McKay's description of the event foreshadows the central conflict with which Bita will struggle throughout the novel: that of living her life according to the mandates of imperial or local worldviews. The cause of her adoption revolves around a sexual encounter she experienced in her early adolescence with the town's local musical savant, Crazy Bow Adair, which thus constitutes Bita's "fall from grace" and consequent need for "salvation" at the hands of missionaries.

Although McKay refers to this experience as a rape, his actual portrayal of the scene suggests his intention that Bita be perceived by readers as a willing participant in the event. He describes her not as attacked by Crazy Bow, but rather as captivated by the beauty of his Orphean music, and as consequently sharing in their mutual seduction through her own sexual overtures. Bita, as she and Crazy Bow played amidst the "caressing fox-tail" along the river, suddenly "got upon Crazy Bow's breast and began rubbing her head against his face."[40] McKay describes Crazy Bow as pushing her away and beginning to play his fiddle, selecting a "sweet tea-meeting love song. And as he played Bita went creeping upon her hands and feet up the slope to him and listened in the attitude of a bewitched being" (9–10). When he finished, McKay describes, Bita "clambered upon him again and began kissing his face. Crazy Bow tried to push her off. But Bita hugged and clung to him passionately. Crazy Bow was blinded by temptation and lost control of himself and the deed was done" (10).

McKay describes Bita's own involvement in the encounter to emphasize what he portrays as her "natural" tendency, as a "primitive" and "instinctive" peasant child, to express her sexuality openly (like the urban drifters of his previous novels)—free from the repressive forces of white "civilization." But the reactions of the community epitomize the cultural conflict that shape Bita's development. Sister Phibby Patroll, who acts as the sometimes accurate observer and sometimes "lying eyes" of the community (as her name suggests), expresses the peasants' perception of the event by considering the encounter simply as "a good thing done early." Missionary Priscilla Craig, on the other hand, who agreed with "her fellow workers in Christ" that the "natives" lacked "that check and control that was supposed to be distinguishing of humanity and of a higher and more complex social order," was filled "with high-class anxiety" and termed Bita's involvement with Crazy Bow as "abuse" (15, 16). In Pygmalion mode, Craig decides to redeem Bita by "taking [her to England] to train as an exhibit" in order to "demonstrate what one such girl might become" with a proper education and "God's help" (17). Bita returns to Jamaica after seven years in Europe and is expected to marry another of the Craigs' colonial "experiments," Harold Newton Day, and to lead the Church with him following the Craigs' deaths or departure from the island. The donnée of the novel focuses on Bita's efforts to comply with the expectations of her Western education while also embracing her origins in the Jamaican peasantry.

The peasants of *Banana Bottom* fall into two categories: the lower class, who are most frequently described with deprecating jocularity; and the upper class, who are portrayed idyllically. Sister Phibby Patroll,

Hopping Dick, Tack Tally, and Yoni Legge represent the lower strata of the peasant social structure in the novel. While the romance genre of *Banana Bottom* allows McKay to display a sense of humor that is less apparent in his more pedantic prose, his representation of these characters goes beyond humor to border on ridicule. Taking a swipe at both "peasant" sexual mores and fundamentalist religion, McKay depicts Hopping Dick, the local dandy who first playfully seduces the higher-classed Bita and then shockingly recants his love for her, as next impregnating "Sister-in-Christ" Yoni Legge under the influence of a Revival Meeting (270–72). Tack Tally, a village legend who returned with riches from his work on the Panama Canal, is stripped of his avowed bravery when he is driven to suicide by his fears of the power of Wumba, the Obeah man. The rather risqué Yoni, whose name recalls a Hindu term for female genitalia, is described as being so preoccupied with her passion for various men that she cannot maintain control of her own life.[41] The "village looselip," Sister Phibby Patroll, is portrayed as obsessively invested in monitoring the activities of all. Granted, McKay uses these figures and incidents to chide organized religion, superstition, and community policing of behavior, but his depiction, characterized by marked comic derision, somewhat startlingly echoes the attitude of the tourist denounced in his own dialect poem twenty years earlier, "Fetchin' Water," who views the "natives" as quaint objects existing primarily for the entertainment of outsiders.

McKay takes this clownish image of peasants to an extreme in his description of Bita's intended, the Reverend-in-training, Harold Newton Day. McKay uses Day as the vehicle through which to expose the hypocrisy of religion, and of missionary religion in particular. While McKay had addressed the issue previously in *Banjo* by conveying through Ray his belief that "the morality of the Christians" is loathsome because it is "false, treacherous, and hypocritical," he posits Day as the fictional personification of these limitations.[42] Day's name facetiously mocks his self-perception as one who will "herald a new day" for islanders by bringing them the white man's Christianity. McKay castigates not only this character who uncritically parrots the teachings of his colonizers from the pulpit, but also Day's followers, the island's "colored elite" (represented in the novel by the Lambert sisters) who perpetuate, through their governmental or religious affiliations, a system intended to repress local inhabitants and indigenous island cultures. By portraying Day monodimensionally, however, McKay denies the character's validity as a serious contender for Bita's affections, and indeed, calls into question his plausibility altogether. In the most artificial event in the tale, the *deus ex machina* seemingly created by McKay to rid Bita (and the author himself perhaps) of Day's presence in order to propel the plot, McKay describes him—wholly unexpectedly—as fornicating with a goat just prior to his marriage, and thus conveniently putting an end to the betrothal (175). The turn of events is so totally out of context given the characterization of Day to this point in the novel that we are led to see it more as a flaw in literary construction than as a realistic or even capricious turn of fictional events. McKay's attempt at humor in this instance, as it is underscored by his own blatant hostility toward missionaries, undermines the credibility not just of Day as a character, but of the author himself as a trustworthy storyteller.

If McKay's descriptions of lower class peasants often seem comical and condescending, his portrayal of Bita and the Plants, members of the upper echelons of the peasant group, seems improbably idealistic. In general, the Plants are imbued with a purity that contrasts startlingly with the alleged wanton sexuality of the lower class peasants. Much like McKay's descriptions of his own parents in *My Green Hills of Jamaica*, Jordan Plant is described as a kind but rigid planter who leads the community by his example of clean living while Bita's foster mother, Anty Nommy (who is notably antinomian in her welcome embrace of all members of the community), serves as the paragon of maternal devotion and integrity for the village.[43] But their striking difference from the other locals thwarts our belief in the authenticity of either group's characterization. McKay struggles with cultural dualism throughout *Banana Bottom*, but in this instance, the challenge he seeks to mount against social constructions of "propriety" and "impropriety," of "upper" and "lower" class, is frustrated by the holes in his literary technique.

The single greatest obstacle to a reading of *Banana Bottom* as a figurative and honorific return by the migrant to his own "imaginary homeland" (to use Salman Rushdie's term in a different context), however, involves his portrayal of the character in the text with whom he might most closely identify: Bita herself. As her name suggests, Bita is intended to represent a small bit of an agrarian ideal who is transplanted into foreign soil but must return to her home in order to flourish fully. McKay first introduces us to Bita in her role as the prodigal daughter:

> Bita's homecoming was an eventful week for the folk of the tiny country town of Jubilee and the mountain village of Banana Bottom. For she was the only native Negro girl they had ever known or heard of who had been brought up abroad. Perhaps the only one in the island. Educated in England—the mother country as it was referred to by the Press and official persons.
> Bita had had some seven years of polite upbringing. And she had never had any contact with her home and her own folk during those

years. And now she was a real young lady wearing a long princess gown and her hair fixed up in style. (1)

McKay's account of Bita's arrival is intended to expose, on one level, colonial bias toward anything British. Bita is emulated by the islanders because of her differences from them, because of her "polite upbringing," her "princess gown" and her "hair fixed up in style." While the peasants admire the Anglicized aspects of Bita's appearance, however, McKay also captures Bita's homesickness for the culture of the folk. Just as the speaker of his poignant poem, "The Tropics in New York," written shortly after McKay's migration to the United States, longs for the glories of the market filled with men and women bartering over "cocoanut drop, banana fritters, ginger nut, . . . congo peas, yams and yampies, breadfruit and the unrefined sugar cane that lay caked rich brown and sweet in upright oblong tins," Bita is literally mesmerized by her reimmersion in the scene upon returning to Jamaica (40). Paralleling McKay's descriptions about the contentment he experienced when "among a great gang of black and brown humanity" in Marseilles whose odors, after "sweating through a day's hard work, like the odor of stabled horses, were not unpleasant even in a crowded café," Bita is described as basking in the "broad warm faces of all colours between brown and black, sweating comfortably, freely in gay calico clothes."[44] To be among these people gave Bita "the sensation of a reservoir of familiar kindred humanity into which she had descended for baptism," much like McKay's feelings upon arriving in Africa, when he describes himself as feeling something "akin to the physical well-being of a dumb animal among kindred animals, who lives instinctively and by sensations only, without thinking."[45] Bita's implied sense of loss while in England and her feelings of renewed kinship upon her return seem to reflect McKay's understanding of the dangerous cultural rift that can result from sustained exile: by losing contact with the folk, he suggests, Bita risks losing a critical element of herself.

But McKay also states in the novel, through his narrator, that if Bita had not "gone abroad for a period so long," she would never have had the opportunity to see the richness of her "native life in perspective" (40). Recalling the sentimental tone of similar passages in *Banjo*, the narrator explains that Bita's joy in the "simple life of her girlhood was childlike and almost unconscious. She could not reason and theorize why she felt that way. It was just a surging free big feeling" (41). Through the depiction of his protagonist, McKay alludes perhaps to his own sense of loss of the culture of his youth, as it is expressed in nearly all of the poems comprising the "Songs for Jamaica" section of his *Selected Poems*. But on another level, his sardonic portraits of peasant culture in *Banana Bottom* reveal his actual affinity with those "young natives" who left the island only to return "aloof from, if not actually despising, the tribal life in which they were nurtured" (41).

Recalling the dilemma that characterizes his poem, "Strokes of the Tamarind Switch," the side of Bita that is most credible to readers is that which most closely resembles McKay himself—the side shaped by exposure to "Western" ideals. He most powerfully convinces us of Bita's authenticity when describing the exile's joy upon submersing herself in the things unique to her native land. She is literally rebaptized into Jamaica's natural world during her swim in Martha's Basin, the pond which she had used as a girl (116–18). She is figuratively rebaptized into African Caribbean culture during her dance at Kojo Jeems' (84–86), as well as during her consumption by the Spirit during a native religious ritual (249–50). These scenes, written from the perspective of a returned (or perhaps longing to return) exile, capture the intense magnetism which "home" holds over all who leave its shelter, and particularly, over dislocated migrants who, due to a history of colonial subjugation, are not wholly certain of where their truthful "home" is: for McKay, Jamaica, the land of his birth; the "mother country," the land of his citizenship; the United States, the land of his adoption; or Africa, the land of his ancestors.

Less convincing are those aspects of Bita's character that are intended to demonstrate her intrinsic links to the peasantry. As the exile, she is depicted as an intelligent, self-possessed, and determined woman; as the peasant, she is incongruously portrayed as a victim of her own romantic impulses and illusions who willingly surrenders her independence to a series of male protectors. Just as McKay was unable to reconcile the voice of standard English with the voice of Jamaican dialect in his early poetry, McKay is comparably unable to reconcile—twenty years later—these competing aspects of this protagonist's identity.

McKay uses the standard literary convention of marriage in his attempt to signify the union of Bita's peasant roots with her Western education, but throughout the novel, the symbolism falls short and borders on cliché. Bita's wish to wed Hopping Dick, for example, strikes us as unlikely, if not altogether impossible within the context of her tale. Her initial infatuation with the dandy seems plausible given both her love for the culture he represents as well as her need to rebel against the restrictions placed on her by the domineering Craigs. Indeed, the coupling of Hopping Dick with Bita corresponds to a general casting and privileging by McKay, as Timothy Chin has provocatively argued, of the sexuality of the "native" peasants as "natural" in contrast to the supposedly "unnatural" sexuality of the repressed "foreigners" from "civilized" England. [46]

That said, however, McKay has also identified his protagonist to this point in the novel as a down-to-earth but highly educated woman who enjoys intellectual discussions with the Craigs, Harold Newton Day, and, most specifically, Squire Gensir. Indeed, Squire Gensir, as her philosophical and intellectual equal on the island, seems a far more likely marriage partner than (a) Hopping Dick. But of course this marriage would be considered impossible by McKay for two reasons. Obviously, due to their racial difference, the marriage of Bita to an older white man would be controversial on the island and would therefore change the point of the entire novel. As importantly, however, since Gensir is based upon Walter Jekyll, the man who McKay implies introduced him to the legitimacy of homosexual love (see chapter two of this study), it is also possible that McKay could not imagine an actual marriage between the two for reasons of sexual orientation—particularly if Bita, although female in the novel, is modeled on McKay himself. While McKay prepares us well for Bita's rejection of suitor Harold Newton Day through numerous descriptions of the characters' disagreements about their roles in the church, their relation to the peasant-parishioners, and their racial identities, his construction of her final choice of Jubban as her husband is far less convincing.

Throughout the novel, McKay relegates Jubban to the periphery of the action, describing him only in secondary relation to the novel's main characters. Extended introduction of Jubban is witheld until approximately a third of the way into the novel, and here McKay informs us only that Jubban was a "poor kid from the country" who wandered about during the dry season trying "to find a home among the better-off peasants," and that, upon being taken in by Jordan Plant, he developed into "one of the best and most reliable of the husky draymen of the region" (114–15).[47] McKay describes Bita's reaction to Jubban quite uneventfully: she simply "became conscious of the existence of her father's drayman for the first time, remarked his frank, broad, blue-black and solid jaws, and thought that it was all right for her father to have confidence in him" (115). As the plot progresses, Jubban recedes further into the background until, seventy pages before the novel's close, he emerges out of the darkness to rescue Bita from the whips of the Rolling Chanters who are possessed by spiritual fury (250). From this point on, McKay attempts to develop Jubban's character in more detail, but this development consists predominantly of descriptions of additional rescues by Jubban of Bita, followed by his final "rescue" of her through marriage. Recalling his earlier vision of women as "passive" figures who "worship the active success of men," McKay casts Jubban predominantly in the role of Bita's savior but provides little information about the drayman's actual character. He does equate the laboring aspects of Jubban's identity with a rather brutish inarticulateness, however, and in so doing not only further diminishes the collective identity of the lower class peasants in *Banana Bottom*, but also causes us to question the validity of Bita's attraction to Jubban and to doubt the character's supposedly heroic proportions.

The literary achievement of *Banana Bottom* is additionally stymied by McKay's inability to create a life for Bita outside of sexual and domestic realms. In contrast to Squire Gensir, the English expatriate who successfully blends his Western and island selves while living alone, Bita, as a woman, is portrayed by McKay as unable to achieve comparable balance independently, and so she must obtain what she lacks through marriage to Jubban. In the most literal terms, McKay's definition of Bita as male-dependent is emphasized by Jubban's seduction of her literally over the dead body of her father. Upon the deaths of Bita's two paternal figures, Jordan Plant and Malcolm Craig, she must be rescued, in McKay's mind, by yet another man.

In an effort to create the balance in his last novel that he had left unresolved in his two previous works of fiction, McKay forces upon Bita not only marriage but motherhood—symbolic of the consummate[d] union of the pastoral and urbane, of the "primitive" and the "civilized." This, too, however, is unbelievable. McKay's description of Bita reading the *Pensées* and reveling in the "rare pleasure" of returning to "the scriptures of [her] formal education" to find "new interest and meaning in old passages" jars discordantly with his depiction of her as the contented farm wife of Jubban, laboring with her husband and child in the fields. The fundamental reason underlying this incongruity is McKay's artificial construction of a false duality in the first place. In *Banana Bottom*, the "civilized" are not at war with the "primitive," but are able to coexist peacefully in a very small place. Within Bita herself, her British training need not be embattled with her peasant background, since in gaining one, she need not necessarily relinquish the other. But McKay's own perception of the irreconcilability of the conflicts he believes are implicit in the return of any exile to his homeland prevents him from envisioning and credibly depicting their harmonious convergence in his final novel.

Thus, *Banana Bottom* neither provides authentic resolution to the conflicts that McKay raised throughout his fiction, nor does it represent his most flawless literary creation, as some critics have argued.[48] Rather, it reveals in subject and structure McKay's continued alienation from the culture of his youth, and affirms his conception of the ultimate incompatibility of the forces of "white civilization" and "primitive black vitality." His return to a traditional literary form, the romance, proves not to be a subversion of that form (as he accomplished with the sonnet) by using it to emphasize the riches of peasant culture in comparison to Western ways; rather, it results in an only moderately successful attempt at fiction that often reads more like parody. *Banana Bottom*, rather than signifying McKay's figurative return to his home, instead actually attests to the sacrifices implicit in his twenty-year exile from Jamaica by revealing that the gulf which began to grow between himself and his peasant peers and family during his youth had only become wider. Thus, his attempt to render them in fiction is perhaps doomed to failure. McKay's negative depiction of nearly all the peasants in *Banana Bottom*, in fact, exposes his own internalization of the very Western ideas of superiority that he wishes to denounce.

Reconsideration of McKay's three novels, particularly within the context of his own migratory journeys, illuminates our understanding of the complexity of both his political and aesthetic visions as well as how his own biographical history influenced these visions. A first-generation, black Caribbean migrant to the United States, McKay in many ways exemplifies what sociologist Robert Park first identified as the "Marginal Man" in his classic 1928 essay, contemporaneous with McKay's own wanderings. According to Park, the very process of migration not only "enlightens" but literally "emancipates" the individual, thereby enabling him to regard his or her home culture with the purported objectivity of a "stranger." No longer bound by community priorities and conventions, the emancipated migrant is able to view his or her surroundings with a critical acuity stemming from "detachment." Emancipation from one's native culture, however, combined with partial if not full exclusion from that of the host society, produced what Park describes as a "cultural hybrid," a person who experiences intimately the customs and traditions of two distinct peoples but belongs intimately to neither. Thus, this "Marginal Man" exists on the peripheries of two cultures and societies, but ultimately remains alienated from both. Park argues that the resulting division of self is fundamentally irreconcilable, leaving the migrant in a state of "profound disillusionment" of a "relatively permanent" nature.[49]

Beginning with McKay's first move away from the country village of Sunny Ville to the more cosmopolitan environment of his brother's home in the city, he did indeed develop a form of liberating "enlightenment" through education and experience which allowed him to view the culture of his youth with relative "detachment." This very "detachment" from peasant life, however, created the barrier that prevented him from successfully capturing the voices of this group in his dialect poetry. Eventually, McKay found himself so alienated from both upper and lower class Jamaicans that "emancipation" could now be found only in escape, and so he began his lifelong journey as a migrant. In the United States, the process of marginalization continued, and McKay began to explore it in more depth in his fiction. His first novel, *Home to Harlem*, considers both the possibilities and limitations that the urban American enclave offers for both the Jakes—those blacks gifted with what McKay considers to be a particularly racially-based form of "instinct" and "primitive vitality"— and the Rays—those who are unduly burdened by the oppressive forces of "intellect" and "education"—of the world. Finding Harlem an unsatisfactory home for either type, McKay unrolls his fictional canvas in his second novel, *Banjo*, to portray the port of Marseilles, a place he configures as an international "free-zone" which enables him to tackle not simply domestic racism as a source of alienation but also ethnocentrism more generally. But again, the beach proves to be a home for neither McKay nor his fictional characters. Finally, McKay gestures fictionally toward his original home in his last novel, *Banana Bottom*, which tells the tale of a returning exile who seeks desperately to reconcile the same dualism with which McKay's first protagonists struggled. While McKay's own "cultural hybridity" allowed him to analyze a variety of cultures with a degree of objectivity unavailable to insiders, however, this same ability to assess the advantages—and what for McKay were more commonly the failings—of the societies on whose margins he stood caused him to dissociate from everything, leaving him most "profoundly disillusioned" and perpetually alone. Both his autobiographical and fictional writings suggest that throughout his life he did indeed feel like the "Outcast" he first described in 1922: "Something in me is lost, forever lost, / Some vital thing has gone out of my heart, / And I must walk the way of life a ghost / Among the sons of earth, a thing apart."[50]

The troubling and interesting question that remains, however, involves the degree to which McKay's literature and life might reflect more generally the dilemma of the Caribbean region itself. As an area of related but also divided people who are separated from one another geographically and culturally, but who also share a common experience of forced migration, displacement, colonization, slavery, indenture, emancipation, nationalism, and neo-colonization, we must ask whether the very "spiritual instability, intensified self-consciousness, restlessness, and malaise" that Park describes as characteristic to the "marginal man" are not characteristic, at this moment at least, of the Caribbean more generally.[51] The question is frightening, for a positive answer would reveal the degree to which the Western world has marginalized an entire society in its midst.

But the more likely response, as a perusal of contemporary Caribbean literature indicates, is that while the region has indeed experienced a history of exploitation and alienation, out of that tragedy come the tools for "connection and reconciliation" that characterize the work of Edward Brathwaite, George Lamming, and most notably, of Paule Marshall.[52]

4

From Dislocation to Dual Location
Paule Marshall's *Brown Girl, Brownstones*

"I NEED THE sense of being *connected* to the women and men, real and imaginary, who make up my being," states Paule Marshall. "Connection and reconciliation are major themes in my work."[1] Indeed, whereas Claude McKay's writings reflect an immigrant experience characterized by dislocation, Paule Marshall's work, in contrast, suggests the possibility of one typified by "dual location"—a pervasive and driving impulse to envision the position of being an immigrant as providing the opportunity to live not between but within two worlds. Her first novel, *Brown Girl, Brownstones* (1959), more than any other text examined in this study, directly addresses the issue of black immigration between the Caribbean and the United States as it chronicles the lives of a Barbadian American family in Brooklyn during the Depression and Second World War. Barbara Christian, herself an immigrant from the Virgin Islands, is one of the few critics to describe the immigrant aspects of the text as those which make it a distinctly "American novel" for it is "the immigrant's experience," according to Christian, "which gives America so much of its uniqueness."[2] Nevertheless, while some attention has been paid to the Barbadian elements of the tale, *Brown Girl, Brownstones* has yet to be read explicitly within the context of migration narratives or ethnic literature more generally. Such a reading, particularly when placed in juxtaposition to the work of Marshall's predecessor Claude McKay, not only reveals the potential range and complexity of literary depictions of black immigrant reactions to the United States but also offers an important alternative to McKay's "internationalism" (which, if interpreted literally, should be seen as ironically reflecting his status as one "between" nations) by presenting a second-generation immigrant character who functions as a "multinational" member of both Barbados and the United States. Throughout her writings, Paule Marshall is concerned with the balance (or lack thereof) between "old world" and "new world" cultural systems within the black diaspora. *Brown Girl, Brownstones* begins Marshall's inquiry into this issue by examining the potential for reconciliation between the more traditional ways of the Barbadian immigrant community in Brooklyn and the paradigm of "progress" embodied by its host society, the United States. While Marshall questions the value of the "American ideal" by revealing the distorting effect that the pursuit of "the almighty dollar" can have on newcomers, she also suggests that the products of this same society—the second-generation or American-born children of Caribbean immigrants—possess the ability to link past with present to create a truly revolutionary, and distinctly black, "new old world" presence in the United States.

The significance of Marshall's own status as a second-generation Barbadian immigrant must not be underestimated when interpreting this text. Like many of McKay's works, Marshall's first novel, in particular, is based significantly upon her own life experiences. Until only recently, in fact, demographic and sociological studies on Caribbean immigration to the United States were so rare that Marshall's fictional literary work was used as documentation of "the Caribbean immigrant experience" by social scientists and historians alike. She herself added to the ambiguity of the novel's classification by contributing essays to social scientific studies which discussed, for example, "Black Immigrant Women in *Brown Girl, Brownstones*," but which referred more directly to her own relatives, the women on whom the characters in her novel are based.[3] While *Brown Girl, Brownstones* is most certainly a finely-crafted fictional depiction of one character's struggle to define for herself what it means to be simultaneously Barbadian, black, and female in 1940s America, it is also important to recognize the novel's value as a partial record of one actual, second-generation Caribbean immigrant's experiences. Doing so allows us to understand both the text's literary value and the transforming impact that race and gender can have upon stereotypical patterns of second-generation immigrant behavior in the United States.

Granted, the attribution of "generational" status to certain patterns of immigrant behavior has been importantly contested. In the end, as Werner Sollors has shown, one's membership in a distinct "generation" is largely a matter of construction: it is determined more by a consensual association of an individual with a figurative or actual ancestor than it is by a relation based on literal, lineal descent.[4] Nevertheless, because of the broad popular and critical use of the concept of the "generation" in interpreting immigrant experiences throughout American history, it remains analytically advantageous to discuss Marshall in generational terms. Thus, for our purposes, while McKay can be considered a (stereo) "typical" first-generation immigrant in his pattern of estrangement from both home and host societies, Marshall, in contrast, should be considered a (stereo) "atypical" second-generation immigrant because of her joint membership in two worlds simultaneously. Indeed, Marshall describes her artistic enterprise as attempting to create a "bridge that joins the two great wings of the black diaspora in this part of the world. . . . My principal imperative [as a writer] is to give expression to the two cultures that created me, and which I really see as one culture. All o' we is one."[5]

According to traditional generational immigration theory, however, Marshall, as a member of the second generation, should also be a "cultural hybrid," an individual poised between two ethnic communities who is never fully able to fuse them into a unifying whole. As historian Oscar Handlin explained in 1966, only seven years after Marshall published *Brown Girl, Brownstones*, the "children of the uprooted" were commonly considered to be

> . . . members of a marginal group standing between two cultures—that of its parents and that of the surrounding native milieu. To some degree, the second generation was alien to both. The culture of the parents was foreign in origin and not altogether comprehensible. On the other hand, residual ethnic traits prevented the native offspring of the immigrants from participating fully in the life about them. Sometimes they acquired a thin veneer of Americanization, changed their names, aped the local dress and manners, and even intermarried. Still they stood apart in their consistent marginality.[6]

The concept of second-generation marginality has been an issue of nearly constant discussion in the field of ethnic theory for half a century. It stems from the work of immigration historian Marcus Hansen, who, based on patterns demonstrated by male, European second-generation immigrants in the early part of the twentieth century, identified in 1937 a behavioral paradigm which he summarized in the phrase, "what the son wishes to forget the grandson wishes to remember." That is to say, members of the second generation commonly discard the ethnic elements of their pasts in an effort toward assimilation, while those of the third generation supposedly attempt to resurrect the ethnic past through revitalizing a series of cultural practices and symbolic markers that signify ethnic association.[7] While subsequent studies have shown that the concepts of second-generation flight and third-generation return have proven to be far more complex than Hansen originally postulated, his thesis nevertheless continues to maintain a critical presence in discussions of immigration. The sheer volume of scholarly discussion generated by "Hansen's law," in fact, caused Sollors, nearly fifty years after its original publication, to describe it as "the best-known modern formulation of generational succession among immigrants."[8] This is due largely, as Peter Kivisto has described, to the revolutionary attention Hansen's argument gave to two aspects of the "ethnic experience" in the United States. First, it called to the foreground the issue of identity as it relates to ethnicity—the "subjective dimension of the ethnic phenomenon"—and in so doing provided the foundation for nearly all subsequent and still ongoing scholarship investigating the relationship between the form and content of ethnicity. Second, it introduced the theme of generations, which has proven to be an important, though increasingly problematic, sociocultural issue for the development of ethnic theory in the United States.[9]

Nevertheless, the Hansen thesis does not hold true for a distinct segment of the American immigrant population: those whose experiences are shaped by racial or gender backgrounds different from Hansen's European "sons." Despite the reassessment of the Hansen thesis from empirical, metaphorical, and even moral angles, few accounts have evaluated the extent to which the factors of race and gender, particularly within the context of the shifting demographies that characterize more recent migrations, pose a challenge to the traditional second-generation assimilationist paradigm.[10] But as Paule Marshall's work graphically demonstrates, these factors do indeed pose a challenge. Long before feminist scholarship provided the tools with which to expose the patriarchal basis of "Hansen's Law," long before post-colonial studies questioned ideas of nation, narration, and linear notions of American immigrant history, long before Nobel laureate Toni Morrison coined the concept of "re-memory" as a means of constructing new identities out of those elements of the past that the dominant group might like to forget, Paule Marshall provided an important revisionist literary record of how the forces of race and gender fundamentally disrupt melting pot models. Analysis of Marshall's entire œuvre, but particularly of her first and most recent novels—*Brown Girl, Brownstones* and *Daughters*—illustrates that she was one of the first to select and reshape elements of both her "immigrant" and "American" histories in order to document, interpret, and inscribe for others like herself—and particularly for the increasing numbers of second-generation Caribbean American women in the United States—both the value and truth of their pasts and the possibilities for their futures. Rather than rejecting the elements of her ethnic past, this particular second-generation immigrant reclaims that past—and she does so through the act of writing itself. Through insistent affirmation of both her Caribbean and African American roots, Marshall's life and writings signal a dramatic shift in the "typical" pattern of second-generation immigrant responses to the United States.

Brown Girl, Brownstones opens in 1939 against the backdrop of the Second World War, and the many invasions and pacts enacted during that year emphasize the centrality of conflict and compromise in the novel.

In March 1939, following rejection of German demands by Poland, the German–Polish Non-Aggression Pact and the Anglo–German Naval Agreement were canceled by Hitler. Throughout the spring and summer, a series of agreements, including the Pact of Friendship and Mutual Aid with Italy ("Pact of Steel"), the non-aggression treaties with Estonia, Latvia, and Denmark, and the German–Soviet Non-Aggression Pact, laid the foundation for the September 1, 1939 German invasion of Poland. This pattern of alliance and betrayal, of retreat and assault, mirrors the action in *Brown Girl, Brownstones*. Seemingly Manichean adversaries—parent and child, husband and wife, male and female, Caribbeaner and American, ethnic and non-ethnic, or first and second generation—shape the novel and create the arena in which Selina fights for individuality in the context of a tightly-knit community.

Upon closer examination, however, these apparently simple contrasts—like those purportedly characterizing ethnic differences—emerge in extraordinary complexity. As Hortense Spillers argues about another of Marshall's novels, "we can expect here no straightforward vindication of various public tastes regarding race, ethos, and gender; no facile condemnation of victors or celebration of victims, but, rather, a staged dialectics of human involvement. . . . "[11] Marshall's skill at capturing the inconsistencies of human behavior prevents us from grouping characters along simple lines of opposition. Rather, *Brown Girl, Brownstones* describes, using Marshall's own metaphor, Selina's delicate dance with the variety of forces that contribute to the shaping of her unique identity and propel her to the position at the novel's end—on the edge of a journey of discovery that will reveal more about herself as a second-generation Barbadian American through revealing more about the *world* of people who "put her so."

In the opening chapter of *Brown Girl, Brownstones*, Marshall introduces each of the forces that affect Selina as she develops from a young girl whose universe is "perfectly bound" by the relative extremes of "Chauncey Street's gentility and Fulton Street's raucousness," to a globally-conscious woman on the verge of undertaking what Marshall believes is the definitive step toward self-possession and understanding, the task of "truly confronting the past, both in personal and historic terms. . . . "[12] As critic Barbara Christian has noted in several of her essays on Marshall, the creation of space is as important to this writer as is the creation of character, and in *Brown Girl, Brownstones*, especially, the houses themselves form figures as influential in the novel as the human beings who live within them.[13] Indeed, the brownstones are the first characters we meet. Symbolizing the strength of the Barbadian American community, these buildings "resemble an army massed at attention" standing "somber[ly], . . . indifferent to the summer's heat and passion," small in truth but giving "the impression of formidable height." The narrator, as though looking through eyes blinded by racism, states that, composed of "all one uniform red-brown stone," the houses look the same; upon closer inspection, however, it becomes clear that "under the thick ivy each house had something distinctively its own." Marshall explicitly describes the stylistic inconsistencies of the houses to symbolize the incongruity both of the buildings' inhabitants and of American culture more generally: "Some touch that was Gothic, Romanesque, baroque or Greek triumphed amid the Victorian clutter. Here, Ionic columns framed the windows while next door gargoyles scowled up at the sun. There, the cornices were hung with carved foliage while Gorgon heads decorated others." But foreshadowing the central tension of the novel, Marshall implies that individuality can be detrimental to a group needing to cohere in order to survive in a nation hostile not only to immigrants but to blacks of all nationalities: while all of the houses are described as "shar[ing] the same brown monotony," they also run the risk of being "doomed by the confusion in their design" (3).

Marshall recounts the history of these brownstones to challenge perceptions of difference that arise from crude definitions of self and other.[14] She describes the pattern of immigration to the area, beginning first with the "Dutch-English and Scotch-Irish who had built the houses." They were followed by generations of descendants whose lives "unravel[ed] in a quiet skein of years behind the green shades," and now, by Caribbeaners. During all of these changes, "behind the grim façades" of the brownstones, "life soared and ebbed." Asserting the unity of all humanity regardless of ethnic, racial, or religious background, Marshall notes that all of the immigrants' lives were comparably punctuated by the rhythms of love-making, child-bearing, living and dying: "Bodies crouched in the postures of love at night, children burst from the womb's thick shell, and death, when it was time, shuffled through the halls" (4). Nevertheless, racial difference dramatically distinguishes the Caribbeaners from their predecessors:

> But now in 1939 the last of [the white immigrants] were discreetly dying behind those shades or selling the houses and moving away. And as they left, the West Indians slowly edged their way in. Like a dark sea nudging its way onto a white beach and staining the sand, they came. The West Indians, especially the Barbadians who had never owned anything perhaps but a few poor acres in a poor land, loved the houses with the same fierce idolatry as they had the land on their obscure islands. But, with their coming, there was no longer tea in the afternoon, and their odd speech clashed in the hushed rooms. (4)

The foreboding tone of this passage alludes to the hostility with which black immigrants to the United States were greeted during the first three decades of this century. Marshall captures the newcomers' dislocation in American culture by describing the Caribbeaners as "edging their way" into unwelcoming territory, as "staining" the American soil with their darkness. Indeed, the appearance of Caribbeaners in the brownstones redefines the very nature of the buildings themselves, as the rituals of "tea in the afternoon" and "mild voices" are usurped by "odd speech" which "clashes" against the "hushed" sounds of "skirts rustling across the parquet floors" (4).

Against the backdrop of this vanguard of living buildings, Marshall introduces Selina Boyce, the central figure to whom all others stand in peripheral relation. The first impression she presents of the "ten-year-old girl with scuffed legs and a body as straggly as the clothes she wore" is of a paradoxical character who is at once wisely mature and naively juvenile. Initiating a reincarnation motif that reappears throughout her works, Marshall describes Selina as possessing

> not the eyes of a child. Something too old lurked in their centers. They were weighted, it seemed, with scenes of a long life. She might have been old once and now, miraculously, young again—but with the memory of that other life intact. She seemed to know the world down there in the dark hall and beyond for what it was. Yet knowing, she still longed to leave this safe, sunlit place at the top of the house for the challenge there.[15] (4)

Marshall's location of Selina "at the top of the house," particularly within the context of her tale of maturation, interestingly suggests a motif common in ethnic literature more generally in which a literal or figurative roof-top serves as the setting for a symbolic juxtaposition of the old world and the new.[16] Alluding to Selina's eventual ambivalence about leaving the Barbadian community of her youth—the "safe, sunlit place at the top of the house"—Marshall describes Selina as at one moment boldly "hurl[ing] herself forward" into the unfamiliar world signified by "the dark hall and beyond," and at the same time as doubting her decision and "reach[ing] back to grasp the bannister." "The contradiction of [Selina's] movement," Marshall explains, "flung her back on the step. She huddled there, rubbing her injured elbow and hating her cowardice" (5). In defiance of her own timidity, and presaging her rejection of the societal racism that will seek to deny her individuality, Selina declares herself to the silent white ghosts by clanging loudly the silver bangles which identify her as a Barbadian American girl.

Despite her apparent independence, Selina feels out of place and lonely in this environment. As with all of Marshall's novels, however, *Brown Girl, Brownstones* suggests a movement toward union with the people comprising one's immediate as well as "extended" family in the broadest sense—a kinship with members of one's blood clan as well as with one's national and racial relatives. In this opening scene, Marshall provides us with inklings of Selina's quest for communion with people beyond her brownstone, beyond Chauncey and Fulton streets, beyond the black immigrant community in Brooklyn. Anticipating her dance of the life-cycle near the novel's end when, lifting a slender arm, Selina "boldly hail[s] the audience, . . . giving each one there something of herself" and "bearing something of them all away with her" in return, a much younger Selina now welcomes with outstretched arms "the white family who had lived here before," greeting them as they glide "with pale footfalls up the stairs" (281–82, 5). Like her later audience at the dance recital, these figures "implore [Selina] to give them a little life," and as she does so they "fus[e] with her" so that "she [is] no longer a dark girl alone . . . but one of them" (5).

But Marshall does not let this early image of interracial harmony stand. Again foreshadowing the climactic life-cycle dance and Selina's subsequent shattering encounter with the racism of her friend Margaret's mother, Selina's "fusion" with people beyond her family and community in this opening scene is suddenly severed when she glimpses her own image:

> . . . the mirror flung her back at herself. The mood was broken. The gown dropped from her limp hands. The illusory figures fled and she was only herself again. A truculent face and eyes too large and old, a flat body perched on legs that were too long. A torn middy blouse, dirty shorts, and socks that always worked down into the heel of her sneakers. That was all she was. She did not belong here. (5–6)

In this passage, Marshall signifies a trope in African American letters in which the protagonist, frequently through glimpsing a visual image of him- or herself, is forced to confront his or her status as an "other" in a world of whites. As did W. E. B. Du Bois, James Weldon Johnson, and Zora Neale Hurston, among others before her, Marshall describes a pivotal moment when her protagonist recognizes her difference from those around her: in this instance, Selina sees her illusion-shattering, dark reflection in the mirror and feels immediately that she "does not belong" in the company of her white ghosts.[17] But Marshall then revises this trope in such a way as to emphasize Selina's isolation even further by describing the young girl as feeling equally alienated from her own kin: she looks at the family photo on the buffet "which did not include her" and decides consequently that the image could never have captured her own family: "The small girl under the drooping bow did not resemble her sister. The young woman in the 1920's dress with a headband around her forehead could not be the mother," and the boy-child whom she had never known sat precisely where her own image should be" (6, 8). Referring to an older brother who died before she was born, the tomboyish Selina contemptuously describes him as looking "like a girl with all that hair." While "he had been frail and dying with a bad heart . . . she had been stirring into life." But when finally "she had come, strong and well-made, to take his place," her family, significantly, "had taken no photographs . . . " (8).

In response to this negation of self, Selina barges in on and beats up her remaining sibling, Ina, in an attempt to affirm her own presence, authority, and difference: "She wanted to leap on Ina, pin her to the bed and then ground her fists and knees in that softness until the tears came and the whimpers and the apologies . . . " (7). In keeping with the series of contrasts that pervade the novel, Marshall describes Ina as being everything that Selina is not. Ina is soft, Selina is bony. Ina is defenseless, Selina is self-sufficient. Ina is passive, Selina is aggressive. While these very differences help Selina carve out her own independent identity, they also suggest at this point certain "outlawed" behaviors and emotions that distance her from the comfort (and approval) of the family—and larger societal— circle. Selina stands as peripheral to the family unit and attributes this status to her own differences from her sibling(s) and parents, but as the novel unfolds, both we and Selina come to recognize that the reason for her exclusion is the absence of a family unit in the first place—and more importantly, that this absence is due to radically different responses to the American environment on the part of each of her immigrant parents.

In this opening scene, Marshall immediately defines Deighton, Selina's father, as the avatar of the islands and uses sun imagery to convey this association. "Stretched dark and limp on a narrow cot like someone drunk with sun," his eyes are "a deeper brown than his skin with the sun in their centers" (8, 9). When Selina shuts her own eyes, "the sun on her lids create[s] an orange void inside her and she want[s] to remain like this always with the sun on her eyes and bound with her father in their circle" (9). When she asks her father whether she can go to a movie with her friends, Deighton wonders what the "New York children," (the name by which the immigrants refer to their American-born offspring), find in "sitting up in a dark place when the sun is shining bright-bright outside," and in response to her query about what could possibly be "better than the movies," he fills her ears with stories of the sea games and sun-bathing he used to enjoy in Barbados (9).[18] Deighton Boyce, who is considered wholly unreliable by his wife and the Barbadian American community, represents for Selina "the one constant in the flux and unreality of life" (8). She adores him and the mere thought of him relieves her alienation: the tone of his greeting upon her entrance to the sun parlor signals "that they had stepped into an intimate circle and were joined together in the pause and beat of life" (9). Through this initial exchange between Deighton and Selina, Marshall carefully sets forth the issue around which the plot revolves—the tension surrounding Deighton's inherited land in Barbados—as well as identifies perhaps the most influential oppositions within Selina's world, those embodied in her father and mother.

As a stark antithesis to these insistent images of sun-induced warmth, relaxation, and leisure, stands Silla, "the mother" who, as she returns home from work, brings "the theme of winter into the park with her dark dress amid the summer green and . . . women lounging on the benches there" (16). Silla is known throughout the novel only as "the mother"; as Deborah Schneider explains, the "language of describing her is used to reject her" as it emphasizes the distance between mother and daughter at the book's beginning.[19] Marshall contrasts Deighton as a town-boy, whose youth was characterized by play, with Silla, who is described as coming "from down some gully or up some hill behind God back and ain use to nothing" but hard work under a sun that brings not pleasure but rather only unbearable heat and exhaustion (10). While Deighton lounges at home fantasizing about the house he wishes to build on the land he has inherited in Barbados, Silla doggedly waits on street corners for day-work as a domestic in order to earn a "few raw-mout' pennies'" to buy a brownstone for her family now living in New York (11). While Deighton is a loner, Selina can "never think of the mother alone" (10).

But these contrasts between father and mother are not as basic as they first appear. As many critics have noted, Marshall deliberately structures differences between Silla and Deighton to reveal the conflicting models on which Selina struggles to configure her own identity, both through acts of alliance and rejection. But Marshall also portrays these two adversaries in such depth that reducing them to simple metaphors for a whole series of oppositions becomes impossible. Despite his "sunny" disposition, Deighton is described as remaining "well-hidden behind" his handsome façade, his eyelids forming "a closed blind over the man beneath" (8). He no longer proclaims himself with the "detached air" and "teasing smile" that Selina observes in the family portrait, but instead has become a man masked by these same images. Silla is no longer the young mother who possessed "a shy beauty" and a "girlish expectancy" in her expression (8), but rather has been transformed into a reprimanding monolith whose "lips, set in a permanent protest against life, implied that there was no time for gaiety" (16). In response to Selina's question about how "the mother" will respond to his plan to buy the land, Deighton laments with "pain darkening his eyes," "How could I know? Years back I could tell but not any more" (12). Deighton, Silla, and the contours of their relationship have obviously changed since the photo of the "neat, young family" was taken years earlier, and it is the task of Selina, a product of their union, to find a way to harmonize for herself the warring forces that embitter her parents (7).

Having introduced us to Selina, her home, and her family, Marshall takes us beyond the walls of the brownstone to meet the other influential figures in Selina's life. In quick succession, we receive glimpses of the new tenant and recent immigrant Suggie Skeete, of Selina's loyal ally Miss Thompson, and of Selina's girlhood soul-mate Beryl Challenor. Suggie Skeete personifies seduction; her "full-fleshed legs and arms, her languorous pose, all the liquid roundness of her body under the sheer summer dress hinted that love, its rituals and its passion, was her domain" (13). Indeed, Suggie will teach Selina, a child of embattled and sexually inimical parents, about erotic love and the pleasures of the body. Next we meet Suggie's counterpart, the African American hairdresser, Miss Thompson. A "tall drawn woman . . . faded brown in color and no longer young" whose "soiled nurse's uniform fell straight down her fleshless body, hiding the bones jutting under the skin," Miss Thompson is appropriately described as the opposite of Suggie, since she teaches Selina about unconditional love—a love that stems from the heart and not from the heat of passion (13).[20] Finally, we meet Beryl Challenor, Selina's best friend and symbol of the customary pattern followed by second-generation immigrants in *Brown Girl, Brownstones*. Portending the prepubescent sexual awakenings Selina will experience with Beryl, the two of them enact a courtship-like ritual of jealousy and reconciliation during which Selina finds Beryl's "tiny breasts" to be "soothing," enjoys feeling Beryl's "warmth [figuratively] rush into her," and wishes that she "could pierce Beryl's skin and roam inside her" (15). Alluding to the dissolution of their friendship that will result from Beryl's unquestioning conformity to the immigrant community's mandates, however, Selina imagines that from the inside Beryl will look rather disappointingly "like a small well-lighted room with the furniture neatly arranged around it" (15).

The first chapter of *Brown Girl, Brownstones* establishes a tone of irreconcilability that is expressed through oppositions between white and black, fusion and fission, "femininity" and "masculinity," leisure and labor, individuality and conformity, and erotic and platonic love. As with most binaries, and especially those based on stereotyped conceptions of race, ethnicity, or gender, increased knowledge about the "other" side improves understanding of the similarities that actually exist. As the opening description of the brownstones indicated, things in this novel are not as obvious as they may initially appear. While Selina is surely, on some levels, suspended between the poles represented by her "Bajan" father and Americanized mother as she (and many critics) so often imagine, in order to understand her maturation fully it is vital to recognize how both she and her parents are influenced by the one character whom Marshall cannot introduce succinctly in the opening chapter: the Barbadian immigrant community. Indeed, this community, which functions as a single entity in the novel, has perhaps the greatest influence of all in terms of shaping the behavior and expectations of both Selina and her parents.

In some ways, to discuss collectively the immigrants in *Brown Girl, Brownstones* who adhere to the tenets of the Barbadian Association is to commit the very error that Marshall cautions us against—that of over-looking individual distinguishing characteristics and seeing the group as "all [of] one uniform red-brown stone" (3). But Marshall's exploration of Selina's identity development within the context of the larger community actually places her squarely within the tradition of Caribbean auto-biographical writing more generally. Critic Sandra Pouchet Paquet explains that the merging of "issues of self-identity" with larger "issues of West Indian identity" is central to "West Indian" autobiographical form: "The individual predicament of the writer as autobiographical subject illuminates the collective predicament of an island community," which is, in this case, the community of transplanted Barbadians living in New York.[21] Barbadian writer George Lamming describes this process similarly in the introduction to his autobiography, *In the Castle of My Skin*, when he argues that Caribbean writers often employ a "method of narration where community and not person is the central character," where "several centers of attention . . . work simultaneously and acquire their coherence from the collective character of the Village." By focusing on "the collective human substance of the Village," Lamming claims, these writers are able to "perceive another dimension to the individual wretchedness of daily living. . . . the dimension of energy, force, a quickening capacity for survival."[22] The articulation of self through articulation of community and the "capacity for survival" based on collective action that Pouchet Paquet and Lamming respectively describe constitute the essence of Marshall's portrayals of both Selina and the immigrant community/character in *Brown Girl, Brownstones.*

The first-generation Barbadian immigrants in the novel are modeled on those described in the first chapter of this study, members of the "first wave" of voluntary Caribbean migration to the United States that occurred roughly between 1885 and 1930. As has been explained, these immigrants were drawn to urban centers by the same forces that pulled

Southern black Americans north during the Great Migration, the search for work and wealth in the land of the "Yankee Dollar." As an exchange between Seifert Yearwood and Deighton Boyce in *Brown Girl, Brownstones* suggests, Marshall's characters encountered the prejudice and squalor that typically greeted newcomers of the period upon their arrival in the United States:

> "Remember," Seifert began, his restive eyes stilled for a moment, "when we first came here in 1920 we was all living in those cold-water dumps in South Brooklyn with cockroaches lifting us up?" He gave a high wheezing laugh but his eyes burned with outrage. "The white people thought they was gon keep us there but they din know what a Bajan does give. We here now and when they run we gon be right behind them. That's why, mahn, you got to start buying. . . . How else a man your color gon get ahead?" (38–39)

Yearwood's comment also indicates, however, that, for a variety of complex reasons, Caribbeaners were able to seize American opportunity as well as challenge inter-group and intra-group racism by assertively forging their own community structures, employment agencies, and social service systems. As is reflected in Yearwood's warning that Deighton must "start buying," the Barbadian Americans in *Brown Girl, Brownstones* understand clearly that one of their greatest weapons with which to combat the poverty and discrimination experienced by most urban African Americans during the period lay in property ownership. Like the actual community on which they are based, Marshall's fictional characters capitalize upon their new-found potential for mobility by working hard, saving money, and eventually establishing a sound economic base of small businesses and professions to serve the black American community.

The acts of distinguishing themselves from the African American community with whom they shared racial similarity, but little else, and operating as a single unit, become essential survival skills for the members of Marshall's Barbadian American Association. Yearwood comments that "they," using the universal referent for the "other" group, in this case African Americans, "lick out their money in the bars and whiskey stores. I tell you, these people from down South does work for the Jew all week and give the money right back to he on Sat'day night like it does burn their hand to keep it" (38). Yearwood's comment reflects a pattern of intra-ethnic "othering" and discrimination that is not uncommon. First, Jews, an ethnic group with whom Caribbeaners were frequently associated because of each group's respective entrepreneurial success, are scapegoated throughout the novel as unduly hard-driving and commerce-oriented. Second, and more important to the argument here, recalling the stereotypes discussed in the first chapter of this study, African Americans (and Southerners in particular) are viewed by their first-generation immigrant peers as less educated, more resigned to powerlessness as second-class citizens in their own country, and therefore collectively as a "keepback" to the Barbadian community.[23] When 'Gatha Steed's daughter wants to marry "some boy from down South, . . . they almost had to tie 'Gatha down with wet sheets when she found out. She want the girl to marry a Bajan boy who's here on the immigration scheme" (73). This resistance to exogamy, common among virtually all first-generation ethnic groups, reflects a larger fear among the Barbadian community of forced inclusion into the systems of oppression that limited the progress of African Americans in the United States. Marshall captures this tension through her depiction of the Barbadian Association's reaction to Claremont Sealy's recommendation that they "strike out that word *Barbadian* and put in *Negro*":

> The silence swept up to him in a cold wind and trailed him out of the room. Then, as rain comes in the West Indies—without warning, to lash the earth in a helpless hysterical deluge—their indignation broke with the same fury. The meeting was at an end. Their set faces were contorted, alive now, with wrath. The women's arms, which had been folded judicially on their high bosoms, now punctured the air with outraged gestures. The dank basement was hot with anger. (222)

For Marshall's Barbadians, including "Negroes" in their Association would signify willful identification with the oppression that African Americans suffered during the interwar years. The goal of the Association members, symbolized by the juxtaposition of their banner to the American flag, is to transcend the barriers of caste and class from which they fled in the islands, to take full advantage of the possibilities in a democratic society to "ascend to great heights," as the Association's motto suggests. In the minds of the Association's members, to identify oneself as black before Barbadian, given the long history of racial discrimination in the United States, is to jeopardize that ascent.

Cecil Osborn, when welcoming new members to the Barbadian Association in *Brown Girl, Brownstones*, summarizes the aspirations of this particular immigrant community. Describing the rotating credit system known to Barbadians as the "susu-hand," Cecil speaks "with fervor of the 'Fund' to which all members contributed and which in turn made small loans to members" (220). Reflecting the strong Caribbean immigrant commitment to and involvement in politics, he tells "of the political ambitions of Percy Challenor and other members and the Association's potential influence in local politics and community affairs. . . . '[W]e got to have a voice at City Hall. . . . And if we have enough pull and enough

money behind us, they gon have to listen . . . !' " (220).[24] By the novel's
end, Percy Challenor has been elected to office. Expressing the key tenet
underlying the Association's philosophy, Cecil describes the group as "a
sign that a people are banded together in a spirit of self-help. A sign that
we are destroying that picture of the poor colored man with his hand
always long out to the rich white one, begging: 'Please, mister, can you
spare a dime?' " (221). Most importantly, however, he affirms the community's faith in the second generation:

> "But tell me why we start this Association now when most of us gon
> soon be giving business to the undertaker? I gon tell you. It's because
> of the young people! Most of us did come to this man country with
> only the strength in we head and hand to make our way, but the young
> people have the opportunity to be professional and get out there and
> give these people big word for big word. Thus, they are our hope. They
> make all the sacrifice, all the struggle worth while." (221)

These notions are crucial to understanding both the community's and
Selina's behavior in this novel. In order to achieve its rather formidable
goals, the community understands that it *must* work together—that each
member must contribute to the formation of a collective identity and
strength. Given the barriers confronting it, the community must be willing to sacrifice the needs of an individual for the needs of the group,
particularly for the benefit of the next generation. No one embraces this
philosophy more earnestly than "the mother," Silla Boyce.

Silla, like the majority of Barbadians in the novel, immigrated to the
United States in order to better her economic position: "You want to see
yourself improve. Isn't that why people does come to this place?" (174).
On one level, her mechanistic drive, compulsion to save money, and virtual
obsession with climbing the ladder of financial and social success suggest that Silla has been wholly consumed by her pursuit of the "American dream." Marshall describes her third novel, *Praisesong for the Widow*
(1983), as focusing on "the materialism of this country, how it often
spells the death of love and feeling and how we, as black people, must
fend it off."[25] In many ways, *Brown Girl, Brownstones* comments equally
profoundly on this same issue. Indeed, Silla openly admits that she is willing "to see [her] soul fall howling into hell" in order to keep pace with
her peers by "buying house" (75). But "buying house" is not motivated
simply by a selfish desire for material gain. Rather, Silla believes that by
achieving a degree of first-generation financial success, she can ensure an
even higher socioeconomic standing for her children. Unlike Deighton,
she is willing to sacrifice the needs of the individual—herself—for the
group—her family.

In order to understand Silla, we must understand her past. Silla's rigorous work ethic is rooted in her status as laborer throughout her life. As a child of the Third Class in the closed society of Barbados, she learned too well the meaning of working for little monetary, social, or personal reward. Describing her youth to the American-born Selina, who thinks that the Third Class must have "something to do with school" Silla painfully explains,

> "The Third Class is a set of little children picking grass in a cane field from the time God sun rise in his heaven till it set. With some woman called a Driver to wash yuh tail in licks if yuh dare look up. Yes, working harder than a man at the age of ten. . . . " Her eyes narrowed as she traveled back to that time and was that child again, feeling the sun on her back and the whip cutting her legs. . . . (45–46)

As "the collective voice of all Bajan women, the vehicle through which their former suffering found utterance," Silla represents the history of this group as laborers (45). Immigration scholar Roy Bryce-Laporte describes Caribbean immigration to the United States as a movement of "induced and recruited *labor* in which women—whether spouses, mothers, daughters, relatives, friends, or neighbors—came as *workers*." Unlike Deighton, whose youth was characterized by games of cricket and the benefits of a formal education, Silla, as part of a long history of black female immigrants, came to the States, as Marshall explains in her essay "Black Immigrant Women in *Brown Girl, Brownstones*," "not for adventure but to perform labor; not for leisure but to gain employment . . . as slaves; as house servants; seamstresses and factory workers; and [more recently] as secretaries, saleswomen, nurses, and other professionals."[26]

This ambitious character covets the monetary fruits of her labor for more than simply financial reasons. In early twentieth-century Barbados, the only way to escape one's class and social "predestination" was to flee the small island for more democratic shores—and to do so required the price of passage. As Marshall describes, "for the women who left Barbados to come to the US in the twenties, the voyage north was financed in a number of ways. Money was borrowed, a bit of family ground was sold, or a relative who had already made his or her way to the 'States' and found work dutifully sent home the money for the ticket."[27] Money was the ticket to escape, but obtaining that ticket often required deep personal hardship, particularly in the case of "Panama money," those funds earned under the harsh labor conditions surrounding the building of the Canal. As was described in the first chapter of this study, thousands of Caribbean workers died from a combination of overwork and unsanitary living conditions, but the money they earned often provided those remaining with the opportunity to migrate. Given this immense toll, Marshall depicts Silla, and the women of her generation in *Brown Girl, Brownstones,* as possessing an appreciation for money that goes far beyond its economic benefits; indeed, the value of riches lay primarily in the sacrifice that goes into acquiring them. As such, money becomes in this novel far more than a means to "buy house"; rather, it is transformed into a culturally revered symbol illustrating one's virtue and personal suffering.

Through the conversations among Silla and her friends in the kitchen of the brownstone, the parameters of both their virtue and suffering are disclosed. Marshall views "common speech and the plain, workaday words that make it up . . . [as] the principal means by which characters . . . reveal themselves and give voice sometimes to profound feelings and complex ideas about themselves and the world."[28] In keeping with the form of immigrant narratives that generally tend both to extol the possibilities offered by the new country as well as to critique the gap between the myths of America and its realities, Silla's passionate and even dogmatic responses to the issues of the day, though simple in language, offer pro-found and complex commentaries on American society in the 1930s as well as suggest much about the factors that pushed her out of the islands and pulled her into a racist but ultimately freer United States.

On the topic of religion, Silla condemns the "hypocrites prostrating themself before the cross each Sunday. The same ones buying house by devious means. Lemme tell you, Iris, you don see God any better by being sanctified. . . . Not everyone who cry 'Lord, Lord' gon enter in . . . Each man got to see God for himself" (69). Of Hitler ("the devil incarnate"), the war, and politicians, Silla cries angrily: "It's these politicians. They's the ones always starting up all this lot of war. And what they care? It's the poor people got to suffer and mothers with their sons" (69). She challenges Iris's willingness to allow her son to fight for England but not for the United States: "What John Bull ever did for you that you's so grateful? You think 'cause they does call Barbados 'Little England' that you is somebody? What the king know 'bout you—or care? . . . You think [he] did care when you was home heading canes? Or when the drought come and not a pot stir 'pon the stove for days . . . ?" (69–70). Silla un-derstands poignantly the nature of British colonial exploitation, and is fully aware of the position of her community as mere underlings of the "mother country." Vehemently, she describes in more detail the isolation, poverty, oppression, and consequent despair that characterize the islands:

> "Iris, you know what it is to work hard and still never make a head-way? That's Bimshire. One crop. People having to work for next skin to noth-ing. The white people treating we like slaves still and we taking it. The rum shop and the church joined together to keep we pacify and in ig-

norance. That's Barbados. It's a terrible thing to know that you gon be poor all yuh life, no matter how hard you work. You does stop trying after a time. People does see you so and call you lazy. But it ain laziness. It just that you does give up. You does kind of die inside." (70)

Silla, however, refuses to "die inside" and risks migration instead. Though she is well aware of the perils of her new world, she is grateful for even just the chance to succeed: "I ain say that we don catch H in this country what with the discrimination and thing and how hard we does have to scrub the Jew floor to make a penny, but my Christ, at least you can make a head-way" (70).

At the same time that Silla capitalizes upon the opportunities available to her in the United States, however, she, like many first-generation immigrants, maintains through custom and confederation her heritage as a Barbadian. Marshall describes her, along with the other black immigrant women in the novel, as "accepting without question the materialistic ethic of this country while at the same time remaining strangely aloof from America. [Her] aloofness, which was perhaps a defensive device, was expressed in the almost contemptuous way [she] insisted on referring to the US as 'this man's country.' It would always, in other words, be foreign territory; someone else's turf."[29] From cooking traditional Barbadian delicacies every Saturday to her passionate affiliation with the nationalist Association, Silla clings defiantly to her Barbadian heritage.

The mornings of making black pudding, souse, and coconut bread follow the familiar immigrant pattern of transporting "foodways" as a means of bringing comfort to those living in a foreign culture, and allow Silla and the women around her table to reconnect themselves to their pasts. The constant stream of conversation, revolving primarily around Barbados, provides the means through which these displaced immigrants affirm both their history and themselves. Marshall describes in more detail the function of these hours of "endless talk" for the women on whom the characters of Silla and her friends are based: "their talk was a refuge. They never really ceased being baffled and overwhelmed by America—its vastness, complexity, and power. Its strange customs and laws. At a level beyond words they remained fearful and in awe." Like all first-generation immigrants, these women were both "confronted . . . by a world they could not encompass, . . . and at the same time . . . permanently separated from the world they had known." In response, they "took refuge in language" which, citing Polish emigré Czeslaw Milosz, Marshall states is ultimately "the only homeland" for the uprooted.[30] In terms of immigrant adjustment patterns, language functions on two levels. First, the use of the "mother tongue" in the presence of those whom one might choose to exclude from understanding allows for the construction of a protective linguistic boundary between insiders and outsiders. Second, language actually helps to constitute and reify a homeland created through imagery, memories, and family stories.

By recreating Barbados through word and memory, Silla and her compatriots define the significance of the island as symbol and reality not only for themselves, but also—and perhaps even more importantly—for the observant members of the second generation, Ina and Selina, for whom the actual reality of Barbados remains distant. In the process, these women contribute fundamentally to the formation of Selina's multinational identity. As Marshall implies in her well-known essay, "Poets in the Kitchen," these gender-based activities held among women in the female and domestic realm of the kitchen inspired her not to reject her ethnic heritage for assimilation into the host society, as has been described as the common pattern among second-generation immigrants, but rather, to record, affirm, and explore the connection between her family's past and her own present through fiction. *Brown Girl, Brownstones,* as a highly autobiographical work, depicts Marshall, through the character of Selina, at the beginning of this long journey of reclamation and discovery.

Despite these efforts at cultural preservation, however, the imposition of American ways of life commonly have created significant tension between first- and second-generation immigrants, and Marshall records this in her novel as well. Early in the book, an exchange between Florrie and Silla about raising children suggests the friction that often arises surrounding parental strictness in the more liberal context of the United States, as well as reveals what Marshall describes elsewhere as the "uneasiness and fear" felt by immigrant parents about the future of the second generation.[31] Admonishing Florrie for giving her son a "cuff that near kill him" because he, as a "New York child," shuns work and listens to "jazz like he's some jazz fiend or the other," Silla warns: "You best watch that heavy hand, . . . 'cause this is New York and these is New York children and the authorities will dash you in jail for them" (68). In addition to fearing the adoption by their children of such black American cultural forms as jazz and the potential assimilation into the African American community that this implies, these women also fear their powerlessness—even in the most personal realm of parenthood—in the American environment where a different cultural system inhibits them from raising their children as they themselves were raised. Indeed, the tension between the ways of the old world and the ways of the new are crystallized in Florrie's response to Silla: "You got to wash their tail in licks. You remember what the old people home did tell us: hard ears you wun hear, own-ways you'll feel" (68).

As Selina begins to realize, Silla's "formidable aspect was the culmination of all that she had suffered" (46). Her drive, her ambition, and her grim diligence do not reflect a woman uninterested in passion or playfulness, but rather stem from a history of unrewarded labor which provoked a profound need to take advantage of the opportunity "to improve." Her myopic pursuit of a brownstone at the expense of Deighton's love reveals less a selfish materialism than a distressing awareness of "the way things arrange." She deports him not out of hatred, but rather out of an inability to watch him suffer at the hands of a racist world (305). She casts him out of the lives of her children in an effort to protect both him and them from the pain of witnessing his humiliation. She herself says "in a very low, pained voice" that "the terrible thing is that . . . People got to make their own way. And nearly always to make your own way in this Christ world you got to be hard and sometimes misuse others, even your own. Oh nobody wun admit it. We don't talk about it, but we does live by it—each in his own way" (224). Silla recognizes what this knowledge has done to her: " 'You think I like myself when I'm in the hall getting on like a black-guard?' . . . Her voice suddenly lapsed, her thick hand lay open and tragic on her lap, her face sank deep into the fur collar. . . . 'We would like to do different. That's what does hurt and shame us so. But the way things arrange we can't, if not we lose out" (224). With a "tragic acceptance" of her personal perversion "lin[ing] her face," Silla tells her friends that "power is a thing that don make you nice," and pleads mutely to Selina "for understanding and tolerance—not only for what she had just said but for all she had ever said or done" (225–26).

Silla's character, then, reveals the larger point that Marshall makes through the text as a whole: the "dead hand of the past," to use ethnic theorists Vladimir Nahirny and Joshua Fishman's phrasing, is not dead at all, but rather plays a vital and continuing role in molding the present.[32] Out of Silla's past come the gifts that she imparts to her daughter—the gifts of ambition, of a belief in her heritage and a curiosity to learn more about her past, and the strength to pursue her goals with undying direction. As Selina herself admits, "Everybody used to call me Deighton's Selina but they were wrong. Because you see I'm truly your child. Remember how you used to talk about how you left home and came here alone as a girl of eighteen and was your own woman? I used to love hearing that. And that's what I want. I want it!" (307).

But in keeping with Marshall's overall authorial strategy, Selina is depicted as not only her mother's child but as a second-generation immigrant negotiating between the "Americanized" and "Bajan" influences of her mother and father, respectively. Selina's father, Deighton Boyce, offers her an entirely different set of values and aspirations which are formed by his past and experiences both in Barbados and upon immigration to the United States. Marshall stated the first time in a 1992 interview how closely the character of Deighton resembles her own father:

> The greatest grief of my childhood was that my father deserted us to become a member of Father Divine's quasi-religious cult, a sect that was popular back in the thirties and forties. My handsome, charismatic father, who was given to wearing silk underwear and spats, who played the trumpet—or tried to for years—and who, like my mother, was a natural-born poet, would say to us in the morning, "Rise and shine and give God the glory!" This father whom I adored became a devotee of someone who decreed there were no more mothers and fathers, parents and children, rather that *he*, Father Divine, was father and mother to *all*. So that Samuel Burke, my father, one day forbade my sister and myself to call him Daddy. Finally, he disappeared out of our lives altogether to go and live in Father Divine's "kingdom" in Harlem, abandoning us to a cycle of poverty and my mother's rapid decline into bitterness, cancer, and an early death.

She goes on to explain that her fiction represents an attempt to "get over [her] anger" at her father, and to "overcome the fear that [she] had been *contaminated* with what [she] saw and sensed as his failure." *Brown Girl, Brownstones* represents Marshall's attempt early in her career to understand her relationship with her father, while her most recent novel and the subject of the next chapter, *Daughters* (1991), signifies "a final purging" of that effort. "I've been able at last," Marshall explains, "to forgive, to bless, and to release Samuel Burke from my life while retaining and honoring the love I still feel for him."[33] In *Brown Girl, Brownstones*, Marshall portrays Deighton Boyce's strengths and weaknesses as, like Silla's, a "culmination of all he has suffered." Based on his personal history in Barbados and the United States, Deighton, rather than being motivated by the opportunity "to rise" in America, is immobilized by the racist barriers that prevent him from realizing his potential in any number of professions he pursues in the novel. The inability to reconcile his dreams with reality destroys him. Continual rejection, including that by his wife, undermines Deighton's confidence on all levels and causes him to retreat repeatedly from what he perceives to be constant assault from the world around him.

In the first interaction between Deighton and Silla in the novel, Marshall employs black and white imagery and its history of connotations to emphasize the gulf that divides husband from wife sexually and symbolically. Deighton's uneasiness in "white" America and the "white" aspects of immigrant culture that are represented by Silla and the Association are reflected in his discomfort in Silla's white kitchen. As he departs for an evening with his lover, in the hall, the smell of Suggie's codfish hung in a dead weight, and he hurried downstairs, afraid that the smell would insinuate itself into his clothes and he would carry it with him all night as the undisputable sign that he was Barbadian and a foreigner. In the basement he paused uneasily at the kitchen door, shaken as always by the stark light there, the antiseptic white furniture and enameled white walls. The room seemed a strange unfeeling world which continually challenged him to deal with it, to impose himself somehow on its whiteness.

His wife stood easily amid the whiteness, at the sink, in the relaxed, unself-conscious pose of someone alone. (22)

Marshall skillfully contrasts Deighton, his romantic intentions, and his female counterpart in the novel, the sensual Suggie Skeete, with the "antiseptic" lightness and "unfeeling" aura of the sexually-distant Silla's kitchen. Marshall captures Deighton's cultural dislocation by describing him as at once not wanting to be recognized as a "Barbadian and a foreigner," and yet at the same time being unable to tolerate the world of "whiteness" in which his wife appears to function so easily. Characteristically, Deighton responds to the "hostile whiteness" of his home by attempting to flee it and his wife who had "ruined" his "elation" about inheriting the land in Barbados, and who had "undermined" his "triumph. . . . with all her doubting" (23, 26). But Deighton's effort to escape is thwarted by Ina, their first child, whom he meets on the way out and whose resemblance to his own mother reminds him of yet another's expectations that he has yet to fulfill. Ina also, in Deighton's eyes, stands as a living symbol of the love, now lost, that he and Silla once shared. Everything Deighton looks upon suggests to him "proof" of his failures.

This sense of inadequacy is only reinforced when Deighton, having left the house, passes a group of men cavorting on the street:

Deighton paused and watched them at a distance, jarred always by the violence in their coarse play, yet strangely envious and respectful. For somehow, even though they were sporting like boys, there was no question that they were truly men; they could so easily prove it by flashing a knife or smashing out with their fists or tumbling one of the whores in the bar onto a bed. But what of those, then, to whom these proofs of manhood were alien? Who must find other, more sanctioned ways? It was harder, that was all . . . None of this ever crystallized for Deighton as he stood watching them, and he would turn away thinking only that they were somehow more fortunate. (37–38)

Indeed, Deighton's manhood is contested terrain in this novel. Many descriptions suggest his literal impotence in contrast to the patriarchal-like power that Silla wields. The reversal of gender roles between these two characters has been the subject of much convincing criticism, but Barbara

Christian provocatively combines an ethnic and gender analysis when she argues that "it is [the] difference in their response to material gain, to America, a difference that has to do partly with their contrasting backgrounds and partly with their order of priorities, that forces them into battle against one another. . . . Their respective responses are what they are because of what a man and woman should be, and because these definitions are threatened by their confusion about what America is and what it promises."[34] Silla's power, as emphasized repeatedly through phallic images of rigidity and force, is expressed ultimately by her usurpation of her husband's supposed patriarchal authority when she forges his signature to sell his (home)land. This constitutes Silla's successful assimilation into the United States because, with the money, she is able to accomplish the immigrant community goal of "buying house." Deighton, by comparison, feels powerless in a society that demands from him—but at the same time denies him—"responsibility" as a male, a husband, a father, and an immigrant.

As he continues down Fulton Street, Deighton confronts yet another reminder of his powerlessness in the form of Seifert Yearwood, a fellow immigrant and owner of a small business. Yearwood, embodying the goals of the Association, "stare[s] unbelievingly" at Deighton when he expresses his disinterest in buying a house; Yearwood's face fills with "tragic concern" when Deighton states that instead he intends "'to get training [as an accountant] and get out there with them!'" (39). "Boyce, mahn," [Yearwood] began softly, "you can know all the accounting there is, these people still not gon have you up in their fancy office and pulling down the same money as them . . . " (39). The truth of Yearwood's statement causes Deighton to recoil physically in terror and shame. Figuratively assaulting Deighton's masculinity,

> Seifert's hand might have penetrated Deighton's shirt to rest hot and offensive on his flesh, for acute physical distaste gripped him. That touch recalled things thrust deep into forgottenness: those white English faces mottled red by the sun in the big stores in Bridgetown and himself as a young man, facing them in his first pair of long pants and his coarse hair brushed flat, asking them for a job as a clerk—the incredulity, the disdain and indignation that flushed their faces as they said no . . . He broke from Seifert Yearwood's hold and before Seifert could recover he was hurrying away, calling back, "I gone." (39)

Again Marshall emphasizes the impact of one's personal history on one's present, as Yearwood's pity recalls for Deighton the humiliation he suffered for even possessing aspirations of success in Barbados. His response in this scene, as well as in many others, reflects a profound desire, like that of Marshall's actual father, to disengage, both figuratively and actually, from a world that will not accept him as he is (39).

When Silla strips Deighton of his land, she not only seizes his patriarchal power, but also seizes the one buffer he created to protect himself from a hostile world—his fantasy of building a house in his homeland. By creating a vision of a house on the islands, Deighton also created a purpose for himself: that of planning, designing, and constructing the ultimate symbol of his wealth and ability to care for his family. More importantly, however, Deighton's dream of building a house reflects his need, like that of so many other displaced immigrants in literature, to find the one safe haven in which he might truly feel at "home." (Recall McKay's poem "My House," as well as V. S. Naipaul's 1961 novel, *A House for Mr. Biswas,* for just two examples.) The Grecian columns and decorative glass he imagines stand in direct contrast to the unadorned and formidable brownstone that Silla intends to purchase to support the family in reality. Upon seeing the land deed in his wife's hands, Deighton "moaned, breaking inside as the dream broke. Yet, as the moan tapered to a sigh, something else emerged. That sigh expressed a profound relief. It was as though Silla, by selling the land, had unwittingly spared him the terrible onus of wresting a place in life. The pretense was over. He was broken, stripped, but delivered . . . " (115). By destroying his dream, Silla does more than simply break Deighton's spirit; indeed, that had been done long ago. By selling Deighton's most valuable material possession— the piece of (home)land that ironically and fantastically assured him of his own validity—Silla strips him most poignantly of his self-possession. As Marshall describes, "the pretense" of trying to find his place in the world "was over." Deighton is at last able to retreat in full.

Following Silla's betrayal, Marshall employs a trope common to immigrant fiction—that of rendering a male newcomer symbolically impotent to the overwhelming forces of a mechanized and modern United States by portraying the severing of a limb or another figurative phallus by some type of machine. Like Henry Roth's character Albert, who is effectively "silenced" in the United States when his thumb is mangled by a printing press—that tool which is able to convey the voice of America—Deighton is similarly made mute when his arm is crushed by a machine. The combination of impotence and loss of voice is made clear earlier in *Brown Girl, Brownstones,* when Selina visits her mother at the factory.

The workers, white and colored, clustered and scurried around the machine-mass, trying, it seemed, to stave off the destruction it threatened. They had built it but, ironically, it had overreached them, so that now they were only small insignificant shapes against its overwhelming complexity. Their movements mimicked its mechanical gestures. They pulled levers, turned wheels, scooped up the metal droppings of the machine as if somewhere in that huge building someone controlled their every motion by pushing a button. And no one talked. Like the men loading the trailer trucks in the streets, they performed a pantomime role in a drama in which only the machines had a voice. (99)

Selina, who has come to confront her mother verbally about betraying Deighton—to "tell her to her face that she can't do it!"—finds herself similarly muted by the "noisy vortex." Suddenly she recognizes her position "in relation to the machine-force: a thin dark girl in galoshes without any power with words. . . . The machines' howling seemed to announce the futility of her mission" (94, 99). Silla, on the other hand, masters both language and the machine. Not only does Silla wield great power with words but she is seen by Selina as a machine herself, beautiful in her power and energy and yet frightening in her frenetic and mechanistic drive (99). The disfiguring tool that injures Deighton is intended to represent the crushing and silencing forces of Silla, the Association, and urban America more generally. It symbolizes all that he has hated in the United States: the technology that defies his natural world, the ideal of "progress" to which he will not aspire, and the perversion of his wife under these powers. Broken now both physically and emotionally, Deighton surrenders to the spiritual refuge of a popular Harlem evangelist named Father Peace (modeled on the actual figure of Father Divine) and in so doing, abdicates all responsibility for his wife and children.[35] In a final blow, like Marshall's own father, he refuses to be called "Daddy" by his family, and leaves them to become "Brother Boyce" in the restaurant of "the only Father," Father Peace (171–72). Deighton's final act of surrender, after being deported by his wife, is to commit suicide in order to avoid the scorn of Barbadian family and friends upon his return.

Thus, Deighton's past failures also shape his present, and the consequences of this teleological relationship—his psychic and literal death—dramatically illustrate for Selina the importance of constructing a meaningful present for herself so that she may have an equally meaningful future. The close of the novel presents Selina on the edge of this journey of exploring her history in order to better understand herself. The process of her reaching this point in the novel is subtle and complex, but two contrasting scenes, both involving the important ritual of dance, dramatically illustrate how Selina mediates not simply the often conflicting influences of her parents, but also those of the immigrant and non-immigrant, and black and white, communities more generally.

The first occurs within the highly loaded ceremonial arena of the Steed daughter's wedding feast. As Eugenia Collier describes, ritual and dance play an essential role in all of Marshall's works in that they provide "an economical way of conveying ideas and emotions that would take . . . pages to communicate" and "more important[ly], . . . evoke responses on a deeply psychic level. . . ."[36] The wedding dance in *Brown Girl, Brownstones* relates powerfully and concisely to Selina the benefits and the dangers of community membership as the group simultaneously supports, disregards, and rejects various members. Silla, having proven her allegiance to the ideals of the Association through her betrayal of her husband in an effort to buy a brownstone, is "consoled" and "praised" for her actions. At the same time, Selina observes the group's disrespect for the wishes of the young bride who, in keeping with common immigrant patterns of endogamy, is forced to marry a man she did not love simply because he was a fellow Barbadian. Marshall describes the bride as "walk-[ing] toward her bridegroom like" the comparably sacrificed "Iphigenia to her death at Aulis" (138). Most importantly, Selina painfully witnesses the community's expulsion of her father.

As the dance begins, Selina senses her own displacement outside the communal value system as she feels a "sharp sense of alienation" from those around her. Recalling her isolation in her own home at the book's beginning, Selina "wanted to leave the table" but finds nowhere to go "in the large hall and belong" (141). Ironically, in the context of this celebration uniting two Barbadians that is intended to symbolize the community's cohesion, Selina's estrangement foreshadows her father's rejection, as well as her own eventual dissociation from her fellow Caribbean immigrants, when she begins to realize "for the first time [that] there was no place for her here . . . " (141). Her discomfort slowly eases, however, at the community's will and insistence. Marshall describes the calypso music played by the wedding band as "binding the dancers together, setting them apart from all other people" (148). She juxtaposes this image of cohesion with the lyrics to a song that lays bare the group's marginality in American culture in order to suggest the necessity of unity within the immigrant community as a weapon against American ethnocentrism. But the community's abrogation and appropriation of the language of their oppressor emphasizes the irony of their rejection of Deighton.

Small Island, go back where you come from.
Small Island, go back where you come from.
You come from Trinidad in a fishing boat,
And now you wearing a great big overcoat!
Small Island, go back where you come from.

> You see them Bajans, they're the worse of them all!
> You hear them say 'I ain't gwine back at all.'
> They come by the one and they come by the two,
> And now you see them all over Lenox Avenue.
> Small Island, go back where you really come from. . . . (148)

Selina, "swaying with the thronged dancers, [feels like] part of a giant amoeba which changed shape yet always remained of one piece" (148). When in the center of this one-celled mass figuratively possessing one heart and one mind, she feels like "the source from which all the movement flowed. When pushed to the periphery, [she feels] like someone clinging to a spinning wheel" (148). But always she is a part of the group, reveling in the ecstatic ritual that "had become a high wave lifting her up" (147).

Her euphoria is ruptured, however, when she witnesses the darker side of this immigrant community's cohesion—its ability to cast out those members who refuse to adhere to its prescribed code of behavior. As Deighton enters and is shunned by all present, Selina struggles to free herself from the group but cannot: " . . . the glaring lights, the loud song and the other dancers seemed to be holding her from him" (149). As her father frantically searches for a welcoming face, the community "closed protectively around Silla and Ina; someone pulled Selina back. Then . . . the dancers turned in one body and danced with their backs to him" (150). In one final act of banishment, all eyes charge Deighton and drive "him from their presence," singing the "Small Island" song (150). As one small child, Selina is powerless to help her father in the face of this collective ostracism. Whereas the general setting of the wedding depicts an Iphegenia-like daughter sacrificed by her father in marriage, however, in this scene (which also evokes the humiliation of the "father" by the "son" in Nathaniel Hawthorne's famous tale "My Kinsman, Major Molineaux"), Selina, the daughter, must sacrifice the father. [37] In so doing, she earns the respect of the community and a degree of authority over Deighton, but for nights afterward her sleep is "marred by the image of her father groping as though blind or drunk from the hall" and the calypso beat that once represented her membership in a clan now only signifies her father's exile from that very same group (151).

Through this ritual Selina becomes aware of the dangerous consequences of community control. In response, she grows increasingly independent from the Barbadian Americans in the novel as she matures. As part of this process, she begins to embrace a larger and more diverse group of people. The second important dance scene in the novel, which takes place years later, when Selina is in college, illustrates the advantages and risks inherent in her movement beyond the confines of her own ethnic enclave. Selina's performance of the "life-cycle" expresses her distance from, as well as her links to, the people who constitute her literal and figurative families. As the recital begins and Selina is alone on the stage, she suddenly realizes "how exposed she would be . . . how utterly dependent she would be upon her own body. It must speak for her and, crouched there, she feared that it would not prove eloquent enough" (280–81). But in contrast to the atmosphere of the wedding dance, Selina feels empowered by her relationship to, rather than her alienation from, those around her:

> . . . the light cascaded down and formed a protective ring around her, [and] as the piano sounded and her body instinctively responded, she thought of [her boyfriend] Clive first, and then of Rachel—how she and Rachel had danced the night before as if guided by a single will, as if, indeed, they were simply reflections of each other. At this, her nervousness subsided, . . . (280–81)

Marshall refers to Clive and Rachel to symbolize Selina's disengagement from the expectations of her mother, the Association, and the immigrant community more generally. Clive, as Selina's first sexual suitor, represents her emergence into womanhood. Rachel, whose Jewish heritage has been repeatedly demeaned by Barbadian Americans in the novel, fuses with Selina "as if guided by a single will" to signify Selina's new association with people beyond the walls of the brownstones and of wholly different backgrounds from her own.

Marshall implies that Selina's experiences will protect her from whatever dangers exist in this new environment by directly paralleling the description of Selina at the recital with one with which the novel began. Marshall first introduced Selina in the context of a dance the young girl imagines involving the immigrant ghosts of her brownstone. Recall that Marshall described Selina in this opening scene as being wiser than her years: "A haze of sunlight . . . caught . . . the eyes set deep in the darkness of her face. They were not the eyes of a child. Something too old lurked in their centers. They were weighted, it seemed, with scenes of a long life. She might have been old once and now, miraculously, young again—but with the memory of that other life intact" (4). Marshall originally characterized this aged child as somehow conscious of the dangers that existed beyond "the safe, sunlit" security of her home and community, and yet at the same time longing to confront them (4). By the novel's end, Selina has taken several steps toward accomplishing that very task. Marshall's description of Selina as she stands before a sea of unfamiliar and expectant faces in the auditorium deliberately resurrects the earlier image: " . . . she rose—sure, lithe, controlled; her head with its coarse hair lifting gracefully; the huge eyes in her dark face absorbed yet passionate, old as they had been old even when she was a child, suggesting always that she had lived before and had retained, deep within her, the memory and scar of that other life" (281). Emphasizing the communal significance of this figurative rite of passage, Marshall describes Selina as hailing the members of the predominantly white audience just as she had hailed the white immigrant ghosts during childhood until, "at the climax, she was dancing, she imagined, in the audience, through the rows of seats, and giving each one there something of herself, just as the priest in Ina's church . . . passed along the row of communicants, giving them the wafer and the transmuted blood . . . " (281). When the applause greets her, it feels "as if the audience was offering her something of itself in exchange for what she had given it." Harkening back to her earlier "fusion" with the white ghosts who once inhabited her home, Selina becomes one with her audience again, "bearing something of them all away with her" (281–82). The image of communion is complete.

In this scene, Selina's dance is not simply about racelessness—about transcending the barriers constructed by a racist society by demanding, through the presentation of the life-cycle, recognition of herself on the basis simply of shared humanity. Rather, Selina's dance is also about claiming authority. Her ability to hold the audience's gaze—to control their attention by forcing them, through the magnetism of her movements, to witness *her* life-cycle—grants her a power of self-definition that she is denied in everyday life as a result of the constant imposition of stereotypes upon her. But, just as her youthful kinship with the white immigrants who previously occupied her brownstone is shattered by the mirror which "flung her [black face] back at herself" and "broke" the "mood," so too is her authority and her kinship with her audience shattered by a cutting encounter with racism following the performance. After the recital, Selina joins the dance troupe at the home of Margaret Benton, a white dancer. Marshall alludes to the theme of transcending ethnic barriers in her description of Selina, Rachel, and Margaret as composing a "startling trio—Selina, in the black leotard, her coat flaring wide, resembling somewhat a cavalier; Rachel, a fabulous sprite and Margaret, her hair catching each passing light, a full-blown Wagnerian heroine" (283). But in this novel of assault and retreat that is so carefully structured against the backdrop of two world wars, Marshall's association of Margaret with Wagner, a composer used throughout the German Third Reich to epitomize Aryan ideals, serves as a clear warning to us: indeed, it is Margaret's mother who is literally unable to see beyond Selina's black skin to the individual person within. Reducing Selina's performance to that of an animal in a circus and reanimating the long-held racist association of blacks with a "natural rhythm" and ability to dance, Mrs. Benton requests a meeting with the "black girl" who danced the life-cycle. Upon determining that Selina is Barbadian rather than African American, she immediately associates her with "Ettie," the West Indian "girl" who "did [her family's] cleaning" (287). Patronizingly praising "Ettie's" efficiency and reliability, Mrs. Benton attempts to prove her "liberalism" to Selina by claiming that Ettie "was just like one of the family." By conflating Selina with her hired help, and recalling Max Eastman's comment upon the occasion of Claude McKay's death that perhaps he should have "kept him as a cook or a maid," Mrs. Benton reduces Selina to the stereotypical role of the maid that has historically plagued black women in the United States. By collapsing Selina and Ettie into one, Mrs. Benton diminishes both to nothing more than blank black entities void of any distinguishing characteristics. At first, Mrs. Benton's comments simply "snuff out the last small flame of Selina's happiness" about her performance, but when she continues saying that even Selina "can't help [her] color," that she "speak[s] so well and [has] such poise," and that she's "taken [her] race's natural talent for dancing and music and developed it" so impressively, Selina recognizes that this woman—and many others in her life who will be equally blinded by racism—will never be able to "*see* . . . that she was simply a girl of twenty with a slender body and slight breasts and no power with words, who loved spring and then the sere leaves falling and dim, old houses, who had tried, foolishly perhaps, to reach beyond herself" (289).[38] Directly recalling the shattering image Selina saw of her face in the hall mirror during the book's opening scene, "when [Selina] looked up and saw her reflection in those pale eyes, she knew that the woman saw one thing above all else. Those eyes were a well-lighted mirror in which, for the first time, Selina truly saw—with a sharp and shattering clarity—the full meaning of her black skin. And knowing was like dying" (289).

But unlike Deighton, who actually does commit suicide, and like Silla, who defies a death imposed by others' visions of herself, Selina rejects this figurative murder of her identity. Terror overtakes her pain at the thought of strangers trying "to rob her of her substance and her self" and, her hate redeeming her, she flees the house and the dancers and the woman (289). Later, peering again at her reflection in a dirty window, Selina considers fully the implications of the world's blindness. She understands

clearly for the first time, the image which the woman—and the ones like the woman—saw when they looked at her. . . . Her dark face must be confused in their minds with what they feared most: with the night, symbol of their ancient fears, which seethed with sin and harbored violence, which spawned the beast in its fen; with the heart of darkness within them and all its horror and fascination. The woman, confronted by her brash face, had sensed the arid place within herself and had sought absolution in cruelty. Like the night, she was to be feared, spurned, purified—and always reminded of her darkness. (291)

Exhausted, Selina collapses against the glass, weeping at her realization that the white world's "idea of her was only an illusion, yet so powerful that it would stalk her down the years, confront her in each mirror and from the safe circle of their eyes, surprise her even in the gleaming surface of a table. It would intrude in every corner of her life, tainting her small triumphs—as it had tonight—and exulting at her defeats" (291).

Not surprisingly, however, given Marshall's artistic goal of joining disparate worlds, the author transforms this devastating moment of rejection into one of ultimate inclusion. Foreshadowing Marshall's nationalistic impulses that emerged through her involvement with the Black Power movement in the sixties, Marshall describes Selina's realization of the strength she can garner from those like herself. Suddenly Selina recognizes that she

was one with Miss Thompson, . . . One with the whores, the flashy men, and the blues rising sacredly above the plain of neon lights and ruined houses. . . . She paused across from the darkened Association building, where the draped American and Association flags billowed from the cornice. And she was one with them: the mother and the Bajan women, who had lived each day what she had come to know. (293)

From the example of these many influences Selina learns how to resist limited definitions of herself. As she walks through her neighborhood at the novel's close, Selina thinks of all—black, white, Barbadian, African American, male, female, young, old—who have shaped her: "Faces hung like portraits in her mind as she walked down Fulton Street: Suggie and her violated body, Miss Mary living posthumously amid her soiled sheets, Miss Thompson bearing the life-sore and enduring, Clive and his benign despair, her father beguiled by dreams even as he drowned in them, the mother hacking a way through life like a man lost in the bush" (307). Selina hopes that somehow these people had "bequeathed her a small strength" to "sustain her all the years." She worries that "it might be quickly spent and she might fall, broken before her time and still far from the center of life. For that was the quest" (308). As the novel ends, Marshall leaves Selina at the beginning of this quest, and it is the same quest which Marshall herself enacts through the process of writing her subsequent novels. In a recent interview, now nearly forty years later,

Marshall evoked a phrase coined by Ralph Ellison which describes the relationship of the writer to her work as the "completion of personality"—as the process, through writing, of "filling in the gaps that can bring a writer closer to wholeness and healing."[39] Fittingly, the final image of *Brown Girl, Brownstones* symbolically reflects the start of that process. Selina, having received something from every individual who has touched her during her brief dance through life, prepares for her journey beyond the brownstones, beyond Brooklyn, and beyond the United States in an effort to better understand herself and her world. But before going, she gives something to those she leaves behind. Recalling her declaration of self at the novel's beginning when she defiantly clanged her silver bangles to the silence, Selina hurls one of her bracelets back into the world of her youth. In so doing, she maintains forever the connection to that community, she preserves that "wholeness," even as she goes on to seek new kinship with other members of the black diaspora in the Caribbean and beyond.

Paule Marshall's first novel, then, offers an alternative paradigm for second-generation immigrant behavior. Whereas for many second-generation immigrants the process of maturation is intimately linked to the process of Americanization, Marshall's protagonist recognizes that in order to move forward she must first move backward. Marshall insists that, instead of rejecting the past and assimilating as quickly as possible into the "American scene" as Marcus Hansen's "law" of second-generation immigrant flight predicted, her character must understand and embrace both the familial as well as collective history of her "people" precisely so that she—and her literal and metaphorical extended kin—might have a meaningful future.

The motivations behind this alternative paradigm stem, at least in part, from the confluence of race and gender in this particular immigrant narrative. As Selina's experience with Mrs. Benton revealed, as a person with black skin she is inevitably linked to all others with black skin: in a society which sees phenotype first, Selina never can "shed" her ethnic past for an assimilated "American" present because her race intervenes in that melting pot process. Thus the "wholesale purging" of the ethnic past that immigration theorists have attributed to "typical" second-generation patterns is neither desirable nor necessarily even possible for *black* immigrants in the United States. Second, as a daughter, and not the son upon which traditional models of immigrant paradigms were based, Selina has been enculturated by other women in distinctly female realms such as the kitchen. While it may have been common for the immigrant son to wish to release himself from the burden of the "dead hand of the past," in

Selina's case, partly because of traditional patterns of gender socialization in which the transference of foodways, for example, commonly exists between women rather than across gender lines, the daughter transforms that "burden" into the very element that can ensure her survival amidst the assaults of a racist nation. For Selina, knowledge about her past serves as a weapon against her own and others' future degradation.

Paule Marshall openly acknowledges that her writing is intended to serve the very purpose of keeping the past alive. By recording and inscribing through fiction both aspects of her ethnic ancestry, she hopes to continue a transference of ethnic knowledge by "creating a body of work that will offer young black women, such as I was years and years ago, a more truthful image of themselves in literature. . . . I believe that literature that speaks to the truth of our lives is an empowering force. It gives us the sense of our right to 'be' in the world, and once you have that sense . . . all positive things follow from that."[40] Having achieved entrée herself, as a second-generation immigrant, into U.S. culture by birthright and into Caribbean culture by socialization, the "truthful image" Marshall seeks to depict is that of an individual who can be intimately linked to both worlds. As she states outright: "I don't make any distinction between African American and West Indian. All o' we is one as far as I'm concerned. And I, myself, am both."[41] The profound sense of "connection and reconciliation" that underscores this comment is expressed dramatically in Marshall's most recent novel, *Daughters.*

5

"All o' we is one"

Paule Marshall's *Daughters*

Paule Marshall's *Brown Girl, Brownstones* ends leaving us at the edge of Selina's impending pilgrimage to Barbados. Like Claude McKay, whose writings move geographically from Jamaica to the United States, then to Europe, to Africa, and finally back to the Caribbean, Marshall's œuvre figuratively extends the travels begun in *Brown Girl, Brownstones* by similarly carrying us on a global journey intended to link diasporic blacks to one another. Barbadian critic and author Edward Brathwaite described her writing as the "literature of *re*connection."[1] Before engaging in a close study of the current end point of these travels, that depicted in Marshall's most recent work, *Daughters*, it is important to trace the voyage on which her previous novels have taken readers.

Marshall's second publication, a collection of novellas titled *Soul Clap Hands and Sing* (1961), moves from "Brooklyn" to "Barbados" to "British Guiana" to "Brazil" (as the titles of each novella indicate). Marshall takes the title of the book from a line in W. B. Yeats's poem "Sailing to Byzantium." Like the poem, many of the novellas explore, within the contexts of each of the four regions in which the stories are set, the position of an older male in relation to the changing societies by which he is surrounded. One might consider these tales as "male" counterparts to Marshall's story, "To Da-duh, in Memoriam," in that they all address the confrontation of an ancestor-figure with the challenges posed by modernity. Marshall believes that *Soul Clap Hands and Sing* represents a shift in her writing from that of *Brown Girl, Brownstones* in that, "in its rejection of America's values, [*Brown Girl, Brownstones*] might be said to be an attempt at a revolutionary statement in individual rather than political terms. It was only in the second book, *Soul Clap Hands and Sing*, that I began consciously reaching for a more expressly political theme." She goes on to describe the collection as "tak[ing] up this dual theme of the emerging third world and a moribund West." In this same essay, Marshall links herself to Claude McKay by noting that they each have been criticized by literary critic and scholar Lloyd Brown for "indulging in a some-

119

what romantic view of West Indian society. As he sees it, in my rejection of Western technology I have, like Claude McKay, with whom he compares me, imbued the islands with an innocence and health which he suggests is both romantic and simplistic." She refutes this by stating that she is well aware of the "social and economic problems of the area where I have lived off and on for the past twenty years, but even more so of the psychological damage brought on by their history."[2] Indeed, that very psychological damage is the subject of her second novel, *The Chosen Place, The Timeless People* (1969).

The Chosen Place, The Timeless People explores in more depth the common histories that bind together people in these seemingly disparate regions of North, Central, and South America. Whereas *Brown Girl, Brownstones* concentrates on Caribbean immigration to the United States, *The Chosen Place, The Timeless People,* set in a fictional island named "Bournehills," reverses that concern by examining the impact of American "development" agendas on the Caribbean. This novel is again characterized by Marshall's self-described "obsession with history" as it emphasizes the need for newly independent nations (and by implication, individuals as well) to reclaim stories of their pasts beyond those taught by their colonizers, and to use this knowledge in the creation of alternative black national identities.[3]

Praisesong for the Widow (1983), Marshall's third novel, tells a different type of coming-of-age story as it chronicles the growth of a middle-aged African American woman during the character's metaphorical and literal journey, via a cruise ship, from White Plains, New York to her ancestral homes in the Caribbean and Africa. Here Marshall suggests that the expedition into the past is ongoing throughout all phases of life, but cautions that the complacency often resulting from success in a capitalist society can serve as a dangerous barrier to the "reconnection" process. As in Leslie Marmon Silko's *Ceremony* (1979), the return journey of this novel is enacted by both *Praisesong*'s protagonist, Avey Johnson, and by Marshall's readers. As critic Abena Busia describes, "to appreciate the widow's experiences fully, the reader must journey with her in the same active process of recognizing and reassembling [the] cultural signs" that will assist Avey in answering the question posed to all of Marshall's characters in some form or another: "What is your nation?" in the words of *Praisesong*'s Lebert Joseph, or "Who put you so?" as it is expressed by Silla Boyce.[4]

This question reappears once again in Marshall's 1991 novel, *Daughters.* The story of Ursa Beatrice Mackenzie picks up the thread of the narrative of Selina Boyce, but places it in the context of contemporary migratory patterns between the Caribbean and the United States.[5] Ursa, as the daughter of an African American woman and a Caribbean man, is clearly, like Selina, a bicultural product of a union of the Caribbean and the United States. But whereas Selina, as a Brooklyn-born, second-generation immigrant, sought a type of cultural and personal reconciliation of the American and Barbadian aspects of her heritage, Ursa, as a first-generation Caribbean immigrant herself, must find a balance between the two worlds which frame her—New York City, her chosen place of residence, and Triunion, the fictional island on which she was raised and where her family still lives. Mirroring the fluidity of current patterns of travel between the two regions, Ursa moves freely between her host and home societies. But this fluidity does not necessarily signal an enhanced sense of liberation for the protagonist, as was the case in *Brown Girl, Brownstones*. Rather, Marshall uses familial and cross-cultural connections in *Daughters* to explore the dangers inherent in relationships that are rooted in dependency.

More specifically, Marshall elevates Selina's quest for personal balance to a political level in *Daughters* by using male/female and parent/child interactions as metaphors through which to examine the often debilitating dependency that has resulted from the unequal, neocolonial relationship between the Caribbean region and its new "mother country," the United States.[6] While her previous novels examine the strength that can be gleaned from recognizing one's ties to others, *Daughters* tests the limits of affiliation based upon inequality and/or obligation. As she describes in a 1991 interview: "One of the principal characters in *Daughters* is dealing with, and I'm quoting T. S. Eliot here, what it means to come out from under the shadow of that red rock, that dependency that gets built in those early relationships."[7] Family ties create the catalyst for a new examination of women's autonomy in *Daughters* as well as provide the backdrop for Marshall's theorizations about how to rectify the negative consequences of the forced kinship between the United States and the Caribbean, a kinship that has resulted from a nearly constant exchange of people, products, and politics over the last fifty years.

Dependency is most cogently symbolized in the novel by childbirth and its permutations, including abortion. Marshall introduces each of the central female characters in relation to her experience with some form of childbirth, thereby linking these women through their reproductive capacities as both mothers and daughters. We are first introduced to Ursa and Astral (Ursa's father's mistress) in the process of abortions; Estelle (Ursa's mother), as she is experiencing a miscarriage; and Celestine (Ursa's father's lifelong nanny), in the context of her abandonment as a child by her own mother. But each woman responds to her maternal and filial responsibilities differently, signifying Marshall's commitment to portraying women's freedom to accept or deny the dependency that can result from procreative potential.

Daughters is not only about motherhood and interaction among women, however. Marshall dedicated *Daughters* to her father and brother, and not surprisingly, the novel is equally concerned with relationships between the sexes. Most centrally, it focuses on those between Primus McKenzie and the "constellation" of "stars" who are drawn to him by a seemingly inescapable pull: Ursa, Estelle, Celestine, and Astral.[8] Indeed, these alliances create the focus for the exploration of another type of dependency between men and women. As Marshall explains:

> "I had an absolute charmer of a father, . . . But he was a man who had great difficulty as a black man dealing with a society that denied him a sense of himself. He was unskilled, not able to find the work that he felt was in keeping with what he was as a person. He eventually abdicated his responsibilities, abandoned us. He fled, and that was exceedingly difficult for me because I so loved him. In many of my relationships along the way there was almost a repeat of that early relationship, always looking for this father in the men that I became involved with, and always preparing myself for the end of that relationship. How long it took me to move away from that and to recover, to insist upon autonomy."[9]

Daughters is modeled in part on Marshall's own experiences as a daughter and lover. She describes it as a novel "about the subtle deferring to men that was so much a part of my childhood and the childhood of many women."[10]

The caretakers of and prototypes for all of the relationships in *Daughters* are the statues of Congo Jane and Will Cudjoe, who are based on the famous Maroon leaders of Jamaican folklore who fought for freedom from British colonizers.[11] Congo Jane and Will Cudjoe, as "coleaders, coconspirators, consorts, lovers, friends," stand frozen in time at the top of Triunion's largest mountain, Gran' Morne, to represent forever an ideal partnership characterized by independence and mutual respect. At moments of crisis in her life, Ursa is revisited by the memory of the first moment she was introduced to these figures:

> "See if you can touch her toes, Ursa-Bea! Reach all the way up and try to touch her toes!" Estelle, her mother, whom she couldn't remember ever calling anything but Estelle, had gotten down on her knees at the base of the statue just minutes ago and put her to stand on her shoulders. Diminutive Estelle down on her knees in slacks—which she got away with wearing because she was the wife the PM went and "find" in America.[12]

Marshall significantly casts Estelle as the person who insists that Ursa physically touch these models of equanimity, for it is Estelle—who breaks convention by wearing slacks and by allowing her daughter to refer to her by first name—who most desires to model both her marital and parental relationships upon the equality and independence that Congo Jane and Will Cudjoe symbolize.[13] "And as Estelle rose to her feet again, both of them wobbling a little, Ursa had felt herself being slowly lifted toward the oversize stone woman in a lace shawl whose head appeared to be grazing the sky. A musket in one hand, a cutlass in the other, the stone woman was marching in place with three stone men on a pedestal that stood about eight feet above the ground." Estelle commands her daughter to "stretch all the way up and touch Congo Jane's toes, Ursa-Bea. Go ahead. Stretch! I'm not going to let you fall!" Ursa, poised somewhat perilously on her mother's small shoulders, reaches up to touch first "the giant foot" of Congo Jane that is defiantly "thrust forward," but also those of Will Cudjoe for "you can't leave him out," according to Estelle. Ursa "did as she was told, leaning dangerously over to her left to get at the other colossal pair of feet. Warmed by the sun, their toes had felt as alive as her own" (13–14). Marshall suggests the difficulty of achieving such balance within oneself and in one's relation to others as she describes Ursa "straining" to touch the toes of the statues, but she implies that Estelle, who encourages her daughter's self-reliance with a vigor that Ursa frequently mistakes for callousness, will support her child in her efforts. Indeed, as the story progresses, it is clear that Ursa must figuratively as well as literally "lean to the left" in order to make the ideal of Congo Jane and Will Cudjoe alive for herself. As a close reading of the novel will show, this memory revisits Ursa throughout her life to serve as the focal point in her quest for comparable balance and equality in her interactions with her parents, lovers, and friends.

Like Marshall's previous novels, *Daughters* is divided into four books. Unlike her earlier works, which tend to follow fairly traditional and linear narrative patterns, however, *Daughters* reflects, both formally and thematically, the more postmodern and post-colonial contexts of its creation. What makes this novel so different from Marshall's earlier writings, in fact, are those characteristics that it shares with so much postmodern and post-colonial fiction including, for example, a fragmentation of narrative voice as well as of geographic and temporal location, which gives the text an ambiguous sense of both self and place. Additionally, the novel follows contemporary patterns of "decanonizing" the authority of cultural and political institutions (particularly those of "the family" and of imperial and colonial governmental structures), of demonstrating a preoccupation with identity in relation to "home," and of embracing a far more "indeterminate" and relative vision of "truth" in which the role of the reader as a participant is vital in interpreting the meaning and significance of the main conflict of the tale.[14] While the goal here is not to make an argument for the novel's classification as either postmodern or post-colonial, it is important to acknowledge these qualities in order to understand the ways in which *Daughters* both marks a departure from and yet also remains quite similar to *Brown Girl, Brownstones* in terms of the development of Marshall's œuvre.

Book I of *Daughters*, titled "Little Girl of All the Daughters," introduces the novel's protagonist, Ursa Beatrice Mackenzie, and is headed by an epigraph to an Alvin Ailey dance: "Little girl of all the daughters, / You ain' no more slave, / You's a woman now." As the epigraph implies, the story of the novel on one level parallels that of Selina in that it chronicles Ursa's psychological journey from childlike servitude to her father to the liberating freedom of adult womanhood. Similar to the introduction of Selina in *Brown Girl, Brownstones*, the first chapter of *Daughters* delineates the important influences in Ursa's life, beginning most startlingly with an abortion she has just had. Marshall begins the novel with this pivotal scene to suggest the centrality of this event as a governing metaphor for the entire novel. Significantly and rather oddly, Ursa feels no pain following her abortion; indeed, she feels so well that she's "game enough to walk the forty-odd blocks to her apartment" through a cutting March wind (5). Upon arriving at home, Ursa is irritated to find urgent phone messages of concern about her prolonged silence from her best friend, Viney Daniels, and she is disappointed not to find a response from the Meade Rogers Foundation, a research group focusing on inner-city development projects, about her inquiry concerning potential employment. Throughout this section, Marshall, in keeping with her preoccupation with physical space, introduces not only the people and things that affect Ursa, but also her surroundings.[15] Marshall depicts New York City in stark terms, firmly locating her character within a postmodern, urban, and distinctly American environment: as Ursa flips through her mail from "The United Way of New York. *Time* magazine . . . The Christian Brothers Cleaning Company. The Council on Economic Priorities. The Literary Guild," the sound of the "planes taking off from Newark Airport" rumbles overhead (8). Still, she feels no pain related to the abortion. In DeLillo-like fashion, Marshall ironically juxtaposes the next catalogue of large impersonal social causes with Ursa's recent personal experience at the doctor's office: "Catholic Charities. Save Our Wildlife. Nuclear Scientists Against War. Committee for Democratic Renewal. The city controller's report. Get thee to the floor!" (9).[16] But suddenly, in the midst of this barrage of mundanity, Ursa spots among the junk mail "the familiar blue airmail envelope with the striped border and the official seal of the government of Triunion. The PM" (9).

The PM is Ursa's father, Primus Mackenzie. Ursa knows that his letter contains a plea for her return to Triunion to assist in his reelection bid to the island's parliament, and she is amazed by what she perceives to be his paternal instincts: "He had known, somehow he had known [about the abortion] and had timed the letter to arrive today" (9). Marshall conflates Ursa's abortion with the PM's request for his daughter's presence to signify Ursa's need metaphorically, having just done so literally, "to cut away those dependencies that can be so crippling."[17] Indeed, immediately following receipt of her father's letter, Ursa recalls another scene from her youth which, serving as counterpoint to her memory of her mother at the statues of Congo Jane and Will Cudjoe, also repeats throughout the novel and suggests the power her father wields over her:

> He used to stand at the edge of the swimming pool everyone said he had installed more for her than for the guests at the so-called hotel he owns, keeping an eye on her while she made like a little chocolate Esther Williams in the water. His shoulders in the shirt-jac suit he wore on Sundays—their day to go to the pool—would look to be a mile wide above her. His head with the high domed forehead she had inherited, and that had earned him the nickname PM when he was a boy, would appear larger than the sun. (9)

While the PM is clearly devoted to his daughter, his very presence and concentrated attention literally block her ability to see the light. He looms above Ursa at pool's edge, assuring her of safety but also denying her vision. Even as a child Ursa felt the PM's presence crowding her and, at times, she seemed willing to risk drowning to escape his control:

> Sometimes, as she glanced up and found she couldn't see the sun or even a blue patch of sky because of his being in the way, she'd do a sudden flip, annoyed, pull the water like a blanket over her head and dive to the bottom of the pool and sit there. Just sit in the watery blue, sunlit silence until the last bubble of air floated up from her lips and disappeared and her lungs ached to breathe in anything, even the blue water. (9–10)

But in the end, Ursa mollified her father by repressing her frustration and "surfacing with a grin and a wink. Then to get back in his good graces, she'd do more minilaps than they had agreed on for the day" (9–10). As an adult, she similarly appeases him by faithfully complying with his requests to return to Triunion at election time, despite the turmoil that this creates within her due to her despair over the island's economic demise, and her forced recognition that her father, despite his supposed authority as "the PM," is ultimately powerless over—and perhaps even complicitous with—the situation. This pattern of affectionate submission to paternal control shapes all elements of Ursa's history, and fundamentally inhibits her from achieving emotional, financial, and psychological independence.

As the introductory chapter continues, Ursa, rifling through the remainder of the mail, discovers the alumni newsletter from her alma mater, Mount Holyoke, and "falls motionless again" at yet another influential memory that suggests the degree to which her dependence upon her father has permeated all other interactions in her life. While in college, Ursa developed a close friendship with one of her teachers, Professor Crowder. Impressed by Ursa's abilities, this man paternalistically took her under his wing and assisted her in getting her first job at the NCRC, a consumer research firm in New York. But when she proposed to write her senior thesis on "the relatively egalitarian, mutually supportive relations that existed between the bondmen and women" of New World slave communities, prompted by her early exposure through Estelle to the statues and lives of Congo Jane and Will Cudjoe, Crowder rejected this without discussion, claiming that its fundamental premise of sexual equality was "highly doubtful" (11). Like Ursa's actual father, who blocked her vision at the pool, Professor Crowder similarly "crowded" Ursa's imaginative and intellectual potential by dismissing her creative impulses. Moreover, he blocked her emotional potential, as well, by reaffirming the culturally-defined "impossibility" of equality between men and women. Not surprisingly, Ursa's immediate fear upon learning of the rejection of her thesis topic by Crowder revolves less around her own sense of betrayal and more around the reaction of her father: "What's the PM gonna say, motherfucker?" (15). Still disturbed by the recurrence of this memory over a decade later, Ursa struggles to understand "why after twelve long years does that thing still rankle so?" (15).

The answer, of course, lies in the fact that Ursa has not yet broken her filial dependence upon her father; she has yet to "insist upon [the] autonomy" that Marshall believes is essential for self-possession in the most literal sense. Equally important, Ursa has also not yet achieved a romantic relationship rooted in the egalitarianism exemplified by Jane and Will. Marshall emphasizes the related significance of these dual barriers to Ursa's development in the final scenes of the chapter. First, Marshall depicts Ursa worrying that the absence of pain from the abortion indicates that "the doctor was some incompetent who only half did the job so that whatever it is, is still there" (18) As she frets, she is bombarded with images of her mother, Estelle, and of her childhood nanny, Celestine.

Marshall superimposes these assaulting images of Ursa's mother-figures with the abortion itself to emphasize that, despite Ursa's abdication of her own maternal potential (note that she refers to the fetus as "it"), she has not yet truly severed the ties that bind her to her own parental figures.[18] Second, Marshall juxtaposes the ignorance of Ursa's lover, Lowell Carruthers, about his own paternity with his weekly, Friday night preparations to catch the train to Philadelphia to act as a "stand-in daddy" for his nephews, whose father is dead. Marshall illustrates the emotional bankruptcy of the bond supposedly linking Ursa and Lowell by portraying Ursa, still feeling no physical evidence of the abortion, recalling amusedly the "love songs, . . . nothing but love songs" which filled the room during the procedure, and remembering that she had burst out with "a laugh that had hurt" at the absurdity of this implicit association of sex with love in the context of an abortion clinic. Ironically, this laugh, which ultimately exposed the emotional barrenness of her own life, was "the closest [Ursa had] come all day to feeling anything like pain" (17).

The reason behind Ursa's mysterious painlessness following her abortion motivates the remainder of the novel. Indeed, recurrently paired throughout Book I of *Daughters* are the issues of whether Ursa will heed her father's request to return to Triunion for the election, and her persistent concern about whether her abortion was actually successfully completed. This is because *Daughters* is, in many ways, a tale about the process of un-becoming a daughter. It is about breaking familial ties. But it is also about breaking colonial ties. It is about nations, and groups within nations, similarly asserting their independence from controlling, if also sometimes benevolent, "paternal" figures. If *Brown Girl, Brownstones* used the context of war (both World War II, during which the novel is set, as well as the cultural "wars" of the late sixties and early seventies which framed its creation) against which to enact its complex series of battles, *Daughters* uses the context of late-twentieth-century postcolonial social and cultural upheaval against which to portray the complex processes of claiming individual and political independence. The relationships of women in the novel to Primus Mackenzie illustrate one level of dependence; the relationship of the "colonized" poor in Triunion and Midland City to "colonizing" developers and politicians illustrates another.

Book II of *Daughters*, titled "Constellation," explores the first level dependence. The constellation of women who surround Primus Mackenzie are all referred to as "stars" (Estelle, Astral, Celestine, and Ursa) to suggest their gravitational attraction to this man who simultaneously represents, yet also obscures, the sun in their lives. As heavenly bodies, the women's names also allude to angelic forms, with the PM acting as a god-like figure in their midst. Indeed, "the PM" is not only the prime minister of Morlands, but he is also the "prime mover," the source of action among his worshipers: as the "*primum mobile*," that which communicates motion to others, Primus's needs and desires determine the re/actions of all the women who love him. Finally, Marshall's use of the letters "PM" also alludes to a theme of increasing importance in her work—aging—as it links Primus to "post meridian," suggesting that Primus Mackenzie must confront the "afternoon" of his life as a political leader and playboy, of sorts, who has passed his prime.

Despite the centrality of the PM in the novel, however, Marshall never allows the character to speak for himself. Instead, she presents all views of him through the eyes of Estelle, Celestine, Astral, and Ursa. That we, as readers, are sympathetic to a character who is never granted his own voice testifies to Marshall's success in taking a risk with form in *Daughters*. By empowering her female characters with the sole authority to relate, in their own words, their attraction to Primus—by trying, as she states in an interview, "in terms of point of view, to blend with the characters" rather than to control description through reliance upon the narrator's voice, as she did in *Brown Girl, Brownstones*, Marshall succeeds brilliantly in depicting the complexity not only of the PM, but of the women who care for him.[19] In this remarkable sense, he is not the center of the novel at all, but rather stands in peripheral relation to the women who define him.

Marshall first introduces Primus Mackenzie through the eyes of his wife in the second chapter of the novel, titled "Estelle Harrison Mackenzie." This is the only chapter in Book I set in the Caribbean and that ostensibly does not directly concern Ursa; but as a brief history of her parents, their relationship, and her conception, it is hardly about the mother at all, and is instead far more about the impact of the parental relationship upon the daughter. Marshall juxtaposes Estelle's memories of her earlier life with depictions of her present circumstances to inform us of the changing nature of Estelle's relationship to Primus during the course of their marriage. The chapter opens with the two rushing across the island to the doctor's office because Estelle, who has a history of miscarriages, is experiencing yet another one. As they drive through the Triunion darkness, Estelle recalls the first time she met Primus at a Carnegie Endowment gathering in her hometown of Hartford, Connecticut. Foreshadowing the storminess of their relationship, their first conversation revolved around the twenty wars in two centuries that shaped Triunion's history. Marshall reveals in this scene Estelle's " 'get up and do' spirit," her love of bringing [things] together and making [them] work," her interest in others, and her down home and down to earth attitude about people and material things as she stands unimpressed and undaunted by the lavish estate which surrounds them (144, 29). In contrast, Marshall portrays the PM as dividing his attention between "the intense buff yellow face raised to his," and the extravagance of the pool, the palazzo, and the important people in their midst, presaging his own desires for status and material gain (30). Finally, through Estelle's memories, Marshall describes their romantic courtship and eventual marriage.

Standing as counterpoint to these visions of the past is the present in which the towns Estelle and Primus drive through slide past just as the fetus slides out of Estelle's body: "Vincennes. Hastings Village. Wellington Town. *Gone!* . . . *Gone!* in minutes. Everything fleeting" (26). Gran' Morne, the mountain which dominates the North district and which Estelle learned from Primus early on was pronounced like "mourn," stands over her "like an anxious mother," not letting "her out of its sight since she stepped in the car an hour ago," seemingly lamenting the loss of yet another child and the deterioration of this troubled couple's love. The PM blames Estelle for causing the miscarriage because of her insistence upon being present at the dedication of a new market shed recently built in Morlands. The two of them together had agitated for its development, and Estelle wanted to be there for the opening, both to partake in the celebration and to ensure that the people wouldn't feel "slighted" by her absence (30). Her interest and participation in island politics is as great as her husband's, yet he seeks to deny her the right to involvement by restricting her to her procreative obligation to him: "'The market would have opened, it would have been dedicated, there would have been the little fete afterward without your being there. You should have stayed in town as I asked you to. As I begged you to'" (31). The gulf between the two could not seem greater.

The relationship between Primus and Estelle began based on the same type of equality reflected by Congo Jane and Will Cudjoe. Following their marriage and Estelle's move to Triunion in 1943, the two campaigned tirelessly together for Primus' first election to parliament. Marshall stages Primus' introduction of his new partner to the people of his home district against the backdrop of the statues of Congo Jane and Will Cudjoe at the Monument of Heroes to emphasize the parity which characterized the early days of their marriage (129). In chapter two of Book II, titled "Primus Mackenzie" but narrated by Estelle in the form of letters home, her contribution to her husband's success is made clear. Estelle describes their honeymoon as consisting not of the typical "mooning and spooning" at sites like Niagara Falls; on the contrary, she states that they have spent "nearly every night tearing around from one little village to another and one small town to the next and up and down mountains and

hills in the pitch darkness trying to get the brand-new husband elected
to public office" (127–28). Estelle revels in the excitement and challenge
of their mission: "*There has never been and there will never be another one
like it*. Period. This honeymoon is not only one for the books, it *is* the
book!" (127). Reflecting her own commitment to improving the welfare
of the people of Morlands, Estelle explains their routine to her "home-
folks":

> We're getting to be quite a team. After Primus finished giving the gov-
> ernment "licks," as they say here, for doing so little for Morlands, I
> usually say a few words. It's not a speech as such, although I also let
> them know how I feel about conditions here. Can you imagine, not a
> single clinic or dispensary in the district, no electricity, not a decent
> road to speak of or a decent drain along the road. And that's not the
> half of it. We're the poorest of the districts. And of course I beat the
> drum for Primus's platform. (131)

Invoking the reincarnation motif that appears throughout Marshall's
work, Estelle goes on to say that "I must have lived here in another life
because I feel so at home already. Everyone seems to like what I have to
say. Only last week an old woman came up after I'd said my piece to tell
me she plans on voting twice, once for Primus and the NPP and a second
time for me. How about that? I love it!" (131). At this point in her life,
Estelle is as blinded as her daughter will eventually be by the splendor of
the PM: as she "stood looking up at him from her scant five feet one, the
top of his head appeared to be grazing the black dome of the sky, while
the white of his eyes was the largest of the stars to be seen there" (137).
The PM, on the other hand, loves his wife for her commitment to him
and to his cause. Imagining how different things would be if he had married a woman of his own class from Triunion, he states that whoever it
might have been certainly "would have scorned going around with me to
these little poor-behind villages in Morlands. I wouldn't even dare ask
her. And as for standing up with me at a meeting and saying a few words
to the people or shaking some fella's rusty hand, not in this life! She'd be
too busy running behind the great people-them!" (132). Rather, Primus
"thank[s] his lucky stars for the Harrison's girlchild," precisely because
she is "not the sort to run behind anybody and who'll see to it that this
country boy in his donkey cart keeps to the straight and narrow" (132).

As important as the partnership conveyed in the above passage is
the possibility Marshall raises about the precise location of one's "homeland." For Estelle, her true place seems to be in Morlands. It is here that
she reaches her potential both personally and politically, as a spousal com-
plement to her intellectual equal and as a grass-roots stump speaker.
Marshall, in contrast to McKay, whose characters are homeless no matter

where they may be, seems to suggest that "home" may very well be where we locate ourselves, regardless of our birthright. The verb "to locate" stems from the Latin *locatus*, meaning both "to settle or be settled" as well as to "let for hire." Indeed, by the novel's end Estelle becomes so firmly settled in and committed to working for the people of Morlands that, forty years and a series of marital and philosophical betrayals later, she must take earnestly her promise to keep her husband to the straight and narrow and protect her "homeland" by deliberately intervening to prevent Primus's reelection to parliament because he himself has now become "too busy running behind the great people-them!" (132). Having endured years of manipulation and inactivity by the ruling party in the government, the elderly Primus has changed from an ambitious and energetic idealist to a complacent and weary old man. He has become more interested in investing in and profiting from a resort scheme initiated by overseas developers than he is in doing anything for the people of Morlands. He is even willing to sacrifice Government Lands, the most beautiful and one of the few remaining public beaches on the island, without even informing his constituents. Much like the male characters in Marshall's collection of short stories, *Soul Clap Hands and Sing*, Primus has indeed become "an aged man" and a "paltry thing / A tattered coat upon a stick," and Estelle sees it as her task to free his soul once again to "clap its hands and sing" by forcing him to confront his betrayal of himself, his ideals, and his (or more accurately, their) constituents. Like Silla Boyce in *Brown Girl, Brownstones*, another of Marshall's strong female characters who usurps her husband's patriarchal authority to ensure a better world for her children, Estelle undermines Primus' power to promote the continuation of oppositional forces on the island, thereby helping to secure a healthier future for the people of Triunion. In so doing, she reveals not her hatred of her husband, but, rather, her profound and redemptive love for him and the people he was elected to serve. At the same time, Estelle shifts the center of power from Primus to herself. She metaphorically seizes the reins of the donkey cart and in taking this action, becomes herself the prime mover, the god-like figure to her husband, as well as the political leader of "her people."

The two other "lovers" of Primus, his maidservant Celestine and his mistress Astral, similarly revel in and yet at the same time transform their love for, and apparent dependence upon, the PM to their own advantages. Celestine, who anticipates his every wish, does indeed move according to the directive of the "*primum mobile*" as she responds to all of Primus' needs without question. Estelle perceives this devotion as not only beyond the call of duty, but also as somewhat degrading to Celestine. She understands the relationship between Celestine and the PM as structured on an inherent imbalance of power in which the PM as "master" wishes and the "servant" complies. A letter from Estelle to her parents expresses her discomfort with this arrangement:

> It's all yours, I've more or less said. . . . if you want to get up at the crack of dawn to make coffee for the PM because you've always done it, fine. If you want to appear like a Johnny-on-the-spot before he even finishes calling your name—which she does all the time—that's fine with me too. It's positively eerie, homefolks. Her name is hardly out of his mouth before she isn't standing there. . . . Not only does she appear almost before he calls her, she seems to know what he wants without him having to say. Which is all the more eerie. So I've called a truce. Why try to take on the Sphinx? (166)

Revealing not only the subtle power struggle raging between the two women concerning the PM's attentions, this passage also exposes the cultural misunderstanding between Triunion native Celestine and U.S.–born Estelle who, like Harriet Shippen in Marshall's *The Chosen Place, The Timeless People*, may ultimately never fully understand certain of the island's traditions because of her ultimate status as an outsider, despite her commitment to the place and its people. To Celestine, however, as for Phyllis Shand Allfrey's character Lally in *The Orchid House*, serving the PM elevates her status both among members of her own community and within the household itself. "Always after me to do this or do that like she feels I missed out on something in this life. What does the woman know!" (345). Celestine Bellegarde, the "good caretaker" as her surname suggests, is motivated by a framework in which not simply working for the PM, but in fact being originally selected by his mother among all the other "door-mouth" or abandoned children to care for him for life, brings honor rather than shame and elevates rather than demeans. Thus, her "dependence" upon the PM actually represents, for her, a type of liberation.

Similarly, Astral Forde's relationship to Primus, though again characterized in one respect by the servitude inherent in being his employee as well as his mistress, is also based, in another respect, upon the promotion of stature she enjoys due to mere association with a figure of such public importance. Not only is the PM a small-business owner, but more significantly, he is a government official. In order to understand the configuration of power which characterizes their relationship, however, we must understand Astral's history. Through the conversations between Astral and Malvern, Astral's friend who lives in Armory Hill, the poorest section of town, Marshall reveals to us Astral's past and why being the "keepmiss" of Primus Mackenzie actually meets all her aspirations.

Astral came from "the country" in her teens in order to make a life in the city, a life in which the implicit goal was finding "somebody that's

in a position to help" her. Her friend Malvern counsels her from the beginning that "with that color you got and that Spanish Bay hair long
down your back, [you] could easy find somebody . . . high up, some big
shot that would send you to learn secretarial or bookkeeping so you could
work in a office or in one the banks, or even help you to open a little shop
of your own. Cause you could run a business" (121). Reflecting the harsh
class structure typical of many Caribbean societies, Malvern counsels her
friend to "Never mind you's not of a class with him, he might still be
willing to married because of the children—you'd make him some pretty-
pretty children. But even if he couldn't see his way to marrying with
you, at least he'd be somebody that could help you" (122). Following
Malvern's advice, Astral pursues this type of relationship with many men
until she finds ultimate satisfaction with Primus Mackenzie. First, she became a concubine of "Mr. Sealy," from whom she received training in
bookkeeping. Next, as companion to "Mr. Sandiford," she got her first
office job. As lover of "Mr. Weekes," she was able to take courses in typing
and secretarial work. Finally, as mistress of Primus Mackenzie, Astral became the sole manager of Mile Trees, his small hotel (177). Consciously
and willingly, she used her beauty to acquire the status and education
required for her vision of success.

In depicting these relationships against the backdrop of Estelle's reactions to them, Marshall again calls into question cultural differences and
American presumptions of morality. Using as her mouthpiece Celestine,
who belittles the light-skinned Estelle for protesting her husband's mistress, she asks: "And what if the woman is his keep-miss? Show me the
man in this place that don't have one and sometimes more than one. This
ain't America where they must do things different. . . . *Mes amis!* He has
a cross to bear in the *blanche neg', oui*" (198–99). On one level Marshall
suggests that all of Astral's hopes, at least as they existed upon entering
the relationship, have been met despite that her lover has never spent and
will never spend more than an afternoon in her company. This is accept-
able to Astral partly because the relationship offers her financial stability
and a degree of social stature. On another level, however, Marshall suggests that Astral is emotionally no more in control of her connection with
the PM than are Ursa and Estelle. Like these two, Astral is blinded by
her attraction to Primus. Repeating and remolding the motif she used in
Brown Girl, Brownstones to describe Deighton's eyes "with the sun in their
centers," Marshall depicts Primus as the sun, the moon, and the stars to
Astral.

He had turned around to face her . . . so that his head, his shoulders
and the top half of his body blocked out everything beyond the win-

dow in back of him. He seemed to fill the entire car. Stay just so, she
almost told him. If possible, she would've had him stay just like that
till Thy Kingdom Come, facing her with the smile and his body shut-
ting out everything beyond the car. (190)

Astral and Primus share a bond, based on a common history, that the PM
cannot enjoy with the American Estelle, a bond that reveals the emotional magnitude of their seemingly utilitarian relationship. As Marshall
explains through Astral, "there wasn't no need for a lot of talk between
them. No need to be always explaining their explanatories. They were
both from the same little two-by-four-place, after all, and knew how
things were done here, were said here . . . " (188). Thus, like Celestine,
Astral has turned the potentially servile aspects of her liaison with the
PM into sources of advantage. Rather than being a poor and truly dependent woman who must rely upon her patron for survival, Astral controls her own business and is surrounded by the "nice things" she sought
as a young woman. Although not married to the PM, she enjoys an intimate and committed relationship that allows her both autonomy and
partnership. Marshall emphasizes these aspects of the relationship between Astral and the PM by linking Astral to Congo Jane via the swatch
of lace (recalling Jane's lace shawl) that is always attached to Astral's
straight black skirt. The goal is balance, and Marshall means to suggest
that Astral has achieved that for herself.

Although each of the PM's lovers, Estelle, Celestine, and Astral, man-
ages at some level her dependence upon this paradoxically seductive yet
childish man, not one is able—nor perhaps chooses—to break fully from
him.[20] None except for his daughter, Ursa, the one woman whom Marshall
names not for a single star but rather for a full constellation. The story
of her severance from her father is actually the most important story of
the novel.

Ursa's love for her father is at once exhilarating and encumbering.
While, on one hand, his love protects her, just as he literally kept her safe
by supervising her at poolside, on the other, it prevents her from entering
fully into new relationships because it is rooted, as Marshall describes, in
a dependency that is "crippling."[21] Indeed, the first time that Ursa meets
her lover, Lowell, following the abortion, she tells him not about her termination of their pregnancy but instead about the PM's request for her
presence at the elections:

She's been waiting all evening to tell Lowell Carruthers this. Waiting
all week, in fact, ever since she woke up last Saturday morning to find
the blue envelope with the Triunion seal lying unopened next to her on
the bed. Seized by guilt she opened and read it before taking off the
heavy coat she had slept in or going to the bathroom. Read the part

about the elections over and over again, becoming more dismayed each time. She finally put the letter in the compartment of her headboard that she reserved for his mail alone. The sound of his voice on paper within easy reach. She had trouble sliding shut the panel, the compartment was so full.

Ever since then she's been waiting to tell Lowell Carruthers that one piece of news. (43–44)

Ursa's need to convey to Lowell the message from the PM—rather than the fact that she aborted their child—strikingly indicates the degree to which her relationship with her father usurps all others in her life. Indeed, the one reason that Ursa cites which might prevent her from accommodating the PM involves neither Lowell nor possible repercussions from the abortion; rather, she cites her employment with the Meade Rogers Foundation as a researcher on a study of economic renewal projects in a poor and predominantly black area called Midland City—a study which, in the end, exposes another type of dependency in the form of "domestic colonization" practices within the United States. Marshall presents Ursa's unshakable deference to her father as a metaphor for Midland City's subjugation by corrupt politicians, developers, and businessmen, and Triunion's forced reliance upon American tourism, industry, and investment, to emphasize the profound danger implicit in any relationship characterized by an imbalance of power. As such, she insures that *Daughters* is not merely an interior, psychological novel about relationships within families; on the contrary, it provides equally forceful political commentary on racism, colonialism, and economic exploitation within and among nations.

After providing the necessary contextual framework for our understanding of each of these three expressions of servitude in the first two books of the novel, Marshall conflates all issues upon one another in Book III of *Daughters*. She titles this book "Polestar" both because it is set in New York, the northernmost point of the novel, and because, like the "polestar" itself, the lessons of this section provide the directive principle or guiding force for the novel's denouement, Ursa's prevention of her father's reelection to parliament. As Book III begins, Ursa prepares for her first day of work on the Midland City project. Reflecting the PM's hold over her, she wears for the first time in months gold earrings and a bracelet he gave her when she got her first job at the NCRC. As she dons these symbolic shackles, she fondly recalls him boasting to his friends, " 'The National Consumer Research Corporation. One of the Fortune 500, bo. She's second only to one of the big directors there,' . . . Pleased. Proud. Her life set to his agenda" (250). On the way to work, Ursa composes in her head the letter she will write to her father to explain that her new job will prevent her from going to Triunion. Importantly, this letter, by containing references both to Midland City and to the resort scheme that will spell her father's demise, again emphasizes the interrelation of these three issues in the novel.

> Been holding off writing you, it'll say, because I didn't know for sure whether I'd be able to come down/say home/ whether I'd be able to come home for the elections next month. I've been waiting around for some definite word on the follow-up study in Midland City . . . when finally, only today, good news! They're going ahead with it after all. And guess who they called right away? The Mackenzies' girlchild. I've just come from a long meeting with the project director. And this time I'm to be one of the key people on the team./He'll like that./ . . . At long last the kind of long-range, in-depth research project I've always dreamed of doing./Don't forget to mention the money./And you'll be pleased to know that I'm being paid well this time, . . . So I'm a respectable working woman again. The only snag is that I have to start work almost immediately, which means I won't be able to get away for a while. I couldn't possibly ask for time off just as the study's getting started. In other words, Mr. Mackenzie, sir, you're going to have to get yourself reelected without my help this time, as difficult as that'll be./ Good. The joke will help. /I know you're going to be annoyed that I won't be there, but I'm sure you'd agree that business comes first and this is where I should be. . . . /What else? Talk about the resort. /By the way, what's the latest on the resort scheme? . . . (250–51)

But suddenly Ursa feels a "flutter kick around her heart at the thought of his face as he reads it. She might not hear from him for months, as happened when she left NCRC" (251). Marshall crafts Ursa's letter to reveal her protagonist's psyche at its most basic level. While Ursa clearly perceives her resistance to her father's request as an act of significant independence, partly enhanced by her recent employment and therefore financial freedom from him, Marshall indicates how obviously labored this supposed liberation truly is. She portrays Ursa simultaneously as an educated professional woman and as an anxious daughter, fearful of a reprisal from her beloved but controlling father.

Marshall also firmly establishes in the first chapter of "Polestar" the interpenetration of the Caribbean and the United States to which she has alluded throughout the book, particularly through the juxtaposition of issues surrounding Midland City and references to Triunion. To celebrate her new job in Midland City, for example, Ursa desires a Cuban dinner complete with "fried plantain," "avocado salad," "*bacalao* in an onion and tomato sauce of king mackerel *ecrevisse*," and "naturally, [some] red or black beans. Everything smelling and tasting as if it's just come out of the kitchen at Morlands" (252). While she revels in the beauty of the

New York spring day, she compares the pale greens to the colors of flora in Triunion and wonders whether the expatriated Estelle ever misses the change of seasons. Finally, she passes Carlos, the Guayabera-shirt clad doorman to Lowell's building, and is reminded of her "uncle Roy and his Spanish Bay shirts" (257). Ursa, despite the letter she has so defiantly drafted in her mind, suddenly "misses them all . . . the PM, Estelle, Celestine, even Astral Forde. Misses the stone faces of Congo Jane and Will Cudjoe and the other two out at the monument. Longs suddenly for the little miserable two-by-four island she's been hiding from with tears in her eyes . . . for the past four years," and "almost wishes for a moment that the study hadn't come through just yet" (257).

The climactic scene establishing Ursa's prolonged and adolescent reliance on her family is fittingly staged in the home of her lover, Lowell Carruthers, the man who feels most profoundly the barrier created by this unusually pronounced father-daughter bond. Marshall describes the view of Harlem that can be seen from Lowell's apartment window as resembling a "bombed-out, burned-out" ruin both to condemn the nationally-condoned racism of the United States and to foreshadow the impending battle between the two lovers. Ursa arrives at Lowell's apartment to find him once again wholly demoralized by his nemesis at work, and attempts to convince him once and for all to quit his job. His furious response exposes the real bone of contention between the two:

> The swollen knot between his eyebrows. The eye of a hurricane. Her little trash house of twigs and dried mud clinging to the side of some mountain in Morlands is about to be swept to the four winds.
>
> "And if I don't make a go of it, if I lose my fucking shirt, I can always go home and take over running Daddy's hotel, right? . . . I've always got that to fall back on." (264)

Lowell's insertion of the PM into a discussion which had nothing to do with Ursa, not to mention her father, indicates the degree to which this man whom he has never met has indirectly scarred his own life. As their conversation escalates into an argument, Lowell holds up an unforgiving mirror to Ursa that reflects the PM at his most vulnerable:

> "First off, since you're being so free with your advice again seems to me you should treat the gentleman I just mentioned to some of it. I'm talking about the gentleman with the hotel. Looks like he could do with some too. Why not write and say look here, Papa-daddy, you've been in that government job too long, it's about time you gave up your seat and let somebody else try to do something for your poor constituents. 'Cause *you's* tired, Papa-daddy. You need to throw in the towel, resign, retire, quit. Now that's some advice that's really needed, if you ask me. You'd be doing Papa-daddy a big favor." (265)

Shifting the focus of his rage to Ursa, Lowell charges that because "ninety-five percent" of her thoughts are of her father, she has room for little else in her life. When she protests that their argument is about Lowell's situation and has nothing to do with the PM, Lowell finally explodes, telling her that "Everything's about him!" (266). He claims that every action she has taken during their relationship has been in response to her father, from quitting the job at NCRC in a feeble effort "to stop always doing what pleased him," to getting another masters degree in order "to make up for having left the job." Marshall suggests through this dialogue that all of Ursa's adult actions, like the extra minilaps she used to do in the pool, consist of attempts to assert her independence followed by conciliatory gestures "to get back in [the PM's] good graces again" when the consequences of her actions become too painful (266). By shifting from first- to third-person narration throughout this scene, Marshall creates ambiguity about who is actually speaking and in so doing, importantly leaves us to question whether the thoughts expressed belong to Lowell or to Ursa herself.

As the battle ensues, Lowell forces Ursa to confront the fact that her resistance to returning to Triunion is intimately linked to the deflation of the PM's image in her own eyes: "It must have finally dawned on you that there's probably no real difference anymore between his so-called opposition party and the ratpack in charge. I suspect the truth came and stared you in the face that last trip, and you've been hiding from it ever since . . . " (266). Finally, he delivers the most piercing blow of all:

> "You're like that place you're from, you know that. Sun Island and all the places you're always criticizing. Independent in name only. Still taking orders from Big Daddy England, America or whoever. Still got that mind-set. Would be scared shitless to stand on their own if they could. That's you all over— . . . You need to come out from under the rock of certain people." (268–69)

Marshall's use of Lowell to convey perhaps the most important message of the novel may appear rather surprising, but when we consider that the central theme of *Daughters* involves balance—between sexes, between nations, within oneself, and in one's relationships with others—Marshall's intentions are more clear. As she herself states: "whatever feminist note is struck in the novel is not meant to obscure what I hope will be seen as a major theme in *Daughters*: the need for black men and women to come together in wholeness and unity. It is this which informs the novel at its deepest level."[22] Ursa's reliance on her family prevents her from loving Lowell fully. At a historical moment in which, as Marshall suggests, black men and women in particular must stand together, Lowell, as Ursa's potential partner and "co-conspirator" (to evoke the model of Jane and Will), is the logical mouthpiece to expose the painful incompleteness of Ursa's life.

Following the destruction of her relationship with Lowell, Ursa sends a letter to the PM informing him that she will not be able to attend the elections, and believes that, as a result, she truly is becoming independent. In keeping with Marshall's belief in the importance of ritual and recalling the significance of the wedding dance scene in *Brown Girl, Brownstones* in which Selina is forcibly severed from Deighton, however, Ursa must actually perform the process of metaphorically cutting the ties with her father in order to attain ultimate freedom. She does so in the concluding Book of *Daughters*, titled "Tin Cans and Graveyard Bones" in reference to a conversation between Ursa and her best friend, Viney, that took place earlier in the novel. After patiently listening to Ursa ruminate about whether she should heed her father's request, Viney had described her as "a cat with a string of tin cans and some bones from a graveyard tied to its tail" when it came to her relationship with her family. "The cans and bones keep up such a racket you can't hear your own self, your own voice trying to tell you which way to go, what to do with your life. . . . You know what you're gonna have to do with all that stuff, don't you?" Then Viney, "her hand turn[ing] into a scalpel" or the cutlass of Congo Jane, held her arm "ramrod straight" and let it fall swiftly down, "slicing the air" and presaging Ursa's most pressing responsibility (112). The occasion is provided by Estelle, who summons Ursa to Triunion following her discovery of the extent to which the PM has become involved with the Planning and Development Board's scheme to build a resort hotel on Government Lands, in the district of Triunion which he represents in parliament, and to restrict public access to its beach. "' . . . I don't think I can manage this one on my own. You have to come down here, Ursa-Bea. Maybe you can think of something. <u>And you have to come right away</u>!' That sentence had been underlined twice" (363). After months, indeed years, of protest over her husband's compliance with overseas investors, whom Estelle believes neither understand nor care about the needs of the island's inhabitants, she learns not only that the PM intends to invest heavily in the resort, but also that he intends to hide the development plans from his constituents until the upcoming election is over. As Estelle explains to Ursa upon her arrival:

> " . . . No experimental farm, Ursa-Bea. No agricultural station. No small farmers' cooperative such as your father and I talked about for years. No model village, housing scheme or hospital. No cannery or sisal plant or any other kind of factory or plant. Instead, Government Lands is to be a playground for the Fortune 500 and friends." (357)

Marshall indicts all tourist establishments, and especially American tourism in the Caribbean, through Estelle's description of the services the resort will provide: "filet mignon flown in fresh every day from Miami," "Dom Perignon served as a matter of course at the built-in bar in the swimming pool," "two huge pools, . . . one saltwater, one fresh, never mind the place will be on a beach that has the best swimming in the world," two eighteen-hole golf courses, tennis courts, health clubs, stables, a yacht marina, and a private airfield for chartered jets (358). These two women, having been trained for the "barricades" by the model of Congo Jane, cannot stand idle while the PM betrays his electors and himself. Becoming "co-conspirators" themselves, moved by their commitment to social activism and their love for Primus Mackenzie, they paradoxically redeem him through betrayal. The process of doing so comprises the ritual of Ursa's liberation.

Through a carefully arranged montage of images, Marshall depicts the final stage of Ursa's evolving separation from her father. Her journey begins after she and Estelle decide to provide the PM's opponent, Justin Beaufils, with a copy of the Planning and Development Board's prospectus to use as arsenal, and it is Ursa's task to deliver the document. Again Marshall's attention to the naming of her characters is evident: Justin Beaufils, as the successor of and adherent to the PM's original ideals, also succeeds the now beleaguered man as the "beautiful son" representing the people of Morlands just as the PM did in his youth. On the way to deliver the document, Ursa stops at the Monument of Heroes, the symbol of independence and equality that has loomed over her since childhood. Imagining the crowds who will stand before it during her father's election rally, Ursa gazes up at "the four who will also be part of this cheering section tomorrow night. The old man, Pere Boussou, . . . Alejandro, the boy-soldier from Spanish Bay, . . . Congo Jane and Will Cudjoe, coleaders, coconspirators, consorts, lovers, friends" (376). Standing before the "four heads graz[ing] the early morning sky" forces Ursa to confront not only her father's hypocrisy but also her own: she recognizes that neither one of them has lived up to the ideals represented by the heroes before her. She recalls Lowell's response upon learning that Congo Jane and Will Cudjoe were "so close" that one couldn't "call her name without calling or at least thinking of" his: " 'We need to get back to thinking like that,' " Lowell had said. To "being like that again if we're ever going to make it' " (377). Ursa finally begins to acknowledge her own role in building a barrier to such unity in her relationship with her lover. As she contemplates the statues further, resentment toward Professor Crowder for denying her the opportunity to tell the world about them floods her mind once again. But "now that she can finally write the paper, she hasn't as yet put down the first word. Reams of notes all over the apartment and not even the introduction written. That part of her life still on hold for some reason" (377). Ursa cannot write the paper, of course, because the process of extolling Congo Jane and Will Cudjoe would painfully expose her own shortcomings. Recognizing this, Ursa "can no longer meet their eyes" and turns away.

Following her interlude at the Monument of Heroes, Ursa goes to the beach at Government Lands, a sacred place which she used to visit with her father alone and which he is now about to destroy. Listening to the waves sounding "Ke'ram," the meditative mantra she uses when she seeks a sense of inner peace, Ursa's mind is bombarded with affirmations of the action she is about to take. First, she recalls the masses of people for whom regular, Sunday baths at the Government Lands beach constitute not merely a physical cleansing but actually a spiritual renewal:

> Sunday is sea-bath day at Government Lands beach. People like peas on the beach from the time God's sun rises. All those who don't spend the day in church coming to have a sea-bath. The children running and flinging themselves half naked into the surf, and the grown-ups—the small farmers, the cane cutters on the big estates, the coffee growers from up Gran' Morne, the men and women who work the rice fields in the wide valley below Bush mountain—all of them performing a careful ritual before actually going for a swim. They will stand waist-deep in the breaking waves, scoop up water in their cupped hands and splash it over their arms and shoulders and chests, and in great handfuls over their heads, while keeping their faces turned to the horizon and beyond. Only after thoroughly splashing themselves will they then go for a swim. Some never even bother. They simply remain in the surf, anointing themselves with seawater until they decide to come out. (378–79)

This vision triggers another memory, equally powerful in its baptismal connotations. Ursa recalls Estelle's assertion one day during her childhood that when one is at Government Lands everything feels like it has "been created no more than ten minutes ago. Everything and everybody's brand-new" (379). These recollections, in addition to confirming the mystical significance of the beach to the people of Triunion, also importantly intimate to Ursa the rebirth she will experience when breaking from her father.

The waves provide another link between past, present, and future as they remind Ursa of the time she and Viney visited the Government Lands beach together, and suddenly she recalls Viney's urging her to attempt to reconcile with Lowell before she left for Triunion on the most recent trip: "I mean you don't just up and walk away from somebody you've been going with for over six years because of a quarrel, I don't care what was said" (382). Marshall identifies Viney as "another Congo Jane who loved pretty things" to emphasize that she, having been betrayed by men she loved and having experienced the difficulties of raising a child alone, can speak with authority about the need to love and be loved in a mutually respectful relationship. Ursa resisted her "sister/friend's" advice to call Lowell, but during the night before she flew to Triunion, her sub- conscious tormented her with a dream that reflected her own ambivalence about her obligation to her estranged partner. Sitting on the beach, Ursa remembers that in the dream Lowell "groped for her arm" as though it "was a stick being held out to someone drowning." She resisted his pull, and the "tug-of-war" between them "soon turned into an all-out brawl." Hordes of people, including Professor Crowder, who "wav[ed] the re- jected [thesis] proposal" in the air, "egg[ed] them on, throwing pen- nies at their feet and taking bets as to which of them would go down first. . . . A battle royal. A nigger show" (383). The fight stopped only when a police officer who had once mistakenly arrested Ursa's young god- son hauled them both away. Marshall explicitly invokes one of the most fa- mous tropes in African American literature—intraracial battles fomented by external forces—to emphasize that the struggles between black men and women in contemporary America are as life-threatening to the race as is racism itself.[23] Indeed, Marshall asserts that the cultural systems that pit black men and women against one another are merely expressions of a new and more insidious form of racism, and she suggests that it is the responsibility of black women, on whose "power" a "society ultimately depends" according to her citation of an African proverb, to reach out to black men in order to defend the children from this omnipresent danger.[24]

The memory of the dream upsets Ursa, and so to rid herself of it, she walks "in the direction of Gran' Morne to the north. With the help of the ground mist, the mountain has begun its morning's levitation, along with everything else. Trees, houses, rocks—all slowly taking to the air" (383). In this novel, as in African American literary and folk traditions more generally, both the North and flight signify liberation; thus, with each step forward, Ursa symbolically moves closer to freedom. She sheds all her belongings: "her sandals," her "beach bag," "no bathing suit, no towel, not even a pair of sunglasses," and walks unencumbered to a large rock on which the children play "Monument" by acting out the story of Congo Jane and Will Cudjoe (383). As she climbs this mini-monument, Ursa notes the sunlight refracting through the bellowsed throat of a liz- ard and thinks how,

> as if by magic their throats . . . swell till they [become] a thin, sheer, translucent fan, and the sunlight passing through it . . . [is] trans- formed. Ke'ram. Thinking: just as the children playing Monument to- morrow will be transformed. . . . I'll come back to see them in the

morning. Thinking too: there won't be many Sundays left for them. The uniformed security guards patrolling the beach will be enough to discourage the rock climbers and everyone else from coming near the place. In short order, Government Lands beach will be the exclusive property of the NCRC types flown in on the private planes. (385)

Marshall first associates the motif of transformation with the figurative Monument of Heroes to symbolize the potential in Ursa to change the parameters of her own life in order to attain greater equanimity in all respects. She then contrasts this image with the ugliness of the resort hotel to motivate Ursa to take action.

Finally, after contemplating her connection to all of the women who love her father—Estelle, Celestine, and Astral—and recognizing their collective responsibility to save him from his own cynicism and self-betrayal, Ursa leaps up at last to deliver the prospectus to her father's challenger. Letting "her legs take off under her," she rushes "downward in a headlong plunge she can't control—that she doesn't want to control—" to the sand below. Marshall illustrates Ursa's newfound freedom by describing her as literally airborne "for seconds at a time" as she speeds to the base of the rock (389). But instead of landing on her feet, Ursa crashes to the ground, striking her right hip on the sharp edges of stone. After a moment of recovery, however, she leaves the beach and completes her mission.

The significance of Ursa's injury remains unclear until the night of her father's election rally. Although she experiences tremendous pain the evening of the fall, pain which sweeps across the well of her stomach in wave-like intervals, "lancing her as if someone had taken a knife to her," she resists awakening either of her mother-figures, Estelle or Celestine, for help and decides simply to stand alone, surrendering to its force (390). Her aching body reminds her of the absence of pain following her abortion, and her concern about whether the operation had been performed correctly: "*Viney, do you think those idiots might've only half done the job, and whatever it is, is still there?* . . . That crazy thought again. Two whole months have passed, and it still comes back from time to time to hag her spirit" (391). But only in the context of the final rally, at which Primus is confronted by his constituents, does Marshall make clear the importance of Ursa's injury: "The worst of the [soreness] had all but disappeared by yesterday morning. Then, . . . just as she was climbing the steps of the monument with Estelle and Celestine, the final meeting about to begin, it flared up again." On this occasion, however, Ursa "welcomes . . . the waves . . . cutting across her stomach" because they "drown out the catcalls and the accusations from the crowd" and "blind her to the sea of flyers being held up in the darkness." Mostly, the pain grants her reprieve from having to see "the PM alone at the front of the platform, under the rigged spotlight. His Gethsemane as he stood there unable to get in a word" (407).

Ursa's anguish, supposedly a result of the hip injury but which Marshall significantly describes as like the lance of a surgical knife, actually stems from her termination of her dependence on her father. It is the delayed pain she did not feel after having a literal abortion at the book's beginning, because the ties she needed most desperately to cut, those binding her to the PM, were not yet severed. Only when Ursa accomplishes this break by distributing the flyers and ultimately saving her father's soul does she feel the results of her actions: " . . . The pain returned last night to blind and deafen her to all that, and then vanished again this evening when the final count came in from the polls" (407).

Equally important, however, is Marshall's association of Ursa's pain with the wave-like contractions of labor. For, as was illustrated by her ritual at the Monument of Heroes and the Government Lands beach, in the process of separating from her father, Ursa also experiences a rebirth which will allow her to attain in her relationships with family, friends, and lovers the harmony and balance exemplified by Congo Jane and Will Cudjoe. In the final scene of the novel, Marshall depicts Ursa partaking in a modern-day ritual cleansing through which she completes her own transformation by shedding the last remnants of her crippling dependence on the PM, and affirming her independent identity: " . . . upon reaching the City after the three hour flight [from Triunion], she'll have the cab bringing her from Kennedy stop off at the natural-foods store not far from her on Broadway. There she'll buy a large packet of herbal mineral salts. . . . And the first thing she'll do when she reaches the apartment is to fill the bathtub with water as hot as she can stand it and take a long, delicious soak in chamomile, rosemary, or comfrey scented salts. To get rid of the last of the soreness. That before anything else. Ke'ram" (408).

Clearly *Daughters* expands upon many of the questions Marshall originally posed in *Brown Girl, Brownstones*. The young Selina Boyce of her first novel in many ways reemerges as the more seasoned, but equally questing, Ursa Mackenzie who similarly struggles to unravel the ways in which history shapes identity, and women's identity in particular. As Marshall explains,

> the characters are all daughters who are in some way connected with the other, back to [Congo Jane]. . . . One of the themes that informs my work is being not only connected with those mother poets who were my mentors and instructors but also with the women who created them. It's part of how we define ourselves as a people. How do black women get a sense of self? How do we create an identity that will permit us to

function? . . . it's all about the creation of a more truthful and liberating identity.[25]

While Marshall once again examines the theme that is implicit in so much of her writing—that of knowing one's past in order to understand the present—she transforms and reinterprets this issue in *Daughters* to consider the ways in which the present, and, specifically, willful action taken in the present, can alter the future. By looking forward, rather than backward, and by emphasizing agency rather than ancestry, Marshall empowers her female protagonist with an ability to control her destiny in a manner that has been only intimated in previous works.

But this novel is not simply about personal freedom. Indeed, the postmodern and post-colonial context in which Ursa's quests for identity and autonomy take place allows Marshall to comment on larger sociopolitical relationships between the Caribbean and the United States as well. She abandons the more traditional temporal scheme that characterized her previous work for a highly fluid chronology that spans two months but which incorporates moments reaching back to the time of slavery in order to obscure the lines between past, present, and future. She alternates settings between New York and Triunion, blurring the boundary between the United States and the Caribbean, in order to emphasize the wave-like movement of cultures and peoples that characterizes contemporary society. While she resolves for Ursa, on a personal level, the issue of dependence in the context of the protagonist's relationship to her family and most particularly to her father, Marshall leaves unanswered the more unmanageable questions of subjugation concerning oppression within and among nations and races. Indeed, in some respects, we are not much further along than we were at the conclusion of Claude McKay's life, and the questions posed earlier still remain. To what degree can a region overcome a history of forced migration, displacement, colonization, slavery, indenture, emancipation, nationalism, and neo-colonization to achieve ultimate independence? Is such independence possible in a modern world characterized by such high degrees of sociocultural, political, and economic interpenetration? Although Marshall does not answer these questions directly, she does powerfully command her readers, as they seek the answers, to adhere to the fundamental principle of mutual respect which stands as the cornerstone of true liberation and independence. *Daughters*, in her mind, is most basically about "the coming together, the working together not only of black men and women, but of the entire black community throughout the world. Idealistic, I know, romantic even—I've been accused of both—yet the possibility, the necessity of that union sustains me."[26]

Afterword

WHEN I FIRST began this project, my goal was to come to a more nuanced understanding of the relationship between African Americans and African Caribbeaners in the United States. My interest in the topic was provoked by two main concerns. First, several years ago, surrounded by the intellectual ferment of the exploding discipline of African American studies and interested in black women's writing and cultural history in particular, I was puzzled by the relatively routine inclusion of Caribbean-born authors like Jamaica Kincaid, Rosa Guy, and Michelle Cliff, for example, in addition to Marshall, on syllabi for courses in African American literature. At that point my interest was cursory and my questions were simple: if these writers were "West Indian," why were they presented as part of the "African American" literary "tradition," and what was the relationship between those two "traditions" anyway? Were not the issues surrounding the experience of immigration and the reality of different national origins to be considered? Were these writers "ethnically" Jamaican or Haitian or Barbadian and "racially" black? Did one take precedence over the other? Indeed, how exactly were race and ethnicity related in the United States?

These questions led me in a number of different directions, including seeking out Caribbean writers and depictions of Caribbeaners in African American fiction. I was surprised to discover repeated portrayals of "West Indians," ranging from Ralph Ellison's Ras the Exhorter to James Baldwin's Mr. Proudhammer to Toni Morrison's Elihue Whitehead, that were less than flattering. Such portrayals caused me to question in more depth, from theoretical and historical angles, processes of identity construction, how race and ethnicity affect these processes, and what consequences these might have for intrarace relations. Believing that in fictional creations can be encoded deeply felt perceptions, attitudes, and occasionally even daily realities that might provide insights into the larger cultural moments framing their creation, I began to tease out the contours of literary depictions of African American/African Caribbean interaction. As is the case with most intellectual enterprises, however, the broader my questions became, the more specific I realized my focus needed to be in order to find the answers. Eventually, what began as a general inquiry into the relationship between the two communities has ended as a study of two specific writers who have traditionally themselves straddled, and whose works have been made to straddle by "canon" constructors, the realms of both African American and African Caribbean literature and culture.

Throughout the project, it has been my contention that the issue of (im)migration, and its concomitant concerns with identity and nationhood, play pivotal roles in the writing of African Caribbean authors in the United States. Accordingly I have traced, through a grounded and historicized analysis of particular texts of two specific Caribbean immigrant authors, a pair of very different responses to the conditions of migrancy and immigration. Claude McKay, in both his autobiographical and fictional writings, expressed a deep sense of perpetual alienation from his home and multiple host societies, while Paule Marshall conveys in her writings a profound and seemingly ever-growing sense of her interconnectedness with both her "homes" in the United States and the Caribbean. A variety of factors beyond each writer's status as an "immigrant," including their immigrant generation, their gender, and the historical and cultural contexts in which their works were produced, have also been considered as influences affecting these responses. Through this examination, I have tried to achieve a number of goals.

First, I have tried most simply to illuminate our understanding of the work of McKay and Marshall by revisiting it from a perspective not previously addressed in criticism. Indeed, I believe that the focus on immigration undertaken here has helped to achieve my second goal of explaining in more depth the complicated web of international critique and affiliation embedded in the work of each writer. Third, I have sought through this process to enrich our understanding of the ways in which the experiences of black immigrants can be both similar to and also radically different from white immigrants' experiences, and in so doing, to suggest the limitations of traditional immigration theory when it is applied specifically to African Caribbeaners but also, by implication, to postcolonial immigrants more generally. Fourth, I have hoped to disrupt the traditional paradigm that has operated in literary studies, which has tended to classify McKay and Marshall as either "African American" or "Caribbean" writers, in favor of a more flexible appreciation of how their work illustrates a relation between the two regions and cultures. Finally and most importantly, through all of these efforts I have attempted to complicate essentialized conceptions of "African American," "black," and "Caribbeaner." But obviously a number of important questions remain.

First and foremost are some basic questions concerning literary history. The alternative poles of dislocation and dual location demonstrated by McKay and Marshall provide just two possible models of immigrant-author reaction to the United States. While the works of these two writers do provide a valuable framing device for understanding patterns in this century, what might the models provided by other earlier, as well as more recent, immigrants look like? How does the work of McKay's contemporary, Eric Walrond, for example, compare to that by McKay? What about similarities and differences between Marshall's writing and that of her contemporaries, Audre Lorde and June Jordan? How do the writings of Jamaica Kincaid, a more recent arrival who moved to the States during the "third wave" of immigration—the largest of the waves and characterized by considerably different "push" and "pull" factors from the previous two—compare to those of McKay and Marshall? Indeed, how might something like Kincaid's relatively immediate entry into the highly literary circles of the New York publishing industry—and also her detachment from them—affect her depiction of the position that African Caribbeaners occupy in U.S. society? Would this have any impact on her work at all? What about the works of Michelle Cliff and Derek Walcott, who claim somewhat similar positions in the American literati? How does the presence of each of these people as professors in academic institutions affect the teaching of Caribbean and African American literature in the United States? What about someone like V. S. Naipaul, who is in some respects "at home" in neither U.S. nor Caribbean literary circles? How might one approach the work of a relative newcomer to the scene, like Edwidge Danticat, who, in contrast to her predecessors, can now see her place in a developing "tradition" of Caribbean American letters? How do the differences in national origins of these writers affect the viability of such a "tradition" in a region that is so radically diverse in language, race, and culture? Is the concept of a "tradition" absurd to ponder at all? Finally, exactly what is it—or is there anything—that binds these writers to one another in the first place, thus warranting discussion of either "tradition" or "group"? The work of all of these authors demands further scrutiny if we are to understand the ways in which the "Caribbeanization" of "America" is shaping contemporary U.S. and Caribbean literary history.

As important to consider are questions about African American authors. Given the racial dichotomy generally at play in the United States, combined with a long history of black nationalist, Pan-African, and, more recently, diasporic interests expressed by the native-born black population, it is important to examine in more depth the nature of cross-racial connections between writers of different national origins. How do the works and experiences of McKay, for example, compare to his compatriot Jean Toomer—a native-born African American who shares McKay's placement within but relative dissociation from the Harlem Renaissance, as well as a history of involvement with a different set of white radicals like Mabel Dodge and Waldo Frank? Indeed, it is not implausible to argue that Toomer also shared with McKay a deep sense of alienation, but for very different reasons. A comparison of these two writers might illuminate what elements of McKay's experience are specific to his status as an immigrant, for example, and what elements might have been characteristic of writers in general during the period, since many modernist authors felt alienated from the larger society and, like Ezra Pound, considered this stance as essential to generating art. Equally constructive comparisons can be drawn between Claude McKay and Langston Hughes, who were deeply sympathetic in terms of certain elements of aesthetics and ideology, but worlds apart in terms of their relation to the African American elite. Similarly, one might gain valuable insights into Marshall's work by holding it up against that by African American women writers of the same generation, like Gayl Jones or Alice Walker, who share Marshall's cross-cultural interest. While some work has begun this line of inquiry, further investigations might demonstrate how the diasporic visions of native-born black writers compare to those with immigrant histories, thereby further illuminating our understanding of the nature of black immigrant versus non-immigrant writing in the United States.[1] Perhaps we will discover that a new category of "black immigrant letters" is required.

Finally, questions surrounding the nature of "ethnic writing" in the United States must be addressed. First, further comparative case studies must be performed on the relationship between "ethnic" writers such as Maxine Hong Kingston, Richard Rodriguez, and Leslie Marmon Silko, to mention those cited in this study, with "racial" writers of African American, African Caribbean, or other black origin in order to further test the relationship between ethnicity and race in the United States. If race and ethnicity are considered to be conceptually distinguished terms, what are the differences and similarities between "ethnic" and "race" writing in this country, both formally and thematically? Are these categories legitimate descriptors of such "genres" of literature at all? If race and ethnicity are considered to stand in relation to one another on a continuum, what then constitutes the larger body of "ethnic" writing in general? Is it literature written by "ethnics"? Is it literature, as Werner Sollors has shown in his insightful reading of Mark Twain's *A Connecticut Yankee in King Arthur's Court*, written by anyone, including "non-ethnics" (if there is such a thing), in which ethnic concepts are embedded? (Indeed, Rey Chow makes a convincing case for the "ethnicity" of the film *Jurassic Park* [Spielberg, 1993], according to this line of reasoning).[2] Or is it simply literature written about "ethnic" topics? Such comparative inquiries will illuminate the theoretical underpinnings of "eth-

nic" writing in the United States as well as help to carve out more precisely the relationships between such routinely categorized, but perhaps
not appropriately problematized, groupings of "Asian American," "African American," "Native American," or "Chicano/a" writers in literature
anthologies and course curricula being produced during this very "multicultural" moment in American history.

   Moving beyond the realms of literature, numerous questions about
immigration history and theory also deserve attention. While I have suggested that race plays a unique role in the way that black immigrants
perceive and are received by American society and that the situation of
African Caribbean immigrants provides a particularly useful example
through which to explore in more depth the relationship between race
and ethnicity in the United States, much more work needs to be done on
precisely how these factors affect processes of identity construction. How
does one's sense of racial or ethnic selfhood change upon moving from
a society in which at least sixty-four different gradations of color exist, as
is the case in certain areas of Latin America, for example, to one in which
the individual is treated as basically "black," "white," or "other"? We must
learn, in much more detail and with sociological grounding, how the experiences of groups of black immigrants differ from those of whites. Are
there important points of distinction between the experiences of black
immigrant groups of different national origins? What is the status of relations, both historically and in contemporary society, between different
black immigrant groups, as opposed to that between black immigrants
in general and African Americans, as has been sketched here? How does
a factor like language enter into these equations? What of the relationship between black immigrants and other "immigrants of color"? What
about that between black immigrants and white immigrants? Again, while
ground-breaking work is being done on certain immigrant groups, more
comprehensive studies that incorporate the data compiled by sociological
investigation with the insights of race and ethnic theory will lead us to an
increasingly clear, if also increasingly complex, vision of the relationship
between immigration, race, ethnicity, and identity in the United States.[3]

   Finally, and perhaps most compellingly, the concept of "home" in
modern society must also be addressed—a concept that is inevitably
linked to key issues in contemporary literary theory. McKay's and
Marshall's differing models have illustrated that the category of "black
immigrant" must be seen as no more stable or uniform than any other
that has been considered. Indeed, as a July 1998 series on "the new immigration" in the *New York Times* so aptly illustrates, the range of responses to the experience of migration and the notions of home embraced
by contemporary immigrants are as multifarious as the individuals are

multiple. Increasing numbers of people, like Marshall, find themselves not living between but actually within two worlds—New York for three weeks a month, Barbados for one. At the same time, increasing numbers of other contemporary Americans, both black and white—many of whom are notably *not* immigrants—find themselves dislocated while even at "home." Clearly, a concern with "home" seems to be a dominant issue for our era. So what might it be that links us to a place and a people, possibly thousands of miles away, which we visit only rarely? What makes the Virgin Islander on the opening page of this study begin his story with an assertion of his identity in relation to his home, but end with a return to New York? What made Colin Powell begin his narrative with a description of his return "home" to Jamaica, even though he had not been there since his childhood and had lived all of his life in the United States? As Emile Durkheim first suggested in 1933, we seem to require some kind of intermediary group between our individual families and the larger apparatus of the state to offer a type of emotional or moral or psychic support that prevents us from lapsing into a condition of anomie.[4] Interestingly, it seems that "home"—the "old country," the "mother land"—whether symbolically, as in the case of Powell and other second- and third-generation immigrants, or literally, as in the case of first-generation immigrants who commute between two nations—seems to serve as that apparatus. To claim membership in a group—"I am a Virgin Islander"—is to assert one's sense of belonging, of kinship, of membership with something that is larger than oneself. It is to have an immediate affinity with other Virgin Islanders, particularly in a foreign environment, even if one has never met them before. Ironically, it is precisely what many immigrants have and what many native-born Americans lack. Thus the experience of being an African Caribbeaner, despite Homi Bhabha's important theorization of the necessary processes of national recreation that occur upon the act of migration, is bound by certain shared realities. There is something that links black immigrants from the Caribbean to one another and stimulates the formation of some type of unit for social and political purposes, and that something seems to be intimately connected to a shared understanding of the significance of the common geographic and cultural home from which Caribbeaners come.

Finally, this concern with "home" can be paralleled to a larger concern with "nation." "What is your nation?" is the question dominating Paule Marshall's *Praisesong for the Widow*. Marshall's protagonist is asked this in an effort to get her to identify and claim her connection to her ancestors. Recall that Claude McKay, when asked a similar question, claimed that he had no connection to a nation or a people, but rather was an "internationalist." While this study has shown that the responses of McKay and Marshall to this type of question seem contradictory, I suggest that they actually illustrate instead comparable efforts to make sense of one of the most salient predicaments of the modern era—the predicament of dislocation. Marshall's response follows what might be called an "affirmative" pattern in African Caribbean writing in which one's sense of relation to others is paramount, while McKay's follows a more "resistant" pattern in which the sense of one's difference from others dominates. Both share distinct features of what is commonly considered post-colonial writing. The strategy of "abrogation" and "appropriation" in which the linguistic dominance of the oppressor is abrogated and its structures appropriated for indigenous or "native" uses is clearly, on some levels, what McKay does with both his more political dialect poetry and with his later sonnets. The postmodern fragmentation of Marshall's latest novel mirrors the post-colonial sense of a fragmented world. The general condition of marginality, of living between two worlds, and of an avowedly "special post-colonial crisis of identity," rooted in preoccupations with place and displacement, certainly thread through the work of both writers.[5] But it is not my purpose here to make a case for the determination of either writer's "post-colonial status." Rather, I wish to suggest that certain features of the post-colonial condition might be inevitable consequences of modernity. Indeed, such feelings and experiences might be inescapable for anyone who chooses to be mobile—to move away from "home"—for whatever reasons. While it is clear that many aspects of post-coloniality are unquestionably rooted in the distinctive experiences, histories, and legacies of imperialization, I suggest that we need a more rigorous inquiry into those aspects of it that resonate with the type of modern marginality first outlined by Robert Park—who, not insignificantly, based his theory in part on Georg Simmel's essay "The Stranger" in which the "Jew" was the model. The Jewish diaspora, the black diaspora, the modern diaspora—"the dispersion of people of one country into other countries"—a word whose synonyms are "exile," "migration," "scattering." Is this the common plight of a modern world—a world in which nationhood is paradoxically both nothing and everything, still? A world in which a sense of "home" continues to ground us, even if we define ourselves in opposition to it? A world in which a "global economy" and a pervasive and invasive popular culture that transcends international borders continually works toward our homogenization, and yet at the same time a world in which our sense of difference from one another continually shapes both personal and geopolitical realities? What does "home" become if all places begin to look the same? Will or can they ever look the same? These are the questions that remain.

Notes

Introduction

1. Ira de Augustine Reid, *The Negro Immigrant: His Background, Characteristics and Social Adjustment, 1899–1937* (1939; reprint, New York: Arno, 1969), 174, 179.

2. These narratives have been republished with a new introduction by Werner Sollors as *The Life Stories of Undistinguished Americans As Told by Themselves* (New York: Routledge, 1990). For an important examination of the African American migration narrative in particular, see Farah Jasmine Griffin's *"Who set you flowin'?": The African-American Migration Narrative* (New York: Oxford University Press, 1995).

3. Maxine Hong Kingston, *Tripmaster Monkey: His Fake Book* (New York: Vintage International, 1990), 307–308.

4. For a valuable overview of these arguments, see Werner Sollors, ed., *Theories of Ethnicity: A Classical Reader* (New York: New York University Press, 1996), xxix–xxxv. See also Sollors, *Beyond Ethnicity: Consent and Descent in American Culture* (New York: Oxford University Press, 1986), 36–39.

5. See Mary C. Waters, "Ethnic and Racial Identities of Second-Generation Black Immigrants in New York City," in *The New Second Generation*, ed. Alejandro Portes (New York: Russell Sage Foundation, 1996), 171–96; T. M. Woldemikael, *Becoming Black American: Haitian and American Institutions in Evanston, Illinois* (New York: AMS Press, 1989); S. Michael, "Children of the New Wave Immigration," in *Emerging Perspectives on the Black Diaspora*, ed. A. V. Bonnett and G. L. Watson (Lanham, Md.: University Press of America, 1990).

6. See Timothy B. Powell, ed. *Beyond the Binary: Reconstructing Cultural Identity in a Multicultural Context* (New Brunswick, N.J.: Rutgers University Press, 1999).

7. Ralph Ellison, *Invisible Man* (New York: Random, 1952), 488.

8. I must thank an anonymous reviewer for suggesting this parallel.

9. Homi K. Bhabha, "Dissemination: Time, Narrative, and the Margins of the Modern Nation," in *The Location of Culture* (New York: Routledge, 1994), 148.

10. I thank Rey Chow for her provocative lecture "The Study of China in the Age of Theory," delivered on September 11, 1998, at the Center for Twentieth Century Studies at the University of Wisconsin–Milwaukee, for stimulating this line of thinking by raising a comparable question concerning the nature of "Chinese cultural studies."

11. Colin L. Powell, with Joseph E. Persico, *My American Journey* (New York: Random House, 1995), viii.

12. Ibid., 3.

13. Herbert Gans, "Symbolic Ethnicity: The Future of Ethnic Groups and Cultures in America," in Sollors, *Theories of Ethnicity*, 436–38.

14. See Paul Gilroy, *There Ain't No Black in the Union Jack* (Chicago: University of Chicago Press, 1991); Gilroy, *Small Acts: Thoughts on the Politics of Black Cultures* (London: Serpent's Tail, 1993); Gilroy, *The Black Atlantic: Modernity and Double Consciousness* (Cambridge: Harvard University Press, 1993); Stuart Hall, ed., *Representation: Cultural*

Representations and Signifying Practices (London: Sage, 1997); Hall and Paul du Gay, eds., *Questions of Cultural Identity* (London: Sage, 1996); Delores Mortimer and Roy S. Bryce-Laporte, eds., *Female Immigrants to the United States: Caribbean, Latin American, and African Experiences* (Washington, D.C.: Smithsonian, 1981); Elsa M. Chaney and Constance R. Sutton, eds., *Caribbean Life in New York City: Sociocultural Dimensions* (New York: Center for Migration Studies, 1987); Philip Kasinitz, *Caribbean New York: Black Immigrants and the Politics of Race* (Ithaca: Cornell University Press, 1992); Mary C. Waters, *Ethnic Options: Choosing Identities in America* (Berkeley: University of California Press, 1990); Irma Watkins-Owens, *Blood Relations: Caribbean Immigrants and the Harlem Community, 1900–1930* (Bloomington: Indiana University Press, 1996).

15. Some attention has also been directed to the image of the Caribbeaner in African American letters: see Melvin B. Rahming, *The Evolution of the West Indian's Image in the Afro-American Novel* (Millwood, N.Y.: Associated Faculty Press, 1986), or Lloyd W. Brown, "The West Indian as an Ethnic Stereotype in Black American Literature," *Negro American Literature Forum* 5.1 (1971): 8–15.

16. For discussions of McKay within the Harlem Renaissance, see Stephen Bronze, *Roots of Negro Racial Consciousness: The 1920's—Three Harlem Renaissance Authors* (New York: Libra, 1964); Nathan Huggins, *Harlem Renaissance* (New York: Oxford University Press, 1971); Amritjit Singh, *Novels of the Harlem Renaissance: Twelve Black Writers, 1923–1933* (University Park: Pennsylvania State University Press, 1973). For an analysis of his "American" poetry, see Jean Wagner, *Black Poets of the United States: From Paul Laurence Dunbar to Langston Hughes*, trans. Kenneth Douglas (Urbana: University of Illinois Press, 1973). For consideration of his political ideologies as expressed through some of his fiction, see Michel Fabre, "Aesthetics and Ideology in *Banjo*," or Liliane Blary, "Claude McKay and Black Nationalist Ideologies (1934–1948)," both in *Myth and Ideology in American Culture*, ed. Regis Durand (Lille, France: Publications de l'Université de Lille, 1976), 195–209. For treatment of his role within Jamaican literary history, see Edward Baugh, *West Indian Poetry 1900–1970: A Study in Cultural Decolonisation* (Kingston, Jamaica: Savacou, 1971); Lloyd Brown, *West Indian Poetry* (Boston: Twayne, 1978); Bruce King, *West Indian Literature* (London: Macmillan, 1979). A notable exception to the more traditional studies of McKay's Jamaican poetry can be found in Michael North's excellent study *The Dialect of Modernism: Race, Language, and Twentieth-Century Literature* (New York: Oxford University Press, 1994).

17. See, for example, John McCluskey, Jr., "And Called Every Generation Blessed: Theme, Setting, and Ritual in the Works of Paule Marshall," in *Black Women Writers (1950–1980): A Critical Evaluation*, ed. Mari Evans (Garden City, N.Y.: Anchor-Doubleday, 1984), 316–34, which comments on the dearth of early criticism of Marshall's work; see also Nick Aaron Ford, "Search for Identity: A Critical Survey of Significant Belles-Lettres by and about Negroes Published in 1961," *Phylon* (1962): 1348, and Darwin Turner, "Introduction," in Paule Marshall, *Soul Clap Hands and Sing* (Washington, D.C.: Howard University Press, 1988), for pieces that discuss Marshall's work within the context of African American letters more generally.

18. Most notable among these texts is Barbara Christian's early study *Black Women Novelists: The Development of a Tradition, 1892–1976* (Westport, Conn.: Greenwood, 1980). The concept of a particular "tradition" of black women's writing on the basis of certain shared attributes, including gender, race, and language, was first asserted by Barbara Smith in her 1977 essay "Toward a Black Feminist Criticism." This view was contested by Deborah McDowell in her 1980 essay "New Directions for Black Feminist Criticism," in which McDowell questioned the existence of some type of monolithic black female language as well as the dangers inherent in correlating the political ide-

ology of a text with its aesthetic value. Hazel Carby, in *Reconstructing Womanhood: The Emergence of the Afro-American Woman Novelist* (New York: Oxford University Press, 1987), similarly challenged the notion of a tradition by arguing that each individual text must be carefully understood within the complex of its historical, cultural, and sociological contexts. Since language represents a negotiation of power between two peoples or groups at a given moment, Carby claimed, no language can be monolithic and shared by people simply on the basis of a common race or gender. In their assertions of the need for historical specificity and analytical treatment of gender and race, McDowell and Carby's works reflect a shift in black feminist criticism from thematic to more theoretical grounds.

19. For writers who focus on diasporic connections in Marshall's works from a more international angle, see, for examples, Abena Busia, "What Is Your Nation? Reconnecting Africa and Her Diaspora through Paule Marshall's *Praisesong for the Widow*," in *Changing Our Own Words: Essays on Criticism, Theory, and Writing by Black Women*, ed. Cheryl Wall (New Brunswick, N.J.: Rutgers University Press, 1989), 196–240; Rhonda Cobham, "Revisioning Our Kumblas: Transforming Feminist and Nationalist Agendas in Three Caribbean Women's Texts," *Callaloo* 16.1 (1993): 44–64; Velma Pollard, "Cultural Connections in Paule Marshall's *Praisesong for the Widow*," *Caribbean Quarterly* 34 (1988): 58–70; or Gay Wilentz, *Binding Cultures: Black Women Writers in Africa and the Diaspora* (Bloomington: Indiana University Press, 1992). For studies which discuss Marshall's international connections in relation to African American writers, see, for examples, Stelamaris Coser, *Bridging the Americas: The Literature of Paule Marshall, Toni Morrison, and Gayl Jones* (Philadelphia: Temple University Press, 1995); Dorothy Hamer Denniston, *The Fiction of Paule Marshall: Reconstructions of History, Culture, and Gender* (Knoxville: University of Tennessee Press, 1995); Joyce Pettis, *Toward Wholeness in Paule Marshall's Fiction* (Charlottesville: University of Virginia Press, 1995).

20. Michelle Cliff teaches writing at the University of California–Santa Cruz and at Trinity College (Hartford), Michael Thelwell at the University of Massachusetts–Amherst, Jamaica Kincaid at Harvard, and Derek Walcott at Boston University, to cite only a few examples.

1. "A Special Issue"

An earlier version of this chapter was first published in *Beyond the Binary: Reconstructing Cultural Identity in a Multicultural Context*, ed. Timothy B. Powell, copyright © 1999 by Rutgers, The State University. Reprinted by permission of Rutgers University Press.

1. Charles S. Johnson was an African American sociologist who played a pivotal role in the Harlem Renaissance through his position as the Urban League's national director of research and investigations and editor of the *Opportunity*. Johnson, "A Caribbean Issue," *Opportunity: A Journal of Negro Life* 4 (1926): 334. All subsequent references will be cited parenthetically in the text.

2. For an important full-length study of this issue from a historical perspective, see Watkins-Owens, *Blood Relations*.

3. Kasinitz, 24. First-generation immigrants are those who actually migrate from a home to a host country; the "second generation" consists of the children born in the host country of these immigrants.

4. Reid, *The Negro Immigrant*, 31–32.

5. Kasinitz, *Caribbean New York*, 24–25. Large groups of black immigrants were also concentrated in Massachusetts and Florida.

6. "Push" factors are those issues considered to drive immigrants out of a home

society (i.e., economic collapse, political turmoil, limited resources), and "pull" factors are those characteristics which draw immigrants to host societies (i.e., economic growth potential, educational or employment opportunities, reunion with immigrated family members).

7. Marshall, "Black Immigrant Women in *Brown Girl, Brownstones,*" in Mortimer and Bryce-Laporte, *Female Immigrants to the United States,* 5.

8. For a more detailed discussion of the significance of the Panama Canal to African Caribbean immigration to the United States, see Watkins-Owens, *Blood Relations,* 11–29.

9. Dawn Marshall, "A History of West Indian Migrations: Overseas Opportunities and 'Safety-Valve' Policies," in *The Caribbean Exodus,* ed. Barry B. Levine (New York: Praeger, 1987), 15–31.

10. Watkins-Owens, *Blood Relations,* 14.

11. Reid, *The Negro Immigrant,* 68.

12. Ibid., 69–70; quoted from original article by Harvey T. Patterson, "American Democracy in the Canal Zone," *The Crisis* 20.2 (1920): 83–85.

13. One of the opportunities Walrond obviously sought was a place in the literary world; six years after immigrating to the Unites States, he earned a position as the business manager of *Opportunity* during the publication of the "Special Caribbean Issue."

14. Peter Linebaugh, "All the Atlantic Mountains Shook," *Labour/Le Travailleur* 10 (1982): 87–121; cited by Paul Gilroy, *The Black Atlantic,* 13.

15. Watkins-Owens, *Blood Relations,* 18.

16. For further information see Joe Trotter, *The Great Migration in Historical Perspective: New Dimensions in Race, Class, and Gender* (Bloomington: Indiana University Press, 1988); Carole Marks, *Farewell— We're Good and Gone: The Great Black Migration* (Bloomington: Indiana University Press, 1989).

17. W. A. Domingo, "The Gift of the Black Tropics," in *The New Negro,* ed. Alain Locke (1925; reprint, New York: Atheneum, 1992), 341.

18. Reid, *The Negro Immigrant,* 84.

19. Shirley Chisolm, *Unbought and Unbossed* (New York: Houghton, 1970), 8.

20. Reid's research showed that between 1931 and 1935, of the roughly 50 percent of immigrants who reported occupations upon arrival, 40.4 percent identified themselves as industrial workers, 28.1 percent as laborers (with the skill level being unspecified), 17.6 percent as previously employed in commerce and finance, and 12 percent as professionals. Reid, 83, 244.

21. George Hutchinson, *The Harlem Renaissance in Black and White* (Cambridge: Harvard University Press, 1995), 443–45. For an extensive treatment of Larsen's biographical history, see Thadious M. Davis, *Nella Larsen, Novelist of the Harlem Renaissance: A Woman's Life Unveiled* (Baton Rouge: Louisiana State University Press, 1994). Carl Van Vechten was a white patron of the arts in Harlem and author of the 1926 novel *Nigger Heaven.*

22. For a more detailed discussion of Caribbean entrepreneurial practices, see Aubrey W. Bonnett, "Structured Adaptation of Black Migrants from the Caribbean: An Examination of an Indigenous Banking System in Brooklyn," *Phylon* 42.4: 346–55; for a discussion of the absence of these systems in the African American community, see Ivan H. Light, *Ethnic Enterprise in America: Business and Welfare among Chinese, Japanese, and Blacks* (Berkeley: University of California Press, 1972), 19–44.

23. For a thorough discussion of Caribbean political involvement in Harlem, see Watkins-Owens, *Blood Relations,* 75–111. She also provides an important analysis of

the ways in which Garvey's presence served to heighten ethnic consciousness in Harlem (112–26). For a complementary study of the political radicalism of more recent immigrants, see Kasinitz, *Caribbean New York* (1992).

24. *New York News*, August 28, 1926, as quoted by Watkins-Owens, *Blood Relations*, 94. See also the discussion of Harrison's centrality in Gilbert Osofsky, *Harlem: The Making of a Ghetto— Negro New York, 1890–1930*, 2nd ed. (New York: Harper, 1971), 132–33.

25. Claude McKay, *Harlem: Negro Metropolis* (New York: Dutton, 1940), 132. Most basically, the "Talented Tenth" is the phrase used by Du Bois to refer to the top ten percent of the race, whom he felt were, by virtue of education and background, most equipped to lead their peers into the 20th century. See Du Bois, *The Souls of Black Folk*, ch. 6: "Of the Training of Black Men" (1903).

26. George Devereux, "Ethnic Identity: Its Logical Foundations and Its Dysfunctions," in Sollors, *Theories of Ethnicity*, 397.

27. Osofsky, *Harlem*, 134–35.

28. Reid, *The Negro Immigrant*, 108. This comment, of course, reflects another equally dangerous stereotype: the widespread Western preoccupation with and fear of the figure of the Jew as merchant and lender combined with African Caribbeaner entrepreneurial success to cause the latter to be labeled "black Jews."

29. Osofsky, *Harlem*, 133.

30. Reid, *The Negro Immigrant*, 107. See also Barbara Christian, "Black, Female, and Foreign-Born: A Statement," in Mortimer and Bryce-Laporte, *Female Immigrants*, 175.

31. For the full catalogue of stereotypes discussed here, see Reid, *The Negro Immigrant*, 107–108.

32. Paule Marshall, "Black Immigrant Women in *Brown Girl, Brownstones*," in Mortimer and Bryce-Laporte, *Female Immigrants*, 8.

33. Mary C. Waters notes the persistence of many of these stereotypes among members of the current second generation in "Ethnic and Racial Identities of Second-Generation Black Immigrants in New York City," in Portes, *The New Second Generation*, 173.

34. Jervis Anderson, *This Was Harlem: A Cultural Portrait, 1900–1950* (New York: Farrar, 1982), 303.

35. The contents of the "Special Caribbean Issue" included pieces by Lucius J. Malmin, judge of the District Court of the U.S. Virgin Islands, and Caspar Holstein, St. Croix native and Harlem businessman, that critiqued the U.S. purchase of and presence in the Virgin Islands in 1917 but that did not address substantively the role of Virgin Islanders in New York. A. M. Wendell Malliet, editor of the *West Indian Statesman*, provided a survey of "Some Prominent West Indians" in England, the Caribbean, and the United States, and Arthur A. Schomburg, founder of the central archive on black studies in this country, the Schomburg Center for Research in Black Culture, allowed the publication of excerpts on "West Indian Composers and Musicians" from an album he had been compiling of historical sketches and essays. Waldo Frank reviewed British Guianan (and *Opportunity* Business Manager) Eric Walrond's collection, *Tropic Death*, and Claude McKay contributed three poems ("Desolate," "My House," and "America in Retrospect"). *Opportunity* also continued its regular features on the arts ("The Ebony Flute"), the "Survey of the Month" which described recent events and people of importance in the black community, an editorial section ranging from a discussion of the cotton market to the rise in lynchings, and "Our Book Shelf." Although the texts reviewed in "Our Book Shelf" were all international in focus, none

of the regularly featured sections was overtly devoted to Caribbean-American concerns.

36. Werner Sollors, "Ethnicity," in *Critical Terms for Literary Study*, ed. Frank Lentricchia and Thomas McLaughlin (Chicago: University of Chicago Press, 1990), 288.

37. Reid, *The Negro Immigrant*, 108–09.

38. Mary C. Waters, "Ethnic and Racial Identities of Second-Generation Black Immigrants in New York City," 178.

39. Paul Gilroy, *Small Acts: Thoughts on the Politics of Black Cultures* (New York: Serpent's Tail, 1993), 2.

2. "A Thing Apart" and "Out of Time"

1. McKay's desired title, "Keep Going," can be found in a letter from Laurence Roberts to McKay dated June 15, 1936 and contained in the McKay correspondence of the James Weldon Johnson collection, Beinecke Rare Book and Manuscript Collection, Yale University, cited by Sister Mary Conroy, "The Vagabond Motif in the Writings of Claude McKay," *Negro American Literature Forum* 5 (1971): 23n7.

2. Some controversy surrounds the exact date of McKay's birth. According to Wayne Cooper, McKay's principal biographer, McKay believed for many years that he was born on September 15, 1889. Not until his birthday in 1920 was he reminded by his sister Rachel of his actual birth date in 1890. Cooper explains that at some point McKay's family had changed his birth date by a year in order to allow him to assist his brother Uriah Theodore (U'Theo) as a teaching assistant. See Cooper, *Claude McKay: Rebel Sojourner*, 7, 377.

3. Jamaica's peasant class during the era was large and encompassed a wide range of economic statuses. People who owned property and engaged in market and export, as well as subsistence farming, were considered peasants, but so too were roving farmhands and landless but home-owning laborers. Other members of the peasantry possessed trade skills or engaged in small scale commerce on the islands, and many children from peasant households performed service jobs that we might now consider working class. Because of their family's landholdings, however, they also continued to be viewed as part of the peasantry. For a more detailed explanation of the socioeconomic structure of Jamaica during the late nineteenth century and of McKay's position within it, as well as an analysis of his attitudes toward class and color conflicts on the island that uses his fictional portrayals as evidence, see Rupert and Maureen Lewis, "Claude McKay's Jamaica," *Caribbean Quarterly* 23.2–3 (1977): 40.

4. McKay, *My Green Hills of Jamaica and Five Jamaican Short Stories*, intro. and ed. Mervyn Morris (Kingston, Jamaica: Heinemann, 1979), 24, 62, 60. McKay, *A Long Way from Home* (New York, 1937; reprint, New York: Harcourt, 1970), 36.

5. McKay, *My Green Hills*, 61. Unfortunately, McKay provides few details about his mother in his memoir, although his poems "My Mother" and "Heritage" suggest his deep respect for her. See *Selected Poems of Claude McKay*, with a biographical note by Max Eastman (1953; reprint, New York: Harcourt, 1981), 22, 29. For the most thorough biographical study of McKay's family and early life, see Cooper, *Claude McKay: Rebel Sojourner*, 1–34. For an assessment of how the qualities displayed by McKay's parents, the prideful independence of his father and the inherent humanism of his mother, shaped McKay's life and work, see John Hillyer Condit, "An Urge toward Wholeness: Claude McKay and His Sonnets," *CLA Journal* 22.4 (1979): 350–64.

6. McKay, *My Green Hills*, 12, 25, 51, 11.

7. Cooper notes that McKay offered various dates at different times in his life for his residence with U'Theo, all of which range roughly between his sixth and fourteenth birthdays. The inconsistencies can be partly explained by McKay's discovery of his real age in 1920. See Cooper, *Claude McKay: Rebel Sojourner*, 11.

8. McKay, *My Green Hills*, 14, 13, 14–15, 15.

9. Ibid., 19. McKay is in error here; Ernst Haeckel is the author of *The Riddle of the Universe* (New York: Harper, 1900). *The History of the Conflict between Religion and Science* was written by the British physician and chemist John William Draper (1811–1882), and was first published in 1875.

10. McKay, *My Green Hills*, 19.

11. Ibid., 21, 22.

12. Ibid., 41.

13. Ibid., 43, 44.

14. Cooper, *Claude McKay: Rebel Sojourner*, 24.

15. McKay, *My Green Hills*, 67.

16. Relatedly, Cooper notes that Jekyll was an acquaintance of Robert Louis Stevenson during the creation of Stevenson's *The Strange Case of Dr. Jekyll and Mr. Hyde* (1886), but he has found no direct evidence to suggest that Stevenson's character was based on Jekyll himself in anything more than name. Nevertheless, it is interesting to reconsider Stevenson's fictional portrayal of his complex, dual-natured character in light of Jekyll's possible homosexuality. Cooper, *Claude McKay: Rebel Sojourner*, 30. For more information about McKay's sexuality, see ibid., 29–32, 75, 131, 149–51, 390; for biographical information on Jekyll, see ibid., 22–25. For an analysis of homophobic elements in McKay's work, see Timothy S. Chin, "'Bullers' and 'Battymen': Contesting Homophobia in Black Popular Culture and Contemporary Caribbean Literature," *Callaloo* 20.1 (1997): 127–41. For further investigation of McKay's and Jekyll's relationship, see the forthcoming dissertation on constructions of masculinity in the 1920s by Michael Maiwald, Ph.D. candidate at Duke University.

17. McKay, *My Green Hills*, 66–67, 113.

18. See P. S. Chauhan, "Rereading Claude McKay," *CLA Journal* 34.1 (1990): 68–80. Chauhan's essay assesses the impact that colonization had upon McKay, arguing that McKay struggles throughout his work with a bipolar allegiance as a colonized subject to Britain and Jamaica. This puts McKay, according to Chauhan, in a position of siding at once with the colonizer and the colonized, with "the victim and the victimizer" (70). See also Chauhan, "Claude McKay: Polarities of the Colonial Imagination," in *Claude McKay: Centennial Studies*, ed. A. L. McLeod (New Delhi: Sterling, 1992), 22–31.

19. McKay, *My Green Hills*, 69.

20. Wayne Cooper suggests another paradigm for this relationship: that between "southern country gentlemen of the United States in the same period" and "their black agricultural laborers" (Cooper, *Claude McKay: Rebel Sojourner*, 381*n*82). Michael North elaborates upon and develops this idea in his excellent study of McKay's linguistic shifts in *The Dialect of Modernism: Race, Language, and Twentieth-Century Literature* (New York: Oxford University Press, 1994), 101.

21. Quoted by Lily J. Shapiro, "Patronage as Peculiar Institution: Charlotte Osgood Mason and the Harlem Renaissance" (senior honors thesis, History and Literature, Harvard University, 1993).

22. Interestingly—but perhaps not surprisingly—McKay included no dialect po-

etry in the collection he compiled shortly before his death for the posthumously published *Selected Poems* (1953).

23. Lloyd W. Brown, *West Indian Poetry* (Boston: Twayne, 1978), 42, 40.

24. Chauhan, "Rereading Claude McKay," 72–73.

25. Claude McKay, *Songs of Jamaica* (1912; reprint, Miami: Mnemosyne, 1969), 7.

26. Brown makes a similar observation in *West Indian Poetry*, 42–43.

27. Jean Wagner, *Black Poets of the United States: From Paul Laurence Dunbar to Langston Hughes*, trans. Kenneth Douglas (Urbana: University of Illinois Press, 1973), 204–205. See also George E. Kent, "The Soulful Way of Claude McKay," *Black World* 20 (1970): 37–50.

28. Claude McKay, *Songs of Jamaica*, 89.

29. The other two poems are "To Bennie" and "A Dream." "To Bennie" consists of an apology on behalf of the speaker to a friend whom he has offended; the poem "Bennie's Departure," contained in McKay's subsequent volume of dialect verse, *Constab Ballads*, suggests that Bennie was a close intimate of McKay's while he worked for the force. "A Dream" describes a nostalgic "dream" of home experienced by the speaker while working in the city.

30. McKay, *Songs of Jamaica*, 113.

31. Ibid., 112.

32. Brown, *West Indian Poetry*, 51.

33. McKay, *Constab Ballads* (London: Watts, 1912), 7.

34. McKay, *My Green Hills*, 82, 86, 86, 84–85. Henrietta Vinton Davis was an African American speaker who performed throughout Jamaica with Madame Naomi Hardy, a vocal soloist. See Cooper, *Claude McKay: Rebel Sojourner*, 56.

35. Although McKay left Tuskegee, he continued to respect greatly the leadership of Booker T. Washington and even composed a sonnet upon Washington's death in 1915 titled "In Memoriam: Booker T. Washington." In this sonnet the speaker, recalling an experience at Tuskegee, praises Washington as "a splendid tower of strength" and commends the unifying ability of the leader's "subtle tact and power"; the speaker also expresses a "fond hope" that Washington's "paternal grace" might have been directed to himself, and laments that the opportunity for this has been denied by Washington's death. McKay's reverence for Washington represents yet another distinctive element of the complex and changing political philosophy that McKay embraced during his lifetime. The original copy of the poem is contained in the William S. Braithwaite Papers in the Houghton Collection of the Harvard University Library. A reprint can be found in Wayne F. Cooper, *The Passion of Claude McKay: Selected Poetry and Prose, 1912–1948* (New York: Schocken, 1973), 116.

36. McKay, *A Long Way from Home* (1937; reprint, New York: Harcourt, 1970), 4.

37. Nathan Huggins, *Harlem Renaissance* (New York: Oxford University Press, 1971), 215–19. See also James Giles, *Claude McKay* (Boston: Twayne, 1976), 42.

38. McKay, *Selected Poems*, 43.

39. For an analysis of the modernist innovations of McKay's sonnets, see Heather Hathaway, "Exploring 'something new': The 'Modernism' of Claude McKay," in *Race and the Modernist Artist*, ed. Jeffrey Melnick (New York: Oxford University Press, forthcoming).

40. McKay, *A Long Way from Home*, 227–28. McKay repeats this sentiment on his recorded reading of the poem for Arna Bontemps's Folkways Album *Anthology of Negro Poets* (FL9791).

41. Numerous scholars claim that Winston Churchill quoted from "If We Must

Die" to the British Commons during World War II in an effort to boost morale, but Wayne Cooper claims that this is apocryphal. See Wayne Cooper, review of *Claude McKay: A Black Poet's Struggle for Identity,* by Tyrone Tillery, *Journal of American History* 79.4 (1993): 1656–57.

42. See Bronze, *Roots of Negro Racial Consciousness,* 74; Brown, *West Indian Poetry,* 39; Huggins, *Harlem Renaissance,* 72, 219. Cooper, *Claude McKay: Rebel Sojourner,* 101.

43. McKay, *Selected Poems,* 42.

44. This line is quoted from the version of "In Bondage" that is contained in McKay's *Selected Poems* (1953). In *Spring in New Hampshire* (1920), however, line 12 reads, "When all that is to-day is ashes and dust."

45. For more information on the influence of McKay on Négritude leaders Aimé Césaire, Léopold Sédar Senghor, and Léon Damas, see Charles R. Larson, "African Afro-American Literary Relationships," *Negro Digest* 19 (December 1969): 35–42. See also Addison Gayle, *Claude McKay: The Black Poet at War* (Detroit: Broadside, 1972); Cooper, *Claude McKay: Rebel Sojourner,* 214–16, 259; Robert P. Smith, Jr., "Rereading *Banjo*: Claude McKay and the French Connection," *CLA Journal* 30.1 (1986): 46–58; Lilyan Kesteloot, *Black Writers in French: A Literary History of Négritude,* trans. Ellen Conroy Kennedy (Philadelphia: University of Pennsylvania Press, 1974).

46. Note that this recalls the peasants of McKay's dialect poetry who are frequently depicted as similarly awaiting their fate, but again, in contrast to these figures, the speaker of "Baptism" takes control of his destiny, while the peasants are denied all agency.

47. McKay, *Selected Poems,* 35.

48. McKay, *A Long Way from Home,* 27. The reliability of *A Long Way from Home* as a source is obviously a complex issue. Like all autobiography, it is a crafted work rather than merely a factual account of McKay's life. In 1937, McKay's career was undergoing significant turmoil. He was having difficulty finding publishers, he was struggling with writing in general, and he was unsuccessful in securing enough money to support his artistic pursuits. *A Long Way from Home* is partly a response to these problems. As such, McKay attempted through his autobiography to embellish his reputation in some areas and to diminish it in others. He denies, for example, his association with Communism, partly because past or present association with the Communist Party in the late thirties could have jeopardized his welcome in the United States by immigration authorities. A close reading of *A Long Way from Home* reveals many similar inconsistencies, as well as actual shifts in McKay's philosophies concerning race and politics.

49. Claude McKay, "To William Stanley Braithwaite," 11 January 1916, William Stanley Braithwaite Papers, bMS Am 1444 (755), Houghton Library, Harvard University, Cambridge, Massachusetts. Quoted with permission.

50. Hutchinson, *The Harlem Renaissance in Black and White,* 152.

51. McKay to Braithwaite, 15 February 1916, Braithwaite Papers, Houghton Library, Harvard University, Cambridge, Massachusetts.

52. McKay, *A Long Way from Home,* 139–40. Michael Gold joined McKay as co-executive editor of *The Liberator* following the departure of Max Eastman in November, 1921. McKay describes Gold as believing that *The Liberator* "should [be] a popular proletarian magazine, printing doggerels from lumberjacks and stevedores and true revelations from chambermaids." McKay explains that he himself "contended that while it was most excellent to get material out of the forgotten numbers of the working class, it should be good stuff that could compare with any other writing. . . . But

Michael Gold preferred sentimentality above intellectuality in estimating proletarian writing and writers." For more information about McKay's conflicts with Gold, and his activities while editor of *The Liberator*, see Cooper, *Claude McKay: Rebel Sojourner* 160–64. For an important assessment of McKay as a key link in the ideological relationship between black writers during the Harlem Renaissance and those of the 1930s, see James A. Miller, "African-American Writing of the 1930s: A Prologue," in *Radical Revisions: Reading 1930s Culture*, ed. Bill Mullen and Sherry Lee Linkon (Urbana: University of Illinois Press, 1996), 78–90.

53. McKay, *A Long Way from Home*, 28.

54. Ibid., 307.

55. McKay explains in his autobiography that "My title was symbolic . . . it had no reference to the official residence of the President of the United States. . . . The title 'White Houses' changed the whole symbolic intent and meaning of the poem, making it appear as if the burning ambition of the black malcontent was to enter white houses in general." He also appended this note to "The White House" in his *Selected Poems*. See McKay, *A Long Way from Home*, 312–14. For more information on the relationship between McKay and Locke, see A. L. McLeod, "Claude McKay, Alain Locke, and the Harlem Renaissance," *Literary Half-Yearly* 27.2 (July 1986) 65–75.

56. See Du Bois's scathing review of *Home to Harlem* in *Crisis* 35 (1928): 202.

57. Cooper, *Claude McKay: Rebel Sojourner*, 113.

58. For a detailed account of McKay's experiences in England, see ibid., 103–133.

59. Max Eastman, introduction to Claude McKay, *Harlem Shadows* (New York: Harcourt, 1922), ix.

60. McKay, *Selected Poems*, 7.

61. Tyrone Tillery, *Claude McKay: A Black Poet's Struggle for Identity* (Amherst: University of Massachusetts Press, 1992), 182.

62. Huggins, *Harlem Renaissance*, 128. Even the comments of John Dewey, whom McKay himself chose to write the "Introduction" to the *Selected Poems*—perhaps for reasons not unlike those which motivated him to invoke Walter Jekyll's voice to introduce his dialect verse—reveal a distance between black poet and white philosopher, as Dewey rather apologetically denies having any authority as a white to comment on a black's poetry. While Dewey attempts to emphasize the universality of McKay's work, his final statement that, "No white man can do more than express his humiliated sympathy" inevitably emphasizes his inability to see beyond racial lines.

63. Langston Hughes capitalized upon the publicity surrounding this incident when he reversed the tables in 1935 during the production of his play, "Mulatto." Arnold Rampersad, Hughes' biographer, relates that Hughes, upon learning that the producer of his play (Martin Jones) intended to segregate the theater, "sent tickets for the most prominent seats to his darkest friends, including the sable Claude McKay." See Rampersad, *The Life of Langston Hughes*, vol. I: *1902–1941* (New York: Oxford University Press, 1986), 314.

64. Cooper, *Passion*, 70.

65. Tillery, *Claude McKay*, 55–57.

66. It should be remembered that McKay's residence in the United States during this era was broken by a two-year period (1919–1921) during which he lived in England and worked for Sylvia Pankhurst on the *Worker's Dreadnought*. McKay first lived in Harlem between 1914 and 1919, again in 1921 and 1922. See Cooper, *Claude McKay: Rebel Sojourner*, for the most detailed account of McKay's biographical history. For a useful chronology, see James Giles, *Claude McKay* (Boston: Twayne, 1976).

67. McKay, *Selected Poems*, 41. On "ghosts," see Maxine Hong Kingston's *The*

Woman Warrior: Memoirs of a Childhood among Ghosts (1976) and Kathleen Bragdon's *Cultural Haunting: Ghosts and Ethnicity in Recent American Literature* (Charlottesville: University Press of Virginia, 1998).

68. McKay, *A Long Way from Home*, 229.

69. The metaphor of the house is used frequently in Caribbean literature to suggest the nearly chronic sense of homelessness among people in the region due to a history of forced resettlement followed by constant migration. See, for example, V. S. Naipaul's novel *A House for Mr. Biswas* (1961), or Paule Marshall's short story "Barbados," contained in *Soul Clap Hands and Sing* (1961).

70. Recall his statement in *My Green Hills* that throughout his life he managed to "preserve some form of personal aloofness" from those around him (41). In *A Long Way from Home*, McKay reiterates this theme when describing his relationship to one of his lovers, Manda, an African American woman from the South. First he notes that "there was always a certain strangeness between Manda and me. Perhaps that helped our getting along comfortably together" (46). Later, referring to their relationship once again, he states that "there is always an unfamiliar something between people of different countries and nationalities, however intimate they may become. And that something between me and Manda helped rather than hindered our relationship" (49). These comments also resonate with the discussions of McKay's putative sexual orientation. His evocation of the "wall" also recalls Du Bois's use of "wall" as an extension of his famous motif of the "veil": see Thomas Holt, "The Political Uses of Alienation: W. E. B. Du Bois on Politics, Race, and Culture, 1903–1940," *American Quarterly* 42.2 (1990): 301–23.

71. Another of McKay's poems published in the November 1926 issue of *Opportunity*, "America in Retrospect," describes the country as creating inspiration, out of its viciousness, for his poetic energies.

72. McKay, *A Long Way from Home*, 277.

3. Searching for That "Strange, Elusive Something"

1. McKay, *A Long Way from Home*, 153. For a detailed study of McKay's journey to Russia and involvement with Communism, see Cooper, *Claude McKay: Rebel Sojourner*, 171–92. See also McKay, *A Long Way from Home* (1937; reprint, New York: Harcourt Brace Jovanovich, 1970), 159–66. For insight into McKay's views during this period about the relationship of race to Communism, see his *The Negroes in America*, trans. Robert Winter, ed. Alan McLeod (Port Washington, N.Y.: Kennikat, 1979). Published in Russia in 1923 and consisting of a series of slightly revised articles McKay had written for the Soviet press during his stay, the volume evaluates black roles in labor, sports, art, music, literature, and the economy from a Marxist perspective. McKay argues that Communism would appeal to blacks in the United States only if it confronted race issues directly and accepted blacks as total equals in the movement. The particular task of black Communists, according to McKay in 1923, was to educate both the black community and the Party heads about the role of blacks historically as workers under white capitalism. As will be discussed later in this chapter, McKay continued this critique in fictional form in *Banjo*. In 1940 McKay produced another socially analytical text, *Harlem: Negro Metropolis*, which, at its most basic level, focused on his belief that the black community needed a stronger, independent infrastructure in order to sustain itself in a racist world. More interesting to note in light of this discussion, however, is McKay's reassessment of the value of Communism to blacks in America: he now argued that the Communist party had held disproportionate power

in Harlem in the thirties, and had thus distracted black leaders from focusing on the pressing economic needs of local African Americans. For more information concerning the production and reception of both of these texts, see Cooper, *Claude McKay: Rebel Sojourner*, 185–88, 340–45.

2. McKay, *A Long Way from Home*, 167, 168, 245, 277, 332. For a detailed study of these travels, see Cooper, *Claude McKay: Rebel Sojourner*, 171–290.

3. McKay also produced during these years three short stories, "Trial By Lynching," "The Mulatto Girl," and "The Soldier's Return," which are self-described in a subtitle as "Stories About Negro Life in North America." These were originally issued by Ogonek Publishing House in Moscow in 1925 under the title *Sudom Lyncha (Trial by Lynching)* and had been written in English and translated into Russian by A. M. and P. Okhrimenko. While the original manuscript has apparently been lost, Wayne Cooper did discover a copy of the initial publication; the stories have since been republished in a collection which has been retranslated by Robert Winter and edited by A. L. McLeod titled *Powre above Powres 2: Trial by Lynching—Stories about Negro Life in North America* (Mysore, India: University of Mysore, 1977). McKay also produced his non-fiction study *The Negroes in America* during this period, which has been described in more detail in note 1 of this chapter and which basically offers a Marxist interpretation of African American history in the United States. He also wrote three more fictional works, a collection of short stories titled *Gingertown* (1933), an unpublished novel, *Color Scheme*, and an unpublished short story, "Romance In Marseilles," that serves as somewhat of a sequel to *Banjo*.

4. For McKay's own comments about the Renaissance and his relationship to it, and more specifically about the conflicts he experienced with both Alain Locke and W. E. B. Du Bois due to his differing views about the relationship between art and politics, see his autobiography, *A Long Way from Home*, 95–150; 307–23.

5. W. E. B. Du Bois, "The Browsing Reader," *Crisis* 35 (1928): 202; Cooper, foreword, in *Home to Harlem* (1928; reprint, Boston: Northeastern University Press, 1987), xvii. For a description of many reviews of *Home to Harlem*, see Cooper, *Claude McKay: Rebel Sojourner*, 241–48.

6. *Nigger Heaven* was published in 1926 by white author and patron of numerous Harlem Renaissance writers, Carl Van Vechten. The novel achieved unusual commercial success during the period largely due to its primitivist rendition of the black community in Harlem; for the same reasons, it evoked considerable controversy concerning the issue of art and representation.

7. Brawley, *The Negro Genius: A New Appraisal of the Achievement of the American Negro in Literature and the Fine Arts* (New York: Dodd, 1937), 245. McKay himself, in his autobiography, *A Long Way from Home*, denies even reading *Nigger Heaven* until *Home to Harlem* was nearly complete: "Many persons imagine that I wrote *Home to Harlem* because Carl Van Vechten wrote *Nigger Heaven*. But the pattern tale of the book was written under the title of 'Home to Harlem' in 1925. When Max Eastman read it he said, 'It is worth a thousand dollars.' Under the same title it was entered in the story contest of the Negro magazine *Opportunity*. But it did not excite the judges. *Nigger Heaven* was published in the fall of 1926. I never saw the book until the late spring of 1927, when my agent, William Aspenwall Bradley, sent me a copy. And by that time I had nearly completed *Home to Harlem*" (282–83). For documentation of this chronology, see Cooper, *Claude McKay: Rebel Sojourner*, 240–45. For comparisons between *Home to Harlem* and *Nigger Heaven*, see Huggins, *Harlem Renaissance*, 121–26.

8. McKay, *Home to Harlem*, 1. All subsequent citations will refer to this edition, and will be cited parenthetically in the text.

9. See R. A. Barksdale, "Symbolism and Irony in McKay's *Home to Harlem*,"

CLA Journal 15 (March 1972): 338–44; Robert Bone, *The Negro Novel in America* (New Haven: Yale University Press, 1958); Robert M. Greenberg, "Idealism and Realism in the Fiction of Claude McKay," *CLA Journal* 24.3 (March 1981): 237–61; Jacqueline Kaye, "Claude McKay's *Banjo*," *Présence Africaine* 73 (1970): 165–69; Kenneth Ramchand, *The West Indian Novel and Its Background* (London: Heinemann, 1983).

10. For more similarities between Jake and McKay himself, see McKay, *A Long Way from Home*: 150 for McKay as a perpetual vagabond; 154 for his period as a stoker; 173 for McKay as "not a joiner kind of fellah" (45, *Home to Harlem*); 228 for McKay as laborer.

11. For examples of McKay's recollections of his boyhood in the Caribbean, see McKay, *My Green Hills of Jamaica*. See McKay, *A Long Way from Home*, 89 and 122, for examples of comparable statements about colonialism and imperialism; 229, about the burdens of British education as a barrier to instinctive living; 55 and 304 about the perils of "civilization." Many of the issues will be discussed in further depth in the section on *Banjo*.

12. For examples of Ray's and McKay's joint literary influences, see McKay, *A Long Way from Home*, 13, 28, 53, and 247.

13. McKay, *A Long Way from Home*, 228.

14. McKay, *The Negroes in America*, 25–36.

15. For a provocative discussion of Jake's "code of order," see Barksdale, "Symbolism and Irony," 338–44.

16. McKay, *A Long Way from Home*, 229.

17. For an interesting analysis of the hog trope, see Charles J. Heglar, "Claude McKay's 'If We Must Die,' *Home to Harlem*, and the Hog Trope," *ANQ: A Quarterly Journal of Short Articles Notes and Reviews* 8.3 (1995): 22–26.

18. In this discussion, as with McKay's use of the term in the novel, "mulatto" refers generally to persons of mixed blood, and is not confined only to those individuals or characters possessing one black and one white parent.

19. Wagner, *Black Poets of the United States*, 216.

20. Hughes examined this theme through a variety of genres ranging from poetry (see "Cross" and "Mulatto"), to short story (see "Father and Son") to play and even opera (see "Mulatto"). For an analysis of the relationship between miscegenation and the oedipal conflict in the short stories of Chesnutt and Hughes, see Heather Hathaway, " 'Maybe Freedom Lies in Hating': Miscegenation and the Oedipal Conflict," in *Refiguring the Father: New Feminist Readings of Patriarchy*, ed. Patricia Yaeger and Beth Kowaleski-Wallace (Carbondale: Southern Illinois University Press, 1989), 153–67.

21. Amiri Baraka (then LeRoi Jones) consciously recalls McKay's antiassimilationist philosophy in his *Tales* (1967). Baraka similarly depicts assimilation as emasculating, equating power with male sexuality and particularly with black male sexuality over white women. He also recalls McKay's struggle with "instinct" and "reason" by lamenting his own compulsion to interpret these sexual actions (like Ray, he claims) rather than to simply act on them (like Jake). Ironically, however, the chapter in which he recalls this old idea, prevalent among much militant writing in the sixties, is titled "New Sense." See Jones, *Tales* (New York: Grove, 1967), 93–97.

22. McKay, "A Negro Writer to His Critics," *New York Herald-Tribune Books*, March 6, 1932; reprinted in Cooper, *Passion*, 135.

23. Carolyn Cooper, "Race and the Cultural Politics of Self-Representation: A View from the University of the West Indies," *Research in African Literatures* 27.4 (1996): 97.

24. Claude McKay, *Banjo: A Story without a Plot* (1929; reprint, New York: Har-

court Brace Jovanovich, 1957), 46. All subsequent quotations will refer to this edition and will be cited parenthetically in the text.

25. McKay, *A Long Way from Home*, 300.

26. For a more detailed account of the disagreements between McKay and Du Bois, see Cooper, *Claude McKay: Rebel Sojourner*, 238–48.

27. W. E. B. Du Bois, "Criteria of Negro Art," in *Within the Circle: An Anthology of African American Literary Criticism from the Harlem Renaissance to the Present*, ed. Angelyn Mitchell (Durham: Duke University Press, 1994), 66.

28. McKay, "A Negro Writer to His Critics," 133.

29. Hughes, in his essay, challenged the African American intelligentsia to "let the blare of Negro jazz band and the bellowing voice of Bessie Smith singing Blues penetrate the closed ears of the colored near-intellectuals until they listen and perhaps understand. Let Paul Robeson singing "Water Boy" and Rudolph Fisher writing about the streets of Harlem, and Jean Toomer holding the heart of Georgia in his hands, and Aaron Douglas drawing strange black fantasies cause the smug Negro middle class to turn from their white, respectable, ordinary books and paper to catch a glimmer of their own beauty. We younger Negro artists who create now intend to express our individual dark-skinned selves without fear or shame. If white people are pleased we are glad, if they are not, it doesn't matter. We know we are beautiful. And ugly too. The tom-tom cries and the tom-tom laughs. If colored people are pleased we are glad. If they are not, their displeasure doesn't matter either. We build our temples for to-morrow, strong as we know how, and we stand on top of the mountain, free within ourselves." Langston Hughes, "The Negro Artist and the Racial Mountain," in Mitchell, *Within the Circle*, 59.

30. McKay to Hughes, 24 April 1926; quoted by Hutchinson in *The Harlem Renaissance in Black and White*, 157.

31. This philosophy is much more complex than the slogan indicates, and cannot be explained fully here. For two excellent biographies of Garvey, see Judith Stein, *The World of Marcus Garvey* (Baton Rouge: Louisiana State University Press, 1986), and Edmund Cronon, *Black Moses* (Madison: University of Wisconsin Press, 1955). For assessments of Garvey's historical and literary impact, see any of the several works by Tony Martin which constitute the New Marcus Garvey Library published by the Majority Press.

32. The new quota immigration laws to which McKay refers were enacted in 1921 and 1924. The first limited immigration in any year to 3 percent of the number of each nationality according to the Census of 1910, with a maximum quota of 375,000. The second further reduced immigration by half of the 1921 quota and limited immigration in any year to 2 percent of the Census of 1890 (in order to reduce entrants from Eastern and Southern Europe). This latter law was intended to remain in force until 1927, when apportionment on the basis of 1920 distribution of "national origins" would serve as the basis for a maximum quota of 150,000 people per year, but due to strong opposition, it was not enforced until July 1929. For a more detailed analysis of immigration patterns, see Dawn Marshall, "A History of West Indian Migrations," 15–31.

33. Apparently McKay wrote a series of articles for the *Negro World* on a club for black soldiers that he frequented in London, but according to Wayne Cooper, only a few assorted copies of the paper have been preserved, and none contain copies of McKay's articles. See Cooper, *Claude McKay: Rebel Sojourner*, 109.

34. McKay, "Garvey as a Negro Moses," *Liberator* 5 (April, 1922): 8–9; reprinted in Cooper, *Passion*, 69.

35. Cooper, *Passion*, 46–47.

36. McKay, "Garvey as a Negro Moses," 69.

37. For a more detailed discussion of McKay's love/hate relationship with France, see Michel Fabre, "Claude McKay and the Two Faces of France," in *From Harlem to Paris: Black American Writers in France, 1840–1980* (Urbana and Chicago: University of Illinois Press, 1991), 92–113. For more examples of McKay's criticism of French liberalism in *Banjo* see *Banjo*, 65, 73–75, 135–36, 267.

38. McKay, *A Long Way from Home*, 354.

39. Cooper, *Claude McKay: Rebel Sojourner*, 282.

40. McKay, *Banana Bottom* (1933; reprint, New York: Harcourt, Brace, Jovanovich, 1961), 9. All subsequent quotations will refer to this edition, and will be cited in the text.

41. I thank Susan Barnett for pointing out the association of Yoni with the Hindu term for female genitalia.

42. McKay, *Banjo*, 268.

43. McKay may also be basing this figure on a "Mr. Plant," identified in *My Green Hills of Jamaica* as one of Jamaica's most renowned educators, who worked with Booker T. Washington for a time and encouraged McKay's enrollment in Tuskegee. See *My Green Hills*, 85.

44. McKay, *A Long Way from Home*, 277; Claude McKay, *Banana Bottom* (New York: Harcourt Brace Jovanovich, 1933), 40.

45. McKay, *Banana Bottom*, 40; *A Long Way from Home*, 300.

46. For an analysis of the way in which binaries of the "natural" and "unnatural" become inscribed respectively onto heterosexual and homosexual love in *Banana Bottom*, see Chin, " 'Bullers' and 'Battymen,' " 130–32.

47. Jubban's name, like so many others in the novel, seems laden with connotation. Most literally it is related to "juba," a word that symbolizes various traits of character including caution and imitativeness. "Jubban" might also be a loose anagram of either "banja," which means to play the fool, or "bungo," which is an insulting term suggesting stupidity, ugliness, or one's status as a "country bumpkin" in Jamaican parlance. Given the care with which McKay named other characters in the novel, it would not be surprising for McKay to have chosen this name deliberately to imply such qualities in the character himself. See Frederic Gomes Cassidy and R. B. LePage, eds., *Dictionary of Jamaican English* (New York: Cambridge University Press, 1980).

48. See, for just one example, Robert A. Bone, *The Negro Novel in America* (New Haven: Yale University Press, 1958).

49. Robert E. Park, "Human Migration and the Marginal Man," in Sollors, *Theories of Ethnicity*, 156–67.

50. McKay, *Selected Poems* (1981), 41.

51. Park, "Human Migration and the Marginal Man," 893.

52. Marshall describes these themes as characterizing all her work in her interview with Dance, 7.

4. From Dislocation to Dual Location

1. Paule Marshall, "An Interview with Paule Marshall," with Daryl Cumber Dance, *Southern Review* 28.1 (1992): 7.

2. Barbara Christian, *Black Women Novelists: The Development of a Tradition, 1892–1976* (Westport, Conn.: Greenwood, 1980), 81. Although *Brown Girl, Brownstones* received positive reviews upon its initial publication in 1959, and was praised early on

by literary critic Robert Bone, it was not until after the success of Marshall's second novel, *The Chosen Place, the Timeless People* (1969), combined with attention given it partly as a result of the developing feminist movement, that *Brown Girl, Brownstones* achieved widespread acclaim as an important coming-of-age tale of a young black woman. Its republication by the Feminist Press in 1981, appended by an important afterword by Mary Helen Washington which both interpreted and situated the novel within Marshall's œuvre, assured *Brown Girl, Brownstones* a secure position in African American and women's studies curricula. For a typical early review of *Brown Girl, Brownstones*, see Carol Field, "Fresh, Fierce and 'First,'" *New York Herald Tribune Book Review* (16 August 1959): 5. For interim studies in which *Brown Girl, Brownstones* is discussed in relation to Marshall's other fiction, see Leela Kapai, "Dominant Themes and Technique in Paule Marshall's Fiction," *CLA Journal* 16.1 (1972): 49–59, or Lloyd W. Brown, "The Rhythms of Power in Paule Marshall's Fiction," *Novel: A Forum on Fiction* 7.2 (Winter 1974): 159–67. For valuable early feminist interpretations, see Christian, *Black Women Novelists* (1980); Washington, Afterword, in Marshall, *Brown Girl, Brownstones* (Old Westbury: Feminist Press, 1981), 311–24. Since the novel's republication in 1981, scholarship on Marshall, and *Brown Girl, Brownstones*, in particular, has abounded.

3. See Marshall, "Black Immigrant Women in *Brown Girl, Brownstones*," in Mortimer and Bryce-Laporte, *Female Immigrants to the United States*, or the same essay in *Caribbean Life in New York City: Sociocultural Dimensions*, ed. Elsa M. Chaney and Constance R. Sutton (New York: Center for Migration Studies). See also Daniel Moynihan and Nathan Glazer, eds., *Beyond the Melting Pot* (Cambridge: MIT Press, 1970), who cite the novel as "remarkably revealing" evidence of the immigrant experience.

4. Sollors, *Beyond Ethnicity*, 210. See especially ch. 7, "First Generation, Second Generation, Third Generation . . . : The Cultural Construction of Descent," 208–36.

5. Marshall, "An Interview with Paule Marshall," 14–15.

6. Oscar Handlin, ed., *Children of the Uprooted* (New York: Braziller, 1966), xv–xvi.

7. Hansen's thesis, delivered in a speech to the Augustana Historical Society in Rock Island, Illinois, did not receive widespread attention until 1952, when it was rediscovered and reprinted by immigration scholar Nathan Glazer. Since then, despite continual contestation of the theory from a variety of disciplines, it has become a classic essay in the field. For a copy of the original speech and several commentaries on its significance, see Peter Kivisto and Dag Blanck, eds., *American Immigrants and Their Generations: Studies and Commentaries on the Hansen Thesis after Fifty Years* (Urbana: University of Illinois Press, 1990).

8. Sollors, *Beyond Ethnicity*, 214.

9. Peter Kivisto, "Ethnicity and the Problem of Generations in American History," in Kivisto and Blanck, *American Immigrants*, 2.

10. For a recent and important collection of essays that begins this process, see *Memory and Cultural Politics: New Approaches to American Ethnic Literatures*, ed. Amritjit Singh, Joseph T. Skerrett, Jr., and Robert E. Hogan (Boston: Northeastern University Press, 1996). For helpful summaries of the empirical, metaphorical, and moral approaches to the Hansen thesis, see Sollors, *Beyond Ethnicity*, 208–36, and Kivisto and Blanck, 3. Stanford M. Lyman, in his article "Hansen's Theory and America's Black Birthright: The Historical Novel as History and Collective Memory," does consider race in terms of the Hansen thesis, but from the perspective of third-generation return. Lyman compares Hansen's use of Margaret Mitchell's *Gone With the Wind* as evi-

dence of third-generation return in 1937 with the situation of third-generation African Americans, descendants of slaves, as depicted in William Wells Brown's historical novel *Clotel; or, The President's Daughter: A Narrative of Slave Life in the United States* (1853), as a means of exposing the limitations of Hansen's notion of birthright. See Lyman in Kivisto and Blanck, *American Immigrants*, 126–41.

11. Hortense J. Spillers, "Chosen Place, Timeless People: Some Figurations on the New World," in *Conjuring: Black Women, Fiction, and Literary Tradition*, ed. Hortense J. Spillers and Marjorie Pryse (Bloomington: Indiana University Press, 1985), 152. Spillers is describing here Marshall's second novel, *The Chosen Place, the Timeless People* (1969).

12. Paule Marshall, *Brown Girl, Brownstones* (1959; reprint, Old Westbury: Feminist Press, 1981) 13. All further quotations from the novel will refer to this edition and will be cited in the text. Marshall, "Shaping the World of My Art," *New Letters* 40.1 (1973): 110–11.

13. See Christian, "Ritualistic Process and the Structure of Paule Marshall's *Praisesong for the Widow*," *Callaloo* 6.2 (1983): 74–83; "Paule Marshall," *Afro–American Fiction Writers after 1955*, vol. 33 of *Dictionary of Literary Biography*, ed. Thadious M. Davis and Trudier Harris (Detroit: Gale, 1984), 161–70; Christian, *Black Women Novelists*, 80–136. For an interesting assessment of the symbolism of architectural motifs throughout the novel, see Kimberly W. Benston, "Architectural Imagery and Unity in Paule Marshall's *Brown Girl, Brownstones*," *Negro American Literature Forum* 9.3 (1975): 67–70.

14. Richard Rodriguez has recently reaffirmed and transformed Marshall's motif and assertion of shared humanity of all "others" in American culture through his interpretation of the gay community's presence in the Victorian mansions of San Francisco. Rodriguez describes the irony implicit in the "coincidence of the market that gay men found themselves living with the architectural metaphor for the family. No other architecture in the American imagination is more evocative of family than the Victorian house. . . . within those same Victorian houses, homosexuals were living rebellious lives to challenge the foundations of domesticity." But he overturns Marshall's description of the inevitability of the progression of the generations in such places by juxtaposing the tragic toll that AIDS has taken on gay men with the "optimism" he believes inherent in the architecture of the house. "The three- or four-story Victorian house, like the Victorian novel, was built to contain several generations and several classes under one roof, behind a single oaken door. . . . Stairs, connecting one story with another, describe the confidence that bound generations through time—confidence that the family would inherit the earth." See Rodriguez, *Days of Obligation: An Argument with My Mexican Father* (New York: Viking, 1992), 30–31.

15. This description foreshadows the closing image of Marshall's autobiographical short story entitled "To Da-duh, In Memoriam" in which a young Barbadian American believes herself to have inherited to some degree her grandmother's spirit upon her grandmother's death. See Paule Marshall, "To Da-duh, In Memoriam," in *Reena and Other Stories* (New York: Feminist Press, 1983). Critic Eugenia Collier assesses Marshall's work chronologically in terms of character progression and describes the young protagonist in "To Da-duh, In Memoriam" as resembling distinctly a younger version of Selina Boyce; see Collier, "The Closing of the Circle: Movement from Division to Wholeness in Paule Marshall's Fiction," in *Black Women Writers (1950–1980): A Critical Evaluation*, ed. Mari Evans (Garden City, N.Y.: Anchor Press/Doubleday, 1984), 295–315. Marshall herself identifies "To Da-duh, In Memoriam" as "the most autobiographical" of those collected in *Reena*, stating that it is a "remi-

niscence largely of a visit I paid to my grandmother (whose nickname was Da-duh) on the island of Barbados when I was nine." She affirms in her own life the idea of the old woman's spirit entering the young girl's soul: "It was as if we both knew, at a level beyond words, that I had come into the world not only to love her and to continue her line but to take her very life in order that I might live." Interestingly, Marshall describes Da-duh as appearing "in one form or another in my other work as well," claiming that in *Brown Girl, Brownstones* she takes the form of "the old hairdresser, Mrs. Thompson, who offers Selina total, unquestioning love" (*Reena*, 95).

16. For a more detailed discussion of this motif, see Werner Sollors, "Literature and Ethnicity," in *Harvard Encyclopedia of American Ethnic Groups*, ed. Stephan Thernstrom (Cambridge, Mass.: Harvard University Press, 1980), 663.

17. Recall, for just a few examples, Du Bois' painful recognition of his race when attempting to give a greeting card to a classmate in *The Souls of Black Folk* (1903), James Weldon Johnson's similar experience when asked to stand along with the black students in class in *The Autobiography of an Ex-Colored Man* (1912), or Janie Starks's sudden comprehension of her race upon seeing herself among whites in a photograph in Zora Neale Hurston's *Their Eyes Were Watching God* (1937). For several provocative assessments of the issue of racial recognition, particularly in relation to Du Bois, see *Lure and Loathing: Essays on Race, Identity, and the Ambivalence of Assimilation*, ed. Gerald Early (New York: Penguin, 1993).

18. As will be discussed in the next chapter, the similarities between Deighton Boyce and Primus Mackenzie, the father in Marshall's latest novel, *Daughters* (1991), are many, including their mutual association with sun imagery. As Marshall explains in her interview with Daryl Cumber Dance, both characters are written in response to the author's relationship with her own father. Marshall, "An Interview with Paule Marshall," with Daryl Cumber Dance, *Southern Review* 28.1 (1992): 7–8.

19. Deborah Schneider, "A Search for Selfhood: Paule Marshall's *Brown Girl, Brownstones*," in *The Afro-American Novel since 1960*, ed. Peter Bruck and Wolfgang Karrer (Amsterdam: Gruner, 1982), 53–73.

20. For an assessment of Suggie Skeete's and Miss Thompson's roles as mother figures to Selina, see Rosalie Riegle Troester, "Turbulence and Tenderness: Mothers, Daughters, and 'Othermothers' in Paule Marshall's *Brown Girl, Brownstones*," *Sage* 1.2 (1984): 13–16.

21. In her article on "West Indian Autobiography" in *African American Autobiography: A Collection of Critical Essays*, ed. William L. Andrews (Englewood Cliffs: Prentice-Hall, 1993), 196–211, Pouchet Paquet examines the similarities and differences in four male, West Indian autobiographical works: George Lamming's *In the Castle of My Skin* (1953), C. L. R. James's *Beyond a Boundary* (1963), Derek Walcott's *Another Life* (1973), and Vidia Naipaul's *Finding the Center* (1984). Interesting to note in the context of this study is Pouchet Paquet's assertion that "the image of the writer as one who writes the self into a specific Caribbean landscape through a process of self-discovery and creation is inverted in [Naipaul's] *Finding the Center* to become a movement out of that landscape," much like the process we have seen in the works of McKay (209).

22. George Lamming, *In the Castle of My Skin* (New York: Schocken, 1983), x.

23. For a discussion of the figure of the Jew in Caribbean literature more generally, see Sue N. Greene, "The Use of the Jew in West Indian Novels," *World Literature Written in English* 26.1 (1986): 150–68.

24. A number of prominent Caribbeaners were active politically in the 1920s and 1930s, including Claude McKay, Richard B. Moore, Otto Huiswood, Caspar Holstein,

W. A. Domingo, and certainly Marcus Garvey. A tradition of community activism has continued among Caribbeaners and has recently been studied by Philip Kasinitz in *Caribbean New York* (1992).

25. As quoted by Christian in "Paule Marshall," 168.

26. Mortimer and Bryce-Laporte, *Female Immigrants*, xxvi, xxvii.

27. Marshall, "Black Immigrant Women in *Brown Girl, Brownstones*," in ibid., 5.

28. Marshall, "Poets in the Kitchen," in *Reena*, 3.

29. Marshall, "Black Immigrant Women in *Brown Girl, Brownstones*," 10.

30. Marshall, "Poets in the Kitchen," in *Reena*, 6–7.

31. Ibid., 7.

32. Vladimir C. Nahirny and Joshua A. Fishman, "American Immigrant Groups: Ethnic Identification and the Problem of Generations," in Sollors, *Theories of Ethnicity*, 266–81. Nahirny and Fishman use this phrase in reference to the typical second-generation immigrant pattern of rejecting the parent's culture in favor of assimilation into the host society.

33. Marshall, "An Interview with Paule Marshall," 8.

34. Christian, *Black Women Novelists*, 90.

35. For more information on Father Divine, see Robert Weisbrot, *Father Divine and the Struggle for Racial Equality* (Urbana: University of Illinois Press, 1983).

36. Collier, "The Closing of the Circle," 296.

37. I thank Werner Sollors for suggesting this interesting inversion.

38. The reference to sight here obviously recalls Ralph Ellison's extended pondering of the theme of invisibility in *Invisible Man* (1952) and anticipates one of the most poignant expressions of the theme (which also interestingly points to aspects of white immigrant experience), the blindness of Mr. Yacobowski when looking at Pecola Breedlove in Toni Morrison's *The Bluest Eye* (New York: Washington Square Press, 1970). "The gray head of Mr Yacobowski looms up over the counter. He urges his eyes out of his thoughts to encounter her. Blue eyes. Blear-dropped. Slowly, like Indian summer moving imperceptibly toward fall, he looks toward her. Somewhere between retina and object, between vision and view, his eyes draw back, hesitate, and hover. At some fixed point in time and space he senses that he need not waste the effort of a glance. He does not see her, because for him there is nothing to see. How can a fifty-two-year-old white immigrant storekeeper with the taste of potatoes and beer in his mouth, his mind honed on a doe-eyed Virgin Mary, his sensibilities blunted by a permanent awareness of loss, *see* a little black girl? Nothing in his life suggested that the feat was even possible, not to say desirable or necessary" (41–42).

39. Marshall, "An Interview with Paule Marshall," 3.

40. Ibid., 17. See also Paule Marshall, "Holding onto the Vision: Sylvia Baer Interviews Paule Marshall," *The Women's Review of Books* 13.10–11 (1991): 24–25.

41. Marshall, "An Interview with Paule Marshall," 7.

5. "All o' we is one"

1. Edward Kamau Brathwaite, "The African Presence in Caribbean Literature," in *Slavery, Colonialism, and Racism*, ed. Sidney Mintz (New York: Norton, 1974), 99; my emphasis.

2. See Marshall, "Shaping the World of My Art," *New Letters* 40.1 (Autumn 1973): 97–112.

3. Marshall, "An Interview with Paule Marshall," 8.

4. Abena Busia, "What Is Your Nation? Reconnecting Africa and Her Diaspora

through Paule Marshall's *Praisesong for the Widow*," in *Changing Our Own Words: Essays on Criticism, Theory, and Writing by Black Women*, ed. Cheryl A. Wall (New Brunswick, N.J.: Rutgers University Press, 1989), 196.

5. A number of characters in *Daughters* recall fictional figures seen in previous works. Compare the psychological journey that Primus Mackenzie experiences from his socialist days in London to his surrender to cynicism about the potential for true independence of the island, for example, with the downfall experienced by Lyle Hutson in *The Chosen Place, the Timeless People*. Similarities of principle and value link Estelle with Merle Kinbona, again of *The Chosen Place, the Timeless People*, while Estelle's ultimate redemption through betrayal of her husband is not unlike that performed by Silla Boyce in *Brown Girl, Brownstones*. Mae Ryland possesses the realism and tenacity of Mrs. Thompson in *Brown Girl, Brownstones*, and the pattern of Lowell Carruthers' life resembles that of Jay Johnson in *Praisesong for the Widow*. Beyond the realms of her own work, many of Marshall's characters in *Daughters* also allude to figures in Caribbean letters. The love triangle between Astral Forde, Primus, and Estelle resembles that portrayed by Phyllis Shand Allfrey in *The Orchid House*, while Celestine recalls both Lally in *The Orchid House* and Pheena in Jean Rhys's *Wide Sargasso Sea*. Marshall denies basing her character on either of these figures, however, and argues instead that Celestine is yet another manifestation of her own maternal grandmother who appeared as "Da-duh" in "To Da-duh, in Memoriam," as Great-Aunt Cuney in *Praisesong for the Widow*, as Leesy Walkes in *The Chosen Place, The Timeless People*, and as Mrs. Thompson in *Brown Girl, Brownstones*. See Marshall, "An Interview with Paule Marshall," 7.

6. Although discussed only briefly in this chapter, the novel also offers, through Ursa's work with the Meade-Rogers Foundation, an important commentary on systems of "domestic colonization" as they operate in contemporary U.S. cities.

7. Marshall, "Holding onto the Vision," 25.

8. Marshall's collection of short stories, *Soul Clap Hands and Sing*, is dedicated to her son, Evan-Keith, and addresses issues of male identity to some degree. In another short story, "Some Get Wasted," she confronts similar issues through the depiction of an adolescent struggling to find a place for himself as a second-generation Caribbean immigrant. (See Marshall, "Some Get Wasted," in *Harlem, U.S.A.*, ed. John Henrik Clarke [Berlin: Seven Seas, 1974]). Marshall has mentioned in a recent interview, however, that her next novel will involve a little boy as the central character: " . . . the entire novel, as I'm thinking, might be told in his voice. . . . All I know about him at this point is the he's the child of some jazz musicians who went to live in Paris, and when they die there, the boy is brought back to the States to be raised by his two rivalrous grandmothers. These two live across the street from each other in Brooklyn and have been at odds for years because of the marriage of their children. It will be a kind of Romeo and Juliet theme, with the old women—one from the South, the other from the Islands—suggesting the warring Montagues and Capulets, with the child, this little boy, caught in the middle of the fray. That's as far as I've gotten." See Marshall, "Interview with Paule Marshall," 13.

9. Marshall, "Holding onto the Vision," 25.

10. Ibid., 25.

11. For more information on the figure of Nanny (who is typified by Congo Jane in the novel) see Lucille Mair, *Women Field Workers in Jamaica during Slavery* (Mona, Jamaica: University of the West Indies, 1987); Michelle Cliff, *Abeng* (New York: Penguin, 1990), 21–22; for information about Jamaican folklore more generally, see Daryl Cumber Dance, *Folklore from Contemporary Jamaicans* (Knoxville: University of Tennessee Press, 1985).

12. Paule Marshall, *Daughters* (New York: Penguin, 1992), 13. All subsequent quotations will be cited parenthetically in the text, and will refer to this edition of the novel.

13. Recall that Silla, in *Brown Girl, Brownstones*, is referred to by Selina only as "the mother," again suggesting a different form of distance between parent and child.

14. For an overview of issues surrounding the relationship between postmodernism and post-colonialism, see Part IV, "Postmodernism and Post-Colonialism," in *The Post-Colonial Studies Reader*, ed. Bill Ashcroft, Gareth Griffiths, and Helen Tiffin (London: Routledge, 1995), 117–50. For the seminal catena of characteristics common to postmodern literature ("indeterminancy, fragmentation, decanonization, selflessness, the unrepresentable, hybridization, carnivalization, and participation"), see Ihab Hassan, "The Culture of Postmodernism," *Theory, Culture, and Society* 2.3 (1985): 119–31.

15. Recall the similar significance placed on space in the beginning of *Brown Girl, Brownstones*. See Christian, *Black Women Novelists*, 80–136.

16. Don DeLillo's *White Noise* (New York: Penguin 1985) contains numerous similar postmodern moments in which profound thoughts and discussions take place in startlingly impersonal and mundane settings. Consider, for just one example, the discussion between Jack Gladney and Murray concerning the nature of death which occurs amidst the material chaos of a grocery store.

17. Marshall, "Holding onto the Vision," 25.

18. This image recalls another scene in African American letters: that in Toni Morrison's *Tar Baby* in which the protagonist, Jadine Childs, is haunted in a dream by women flaunting breasts and eggs as a similar reminder of fertility and supposed female obligation. See Morrison, *Tar Baby* (New York: Signet, 1981), 222–23.

19. Marshall, "Holding onto the Vision," 25.

20. Although she only alludes to this in the novel (348), Marshall states directly in an interview that Celestine "initiated the PM sexually when he was a boy." See Marshall, "Interview with Paule Marshall," 7.

21. Marshall, "Holding onto the Vision," 25.

22. Marshall, "Interview with Paule Marshall," 20.

23. Ralph Ellison, in *Invisible Man* (1952), gives this issue considerable attention throughout the novel but most explicitly in the first chapter of the text, which is titled "Battle Royal."

24. Marshall, "Interview with Paule Marshall," 20.

25. Marshall, "Holding onto the Vision," 25.

26. Marshall, "Interview with Paule Marshall," 4.

Afterword

1. I thank an anonymous reviewer for suggesting the value of a comparison between McKay and Toomer, and Marshall and Jones. Stelamaris Coser has already done important work on Marshall and Jones in *Bridging the Americas: The Literature of Toni Morrison, Paule Marshall, and Gayl Jones* (Philadelphia: Temple University Press, 1994).

2. Rey Chow, *Ethics after Idealism: Theory–Culture–Ethnicity–Reading* (Bloomington: Indiana University Press, 1998), 108–12.

3. For examples of work done on specific immigrant groups, see Mary Waters's several studies on English-speaking Caribbean immigrants to the United States; Glenn Hendricks, *The Dominican Diaspora: From the Dominican Republic to New York City—Vil-*

lagers in Transition (New York: Teachers College Press, 1974); Michael S. Laguerre, *American Odyssey: Haitians in New York City* (Ithaca: Cornell University Press, 1984). For a study of African American reactions to white immigrants, see Arnold M. Shankman, *Ambivalent Friends: Afro-Americans View the Immigrant* (Westport, Conn.: Greenwood, 1982).

4. Emile Durkheim, *The Division of Labor in Society* (New York: Free Press, 1933).

5. For an attribution of these concepts to post-colonial writing, see Bill Ashcroft, Gareth Griffiths, and Helen Tiffin, eds., *The Empire Writes Back: Theory and Practice in Post-Colonial Literatures* (London: Routledge, 1989).

Bibliography

Abruña, Laura Niesen de. "The Ambivalence of Mirroring and Female Bonding in Paule Marshall's *Brown Girl, Brownstones.*" In *International Women's Writing: New Landscapes of Identity*, ed. Anne E. Brown and Marjanne E. Goozé. Westport, Conn.: Greenwood, 1995. 245–52.

——. "Twentieth-Century Women Writers from the English-Speaking Caribbean." In *Caribbean Women Writers: Essays from the First International Conference*, ed. Selwyn R. Cudjoe. Wellesley: Calaloux, 1990.

Allfrey, Phyllis Shand. *The Orchid House.* Washington, D.C.: Three Continents, 1985.

Allis, Jeannette B. *West Indian Literature: An Index to Criticism, 1930–1975.* Boston: Hall, 1981.

Anderson, Jervis. *This Was Harlem: A Cultural Portrait, 1900–1950.* New York: Farrar, 1981.

Andrews, William L., ed. *African American Autobiography: A Collection of Critical Essays.* Englewood Cliffs, N.J.: Prentice, 1993.

Arden, Eugene. "The Early Harlem Novel." *Phylon* 20 (Spring 1959): 25–31.

Aronson, Dan R. "Ethnicity as a Cultural System: An Introductory Essay." In *Ethnicity in the Americas*, ed. Frances Henry. The Hague: Mouton, 1976. 9–22.

Ascher, Carol. "Compromised Lives." *The Women's Review of Books* 9.2 (1991): 7.

Ashcroft, Bill; Gareth Griffiths; and Helen Tiffin, eds. *The Empire Writes Back: Theory and Practice in Post-Colonial Literatures.* London: Routledge, 1989.

——. *The Post-Colonial Studies Reader.* London: Routledge, 1995.

Baker, Houston A., Jr. *Modernism and the Harlem Renaissance.* Chicago: University of Chicago Press, 1987.

Baldwin, James. *Tell Me How Long the Train's Been Gone.* New York: Dell, 1968.

Balutansky, Kathleen M. "Naming Caribbean Women Writers." *Callaloo* 13.3 (1990): 539–50.

Bammer, Angelika. *Displacements: Cultural Identities in Question.* Bloomington: Indiana University Press, 1994.

Barksdale, R. A. "Symbolism and Irony in McKay's *Home to Harlem.*" *CLA Journal* 15 (March 1972): 338–44.

Barthold, Bonnie J. *Black Time: Fiction of Africa, the Caribbean, and the United States.* New Haven: Yale University Press, 1981.

Bartkowski, Francis. *Travelers, Immigrants, Inmates: Essays in Estrangement.* Minneapolis: University of Minnesota Press, 1995.

Baugh, Edward. *West Indian Poetry 1900–1970: A Study in Cultural Decolonisation.* Kingston: Savacou, 1971.

Benston, Kimberly W. "Architectural Imagery and Unity in Paule Marshall's

Brown Girl, Brownstones." *Negro American Literature Forum* 9.3 (1975): 67–70.

Bernabé, Jean; Patrick Chamoiseau; and Raphael Confiant. "In Praise of Creoleness." *Callaloo* 13.4 (1990): 886–909.

Bhabha, Homi K. *The Location of Culture.* New York: Routledge, 1994.

Blary, Liliane. "Claude McKay and Black Nationalist Ideologies (1934–1948)." In *Myth and Ideology in American Culture*, ed. Regis Durand. Lille, France: Publications de l'Université de Lille III, 1976. 211–31.

Bone, Robert. "Merle Kinbona Was Part Saint, Part Revolutionary, Part Obeah-Woman." *New York Times Book Review* (30 Nov. 1969): 4, 54.

———. *The Negro Novel in America.* New Haven: Yale University Press, 1958.

Bonnett, Aubrey W. "Structured Adaptation of Black Migrants from the Caribbean: An Examination of an Indigenous Banking System in Brooklyn." *Phylon* 42.4: 346–55.

Bontemps, Arna. *Anthology of Negro Poets.* FL9791. A Folkways Recording.

Bragdon, Kathleen. *Native People of Southern New England, 1500–1650.* Norman: University of Oklahoma Press, 1996.

Brathwaite, Edward Kamau. "The African Presence in Caribbean Literature." In *Slavery, Colonialism and Racism*, ed. Sidney Mintz. New York: Norton, 1974. 73–110.

———. *The Arrivants: A New World Trilogy.* London: Oxford, 1973.

———. "History, the Caribbean Writer and X/Self." In *Crisis and Creativity in the New Literatures in English*, ed. Geoffrey V. Davis and Hena Maes-Jelinek. Amsterdam: Rodopi, 1990. 23–46.

———. "West Indian History and Society in the Art of Paule Marshall's Novel." *Journal of Black Studies* 1 (Dec. 1970): 225–38.

Brawley, Benjamin. *The Negro Genius: A New Appraisal of the Achievement of the American Negro in Literature and the Fine Arts.* 1937. Reprint, New York: Biblo and Tannen, 1972.

Bröck, Sabine. "Transcending the 'Loophole of Retreat': Paule Marshall's Placing of Female Generations." *Callaloo* 10.1 (1987): 79–90.

Bronze, Stephen. *Roots of Negro Racial Consciousness: The 1920's—Three Harlem Renaissance Authors.* New York: Libra, 1964.

Brown, Claude. *Manchild in the Promised Land.* New York: Macmillan, 1966.

Brown, Lloyd W. "The Expatriate Consciousness in Black American Literature." *Studies in Black Literature* 3 (Summer 1972): 9–11.

———. "The Rhythms of Power in Paule Marshall's Fiction." *Novel: A Forum on Fiction* 7.2 (1974): 159–67.

———. "The West Indian as an Ethnic Stereotype in Black American Literature." *Negro American Literature Forum* 5.1 (1971). 8–14.

———. "West Indian Literature: Road to a 'New World' Sensibility." *Journal of Black Studies* 7.4 (1977): 411–36.

———. *West Indian Poetry.* Boston: Twayne, 1978.

Brown, Lyn Mikel, and Carol Gilligan. *Meeting at the Crossroads: Women's Psychology and Girls' Development.* Cambridge: Harvard University Press, 1992.

Bruck, Peter, and Wolfgang Karrer, eds. *The Afro-American Novel since 1960.* Amsterdam: Gruner, 1982.

Bryce-Laporte, Roy S. "Black Immigrants: The Experience of Invisibility and Inequality." *Journal of Black Studies* 3: 29–56.

———. "The New Immigration: The Female Majority." In *Female Immigrants to the United States: Caribbean, Latin American, and African Experiences*, ed. Delores M. Mortimer and Roy S. Bryce-Laporte. Washington, D.C.: Smithsonian, 1981. vii–xl.

Bryce-Laporte, Roy S., and Delores M. Mortimer, eds. *Caribbean Immigration to the United States*. Washington, D.C.: Smithsonian, 1976.

Busia, Abena P. A. "What Is Your Nation? Reconnecting Africa and Her Diaspora through Paule Marshall's *Praisesong for the Widow*." In *Changing Our Own Words: Essays on Criticism, Theory, and Writing by Black Women*, ed. Cheryl A. Wall. New Brunswick, N.J.: Rutgers University Press, 1989. 196–211.

Callahan, John F. *In the African-American Grain: Call-and-Response in Twentieth-Century Black Fiction*. Middletown: Wesleyan University Press, 1988.

———. "'A Long Way from Home': The Art and Protest of Claude McKay and James Baldwin." *Contemporary Literature* 34.4 (1993): 767–77.

Carby, Hazel V. *Reconstructing Womanhood: The Emergence of the Afro-American Woman Novelist*. New York: Oxford University Press, 1987.

Carnegie, Charles V. "A Social Psychology of Caribbean Migrations: Strategic Flexibility in the West Indies." In *The Caribbean Exodus*, ed. Barry B. Levine. New York: Praeger, 1987. 32–43.

Cartey, Wilfred. "Four Shadows of Harlem." *Negro Digest* 18 (1969): 22–25, 83–92.

Cassidy, Frederic Gomes, and R. B. LePage, eds. *Dictionary of Jamaican English*. New York: Cambridge University Press, 1980.

Cataliotti, Robert H. *The Music in African American Fiction*. New York: Garland, 1995.

Chambers, Iain. *Migrancy, Culture, Identity*. New York: Routledge, 1994.

Chaney, Elsa M., and Constance R. Sutton, eds. *Caribbean Life in New York City: Sociocultural Dimensions*. New York: Center for Migration Studies, 1987.

Chauhan, P. S. "Claude McKay: Polarities of the Colonial Imagination." In *Claude McKay: Centennial Studies*, ed. A. L. McLeod. New Delhi: Sterling, 1992. 22–31.

———. "Rereading Claude McKay." *CLA Journal* 34.1 (1990): 68–80.

Childress, Alice. *A Short Walk*. New York: Avon, 1979.

Chin, Timothy S. "'Bullers' and 'Battymen': Contesting Homophobia in Black Popular Culture and Contemporary Caribbean Literature." *Callaloo* 20.1 (1997): 127–41.

Chisolm, Shirley. *Unbought and Unbossed*. New York: Houghton, 1970.

Chodorow, Nancy. *The Reproduction of Mothering: Psycholanalysis and the Sociology of Gender*. Berkeley: University of California Press, 1978.

Chow, Rey. *Ethics after Idealism: Theory–Culture–Ethnicity–Reading*. Bloomington: Indiana University Press, 1998.

Christian, Barbara T. "Black, Female, and Foreign-Born: A Statement." In *Female Immigrants to the United States: Caribbean, Latin American, and African Experiences*, ed. Delores M. Mortimer and Roy S. Bryce-Laporte. Washington, D.C.: Smithsonian, 1981. 172–76.

———. *Black Women Novelists: The Development of a Tradition, 1892–1976*. Westport, Conn.: Greenwood, 1980.

———. "Paule Marshall." In *Afro-American Fiction Writers after 1955*, vol. 33 of *Dictionary of Literary Biography*, ed. Thadious Davis and Trudier Harris. Detroit: Gale, 1984. 161–70.

———. "Ritualistic Process and the Structure of Paule Marshall's *Praisesong for the Widow*." *Callaloo* 6.2 (1983): 74–83.

Christol, Hélène. "Paule Marshall's Bajan Women in *Brown Girl, Brownstones*." In *Women and War: The Changing Status of American Women from the 1930s to the 1950s*, ed. Maria Deidrich and Dorothea Fischer-Hornung. Berg, 1990. 141–53.

Clarke, John Henrik, ed. *Harlem: A Community in Transition*. New York: Citadel, 1964.

———. *Harlem, U.S.A*. Berlin: Seven Seas, 1974.

Cliff, Michelle. *Abeng*. New York: Penguin, 1984.

———. *No Telephone to Heaven*. New York: Vintage, 1987.

Cobham, Rhonda. "Revisioning Our Kumblas: Transforming Feminist and Nationalist Agendas in Three Caribbean Women's Texts." *Callaloo* 16.1 (1993): 44–64.

Colen, Shellee. "'Just a Little Respect': West Indian Domestic Workers in New York City." In *Muchachas No More: Household Workers in Latin America and the Caribbean*, ed. Elsa M. Chaney and Mary Garcia Castro. Philadelphia: Temple University Press, 1989. 171–94.

Collier, Eugenia. "The Closing of the Circle: Movement from Division to Wholeness in Paule Marshall's Fiction." In *Black Women Writers (1950–1980): A Critical Evaluation*, ed. Mari Evans. Garden City: Anchor, 1984. 295–315.

———. "The Four Way Dilemma of Claude McKay." *CLA Journal* 15 (Mar. 1972): 345–53.

———. "Heritage from Harlem." *Black World* 20 (Nov. 1970): 52–59.

Condit, John Hillyer. "An Urge toward Wholeness: Claude McKay and His Sonnets." *CLA Journal* 22.4 (1979): 350–64.

Conroy, Sister Mary. "The Vagabond Motif in the Writings of Claude McKay." *Negro American Literature Forum* 5 (1971): 15–23.

Coombs, Orde. *Do You See My Love for You Growing?* New York: Dodd, 1970.

Cooper, Carolyn. "Race and the Cultural Politics of Self-Representation: A View from the University of the West Indies." *Research in African Literatures* 27.4 (1996): 97–105.

Cooper, Wayne F. *Claude McKay: Rebel Sojourner in the Harlem Renaissance*. New York: Schocken, 1987.

———. "Claude McKay and the New Negro of the 1920s." *Phylon* 25 (1964): 297–306.

———. Review of *Claude McKay: A Black Poet's Struggle for Identity*, by Tyrone Tillery. *Journal of American History* 79.4 (1993): 1656–57.

Cooper, Wayne F., ed. *The Passion of Claude McKay: Selected Poetry and Prose, 1912–1948*. New York: Schocken, 1973.

Cooper, Wayne F., and Robert C. Reinders. "A Black Briton Comes 'Home.'" *Race* 9 (July 1967): 67–83.

Coser, Stelamaris. *Bridging the Americas: The Literature of Paule Marshall, Toni Morrison, and Gayl Jones.* Philadelphia: Temple University Press, 1995.

Coulthard, G. R. "The West Indian Novel of Immigration." *Phylon* 20 (Spring 1959): 32–41.

Cronon, Edmund. *Black Moses.* Madison: University of Wisconsin Press, 1955.

Cruse, Harold. *The Crisis of the Negro Intellectual.* 1967. Reprint, New York: Quill, 1984.

———. "Harold Cruse: An Interview." With C. W. E. Bigsby. In *The Black American Writer*, vol. II: *Poetry and Drama*, ed. C. W. E. Bigsby. Deland: Everett, 1969.

Cudjoe, Selwyn R., ed. *Caribbean Women Writers: Essays from the First International Conference.* Wellesley: Calaloux, 1990.

Dabydeen, David, and Nana Wilson-Tagoe. *A Reader's Guide to West Indian and Black British Literature.* Kingston-upon-Thames: Dangaroo, 1987.

Dance, Daryl Cumber. *Folklore from Contemporary Jamaicans.* Knoxville: University of Tennessee Press, 1985.

Dance, Daryl Cumber, ed. *Fifty Caribbean Writers: A Bio-Bibliographical and Critical Sourcebook.* New York: Greenwood, 1986.

Dash, J. Michael. *Haiti and the United States: National Stereotypes and the Literary Imagination.* London: Macmillan, 1988.

Dathorne, O. R. *Dark Ancestor: The Literature of the Black Man in the Caribbean.* Baton Rouge: Louisiana State University Press, 1981.

Davies, Carole Boyce. *Black Women, Writing, and Identity: Migrations of the Subject.* New York: Routledge, 1994.

Davis, Arthur P., and Saunders Redding, eds. *Cavalcade: Negro American Writing from 1760 to the Present.* Boston: Houghton, 1971.

Davis, Thadious M. *Nella Larsen, Novelist of the Harlem Renaissance: A Woman's Life Unveiled.* Baton Rouge: Louisiana State University Press, 1994.

Davis, Thadious M., and Trudier Harris, eds. *Afro-American Fiction Writers after 1955.* Vol. 33 of *Dictionary of Literary Biography.* Detroit: Gale, 1984. 161–70.

Delany, Martin R. *Blake, or The Huts of America.* Ed. Floyd J. Miller. Boston: Beacon, 1970.

DeLillo, Don. *White Noise.* New York: Penguin, 1985.

Denniston, Dorothy Hamer. *The Fiction of Paule Marshall: Reconstructions of History, Culture, and Gender.* Knoxville: University of Tennessee Press, 1995.

Denniston, Dorothy L. "Early Short Fiction by Paule Marshall." *Callaloo* 6.2 (1983): 31–45.

Devereux, George. "Ethnic Identity: Its Logical Foundations and Its Dysfunctions." In Werner Sollors, ed., *Theories of Ethnicity: A Classical Reader.* New York: New York University Press, 1996.

Dewey, John. "Introduction." In *Selected Poems by Claude McKay.* New York: Bookman, 1953.

Diawara, Manthia. "Englishness and Blackness: Cricket as Discourse on Colonialism." *Callaloo* 13.3 (1990): 830–44.

Domingo, W. A. "Gift of the Black Tropics." In *The New Negro*, ed. Alain Locke. 1925. Reprint, New York: Johnson Reprint Corporation, 1968. 341–49.

Dominguez, Virginia R. *From Neighbor to Stranger: The Dilemma of Caribbean Peoples in the United States.* New Haven: Antilles Research Program, Yale University, 1970.

Dorris, Ronald. "Claude McKay's *Home to Harlem.*" *McNeese Review* 29 (1982–83): 53–62.

Drake, St. Clair. *Black Folk Here and There: An Essay in History and Anthropology.* Vol. 1. Los Angeles: UCLA, 1987.

Drayton, Arthur. "McKay's Human Pity: A Note on His Protest Poetry." *Black Orpheus* 17 (June 1965): 39–48.

Du Bois, W. E. B. "The Browsing Reader." *Crisis* 35 (1928): 202.

———. "Criteria of Negro Art." In Angelyn Mitchell, ed., *Within the Circle: An Anthology of African American Literary Criticism from the Harlem Renaissance to the Present.* Durham: Duke University Press, 1994.

———. *Dark Princess: A Romance.* 1928. New York: Kraus Thompson Organization, 1974.

———. *The Souls of Black Folk.* Introduction by Donald B. Gibson. New York: Penguin, 1989.

Durand, Regis, ed. *Myth and Ideology in American Culture.* Lille, France: Publications de l'Université de Lille, 1976.

Durkheim, Emile. *The Division of Labor in Society.* New York: Free Press, 1933.

Early, Gerald, ed. *Lure and Loathing: Essays on Race, Identity and the Ambivalence of Assimilation.* New York: Penguin, 1993.

Eastman, Max. "Introduction." In Claude McKay, *Harlem Shadows.* New York: Harcourt, 1922.

Edwards, Rhonda M. "Strained Bedfellows: Black Ethnic Plurality Explored through Afro-American and West Indian Relations." Senior honors thesis, Department of Sociology, Harvard University, 1989.

Eko, Ebele. "Beyond the Myth of Confrontation: A Comparative Study of African and African-American Female Protagonists." *Ariel: A Review of International English Literature* 17.4 (1986): 139–52.

Elimimian, Isaac I. "Theme and Technique in Claude McKay's Poetry." *CLA Journal* 25.2 (1981): 203–11.

Ellison, Ralph. *Invisible Man.* New York: Random, 1952.

Emanuel, James A., and Theodore L. Gross, eds. *Dark Symphony: Negro Literature in America.* New York: Free Press, 1968.

Emerson, O. B. "Cultural Nationalism in Afro-American Literature." In *The Cry of Home: Cultural Nationalism and the Modern Writer,* ed. Ernest H. Lewald. Knoxville: University of Tennessee Press, 1972. 211–44.

Fabre, Michel. "Aesthetics and Ideology in *Banjo.*" In *Myth and Ideology in American Culture,* ed. Regis Durand. Lille, France: Publications de l'Université de Lille, 1976. 195–209.

———. *From Harlem to Paris: Black American Writers in France, 1840–1980.* Urbana: University of Illinois Press, 1991.

Fairbanks, Carol. *Black American Fiction: A Bibliography.* Metuchen: Scarecrow, 1978.

Felgar, Robert. "Black Content, White Form." *Studies in Black Literature* 5 (Spring 1974): 28–31.

Ferraro, Thomas J. *Ethnic Passages: Literary Immigrants in Twentieth-Century America*. Chicago: University of Chicago Press, 1993.

Field, Carol. "Fresh, Fierce and 'First.'" *New York Herald Tribune Book Review* (16 August 1959): 5.

Fishman, Joshua; Vladimir C. Nahirny; John E. Hofman; and Robert G. Hayden. *Language Loyalty in the United States*. The Hague: Mouton, 1966.

Fogelson, Robert M., and Richard Rubenstein, eds. *Mass Violence in America: The Complete Report of Mayor LaGuardia's Commission on the Harlem Riot of March 19, 1935*. New York: Arno, 1969.

Ford, Nick Aaron. "Search for Identity: A Critical Survey of Belles-Lettres by and about Negroes Published in 1961." *Phylon* (1962): 1348.

Forsythe, Dennis. "West Indian Radicalism in America: An Assessment of Ideologies." In *Ethnicity in the Americas*, ed. Frances Henry. The Hague: Mouton, 1976. 301–32.

French, William P. *Afro-American Poetry and Drama, 1760–1975: A Guide to Information Sources*. Detroit: Gale, 1979.

Friedman, Susan Stanford. "Women's Autobiographical Selves: Theory and Practice." In *The Private Self: Theory and Practice of Women's Autobiographical Writings*, ed. Shari Benstock. Chapel Hill: University of North Carolina Press, 1988. 34–62.

Fullinwider, S. P. *The Mind and Mood of Black America: 20th Century Thought*. Homewood, Ill.: Dorsey, 1969.

Gans, Herbert. "Symbolic Ethnicity: The Future of Ethnic Groups and Cultures in America." In *Theories of Ethnicity: A Classical Reader*, ed. Werner Sollors. New York: New York University Press, 1996. 425–59.

Gates, Henry Louis, Jr. *Figures in Black: Words, Signs, and the "Racial" Self*. New York: Oxford University Press, 1987.

———. *The Signifying Monkey: A Theory of African-American Literary Criticism*. New York: Oxford University Press, 1988.

Gayle, Addison. *Claude McKay: The Black Poet at War*. Detroit: Broadside, 1972.

Gikandi, Simon. "The Circle of Meaning: Paule Marshall, Modernism, and the Masks of History." In *Of Dreams Deferred: Dead or Alive—African Perspectives on African-American Writers*, ed. Femi Ojo-Ade. Westport, Conn.: Greenwood, 1996. 143–55.

Giles, James. *Claude McKay*. Boston: Twayne, 1976.

Gilligan, Carol. *In a Different Voice: Psychological Theory and Women's Development*. Cambridge: Harvard University Press, 1982.

Gilroy, Paul. *The Black Atlantic: Modernity and Double Consciousness*. Cambridge, Mass.: Harvard University Press, 1993.

———. *Small Acts: Thoughts on the Politics of Black Cultures*. New York: Serpent's Tail, 1993.

———. *There Ain't No Black in the Union Jack*. Chicago: University of Chicago Press, 1991.

Gloster, Hugh M. *Negro Voices in American Fiction*. Chapel Hill: University of North Carolina Press, 1948.

Gowda, H. H. Anniah. *The Colonial and the Neo-Colonial Encounters in Commonwealth Literature*. Mysore, India: University of Mysore, 1983.

Green, Vera. "Racial versus Ethnic Factors in Afro-American and Afro-Caribbean Migration." In *Migration and Development: Implications for Ethnic Identity and Political Conflict*, ed. Helen I. Safa and Brian M. DuToit. The Hague: Mouton, 1975. 83–96.

Greenberg, Robert M. "Idealism and Realism in the Fiction of Claude McKay." *CLA Journal* 24.3 (1981): 237–61.

Greene, Sue N. "The Use of the Jew in West Indian Novels." *World Literature Written in English* 26.1 (1986): 150–68.

Griffin, Barbara J. "Claude McKay: The Evolution of a Conservative." *CLA Journal* 36.2 (1992): 157–70.

———. "The Last Word: Claude McKay's Unpublished 'Cycle Manuscript.'" *MELUS* 21 (Spring 1996): 41–57.

Griffin, Farah Jasmine. *"Who set you flowin'?": The African-American Migration Narrative*. New York: Oxford University Press, 1995.

Hall, Stuart, ed. *Representation: Cultural Representations and Signifying Practices*. London: Sage, 1997.

Hall, Stuart, and Paul du Gay, eds. *Questions of Cultural Identity*. London: Sage, 1996.

Handlin, Oscar, ed. *Children of the Uprooted*. New York: George Braziller, 1966.

Hannerz, Ulf. "Some Comments on Race and Ethnicity in the United States." In *Ethnicity in the Americas*, ed. Frances Henry. The Hague: Mouton, 1976. 429–38.

Harris, Trudier. "No Outlet for the Blues." *Callaloo* 6.2 (1983): 57–67.

———. "Three Black Women Writers and Humanism: A Folk Perspective." In *Black American Literature and Humanism*, ed. R. Baxter Miller. Lexington: University of Kentucky Press, 1981. 50–74.

Harris, Wilson. *The Womb of Space: The Cross-Cultural Imagination*. Westport, Conn.: Greenwood, 1983.

Hart, Robert C. "Black–White Literary Relations in the Harlem Renaissance." *American Literature* 44 (Jan. 1973): 612–28.

Hassan, Ihab. "The Culture of Postmodernism." *Theory, Culture, and Society* 2.3 (1985): 119–31.

Hathaway, Heather. "Exploring 'something new': The 'Modernism' of Claude McKay." In *Race and the Modernist Artist*, ed. Jeffrey Melnick. New York: Oxford University Press, forthcoming.

———. "Maybe Freedom Lies in Hating': Miscegenation and the Oedipal Conflict." In Patricia Yaeger and Beth Kowaleski-Wallace, eds., *Refiguring the Father: New Feminist Readings of Patriarchy*. Carbondale: Southern Illinois University Press, 1989. 153–67.

Hedetoft, Ulf. *British Colonialism and Modern Identity*. Aalborg: Aalborg University Press, 1985.

Heglar, Charles J. "Claude McKay's 'If We Must Die,' *Home to Harlem*, and the Hog Trope." *ANQ: A Quarterly Journal of Short Articles, Notes, and Reviews* 8.3: 22–25.

Helbling, Mark. "Claude McKay: Art and Politics." *Negro American Literature Forum* 7 (Summer 1973): 49–52.

Hendricks, Glenn. *The Dominican Diaspora: From the Dominican Republic to New York City— Villagers in Transition*. New York: Teachers College Press, 1974.

Henri, Florette. *Black Migration: Movement North, 1900–1920.* Garden City: Anchor, 1975.

Henry, Frances, ed. *Ethnicity in the Americas.* The Hague: Mouton, 1976.

Hogue, W. Lawrence. *Discourse and the Other: The Production of the Afro-American Text.* Durham: Duke University Press, 1986.

Holt, Hamilton, ed. *The Life Stories of Undistinguished Americans As Told by Themselves.* Introduction by Werner Sollors. New York: Routledge, 1990.

Holt, Thomas. "The Political Uses of Alienation: W. E. B. Du Bois on Politics, Race, and Culture, 1903–1940." *American Quarterly* 42.2 (1990): 301–23.

Huggins, Nathan Irvin. *Harlem Renaissance.* New York: Oxford University Press, 1971.

Hughes, Carl Milton. *Negro Novelist: A Discussion of the Writings of American Negro Novelists, 1940–1950.* New York: Citadel, 1953.

Hughes, Langston. "The Negro Artist and the Racial Mountain." In Angelyn Mitchell, ed., *Within the Circle: An Anthology of African American Criticism from the Harlem Renaissance to the Present.* Durham: Duke University Press, 1994.

Hull, Gloria T. "The Black Woman Writer and the Diaspora." *Black Scholar* 17.2 (1986): 2–4.

———. " 'To Be a Black Woman in America': A Reading of Paule Marshall's 'Reena.' " *Obsidian* 4.3 (1978): 5–15.

Hurston, Zora Neale. *Their Eyes Were Watching God.* 1937. Reprint, Westport, Conn.: Greenwood, 1969.

Hutchinson, George. *The Harlem Renaissance in Black and White.* Cambridge, Mass.: Harvard University Press, 1995.

Ikonne, Chidi. *From Du Bois to Van Vechten: The Early New Negro Literature, 1903–1926.* Westport, Conn.: Greenwood, 1981.

Isaacs, Harold R. "Five Writers and Their African Ancestors." *Phylon* 21 (Fall 1960): 243–65.

Jackson, Blyden. "Claude McKay and Langston Hughes: The Harlem Renaissance and More." *Pembroke Magazine* 6 (1975): 43–8.

———. "The Essential McKay." *Phylon* 14 (1953): 216–17.

———. "The Harlem Renaissance." In *The Comic Imagination in American Literature,* ed. Louis D. Rubin. New Brunswick, N.J.: Rutgers University Press, 1973. 295–303.

Jackson, Miles M. "Literary History: Documentary Sidelights—James Weldon Johnson and Claude McKay." *Negro Digest* 17 (June 1968): 25–29.

James, C. L. R. *Beyond a Boundary.* London: Hutchinson, 1963.

Johnson, Barbara. *A World of Difference.* Baltimore: Johns Hopkins University Press, 1987.

Johnson, Charles. "A Caribbean Issue." *Opportunity: A Journal of Negro Life* 4 (1926).

Johnson, James Weldon. *The Autobiography of an Ex–Colored Man.* Boston: Sherman, French and Co., 1912.

———. *Black Manhattan.* 1930. Preface by Allan H. Spear. New York: Atheneum, 1968.

Jones, LeRoi (Baraka, Amiri). *Tales.* New York: Grove, 1967.

Jordan, June. *Things That I Do in the Dark*. New York: Random, 1967.

Kapai, Leela. "Dominant Themes and Technique in Paule Marshall's Fiction." *CLA Journal* 16.1 (1972): 49–59.

Kasinitz, Philip. *Caribbean New York: Black Immigrants and the Politics of Race*. Ithaca: Cornell University Press, 1992.

Kaye, Jacqueline. "Claude McKay's *Banjo*." *Présence Africaine* 73 (1970): 165–69.

Keizs, Marcia. "Themes and Style in the Works of Paule Marshall." *Negro American Literature Forum* 9.3 (1975): 67, 71–76.

Keller, James R. " 'A chafing savage down the decent street': The Politics of Compromise in Claude McKay's Protest Sonnets." *African American Review* 28.3 (1994): 447–56.

Kellner, Bruce, ed. *The Harlem Renaissance: A Historical Dictionary for the Era*. New York: Methuen, 1987.

Kent, G. E. *Blackness and the Adventure of Western Culture*. Chicago: Third World Press, 1972.

———. "Claude McKay's *Banana Bottom* Reappraised." *CLA Journal* 18 (Dec. 1974): 222–34.

———. "The Soulful Way of Claude McKay." *Black World* 20 (1970): 37–50.

Kesteloot, Lilyan. *Black Writers in French: A Literary History of Négritude*. Trans. Ellen Conroy Kennedy. Philadelphia: University of Pennsylvania Press, 1974.

Killens, John Oliver. *The Cotillion; or, One Good Bull Is Half the Herd*. New York: Trident, 1971.

Kincaid, Jamaica. *Annie John*. New York: Penguin, 1983.

———. *At the Bottom of the River*. New York: Vintage, 1985.

———. *Lucy*. New York: Farrar, 1990.

———. *A Small Place*. New York: Penguin, 1988.

King, Bruce, ed. *The Commonwealth Novel since 1960*. London: Macmillan, 1991.

———. *West Indian Literature*. London: Macmillan, 1979.

King, Deborah K. "Multiple Jeopardy, Multiple Consciousness: The Context of A Black Feminist Ideology." *Signs* 14.1 (1988): 42–72.

Kingston, Maxine Hong. *Tripmaster Monkey: His Fake Book*. New York: Vintage, 1990.

———. *The Woman Warrior: Memoirs of a Childhood among Ghosts*. New York: Vintage, 1977.

Kivisto, Peter, and Dag Blanck, eds. *American Immigrants and Their Generations: Studies and Commentaries on the Hansen Thesis after Fifty Years*. Urbana: University of Illinois Press, 1990.

Kolodny, Annette. "The Integrity of Memory: Creating a New Literary History of the United States." *American Literature* 57.2 (1985): 291–307.

Kuntz, Joseph M. *Poetry Explication: A Checklist of Interpretation since 1925 of British and American Poems, Past and Present*. Boston: Hall, 1980.

Lacovia, R. M. "Migration and Transmutation in the Novels of McKay, Marshall, and Clarke." *Journal of Black Studies* 7.4 (1977): 437–54.

Laguerre, Michael S. *American Odyssey: Haitians in New York City*. Ithaca: Cornell University Press, 1984.

Lamming, George. *In the Castle of My Skin*. New York: Schocken, 1983.

———. *The Pleasures of Exile*. London: Allison, 1960.

Lamur, Humphrey E., and John D. Speckman, eds. *Adaptation of Migrants from the Caribbean in the European and American Metropolis.* Amsterdam: University of Amsterdam, 1975.

Lang, P. M. "Claude McKay: Evidence of a Magic Pilgrimage." *CLA Journal* 16 (June 1973): 475–84.

Larson, Charles R. "African Afro-American Literary Relationships." *Negro Digest* 19 (Dec. 1969): 35–42.

———. "Three Harlem Novels of the Jazz Age." *Critique* 11 (1969): 66–78.

Lederer, Richard. "The Didactic and the Literary in Four Harlem Renaissance Sonnets." *EJ* 62 (1973): 219–23.

Lee, R. A. "On Claude McKay's 'If We Must Die.'" *CLA Journal* 18 (Dec. 1974): 216–17.

Lee, Robert A., and Graham Clarke, eds. "Harlem on My Mind: Fictions of a Black Metropolis." In *The American City: Literary and Cultural Perspectives.* New York: St. Martin's, 1988.

Lentricchia, Frank, and Thomas McLaughlin, eds. *Critical Terms for Literary Study.* Chicago: University of Chicago Press, 1990.

LeSeur, Geta. "Claude McKay's Marxism." In *The Harlem Renaissance: Reevaluations,* ed. Amritjit Singh, William S. Shiver, and Stanley Brodwin. New York: Garland, 1989. 219–32.

———. "Claude McKay's Romanticism." *CLA Journal* 32.3 (1989): 296–308.

———. "One Mother, Two Daughters: The Afro-American and the Afro-Caribbean Bildungsroman." *Black Scholar* 17.2 (1986): 26–33.

———. *Ten Is the Age of Darkness: The Black Bildungsroman.* Columbia: University of Missouri Press, 1995.

Leuth, Elmer. "The Scope of Black Life in Claude McKay's *Home to Harlem.*" *Obsidian II* 5.3 (1990): 43–52.

Levine, Barry B., ed. *The Caribbean Exodus.* New York: Praeger, 1987.

Lewald, Ernest H., ed. *The Cry of Home: Cultural Nationalism and the Modern Writer.* Knoxville: University of Tennessee Press, 1972.

Lewis, David Levering. *When Harlem Was in Vogue.* New York: Knopf, 1981.

Lewis, Rupert, and Maureen Lewis. "Claude McKay's Jamaica." *Caribbean Quarterly* 23.2–3 (1977): 38–53.

Light, Ivan. *Ethnic Enterprise in America: Business and Welfare among Chinese, Japanese, and Blacks.* Berkeley: University of California Press, 1972.

Lindberg-Seyersted, Brita. *Black and Female: Essays on Writings by Black Women in the Diaspora.* Oslo: Scandinavian University Press, 1994.

Linebaugh, Peter. "All the Atlantic Mountains Shook." *Labour/Le Travailleur* 10 (1982): 87–121.

Lively, Adam. "Continuity and Radicalism in American Black Nationalist Thought, 1914–1929." *Journal of American Studies* 18.2 (1984): 207–35.

Locke, Alain, ed. *The New Negro.* 1925. Reprint, New York: Atheneum, 1992.

Locke, Alain, and Bernhard J. Stern, eds. *When Peoples Meet: A Study in Race and Culture Contacts.* New York: Progressive Education Association, 1941.

Long, Richard A., and Eugenia W. Collier, eds. *Afro-American Writing: An Anthology of Prose and Poetry.* Vol. II. New York: New York University Press, 1972.

Lorde, Audre. "Sisterhood and Survival." *Black Scholar* 17.2 (1986): 5–7.

Lyman, Stanford. "Hansen's Theory and America's Black Birthright: The Historical Novel as History and Collective Memory." In Peter Kivisto and Dag Blanck, eds., *American Immigrants and Their Generations: Studies and Commentaries on the Hansen Thesis after Fifty Years.* Urbana: University of Illinois Press, 1990. 126–41.

Mair, Lucille. *Women Field Workers in Jamaica during Slavery.* Mona, Jamaica: University of the West Indies, 1987.

Major, Clarence. "Dear Jake and Ray." *American Poetry Review* 4 (1975): 40–42.

Margolies, Edward. *Native Sons.* New York: Lippincott, 1968.

Marks, Carole. *Farewell—We're Good and Gone: The Great Black Migration.* Bloomington: Indiana University Press, 1989.

Marshall, Dawn. "A History of West Indian Migrations: Overseas Opportunities and 'Safety-Valve' Policies." In *The Caribbean Exodus*, ed. Barry B. Levine. New York: Praeger, 1987. 15–31.

Marshall, Paule. "Black Immigrant Women in *Brown Girl, Brownstones.*" In *Female Immigrants to the United States: Caribbean, Latin American, and African Experiences*, ed. Delores M. Mortimer and Roy S. Bryce-Laporte. Washington, D.C.: Smithsonian, 1981. 3–13.

———. *Brown Girl, Brownstones.* 1959. Reprint, Old Westbury: The Feminist Press, 1981.

———. *The Chosen Place, the Timeless People.* New York: Random, 1969.

———. *Daughters.* 1991. Reprint, New York: Penguin, 1992.

———. "Holding onto the Vision: Sylvia Baer Interviews Paule Marshall." *The Women's Review of Books* 13.10–11 (1991): 24–5.

———. "An Interview with Paule Marshall." With Daryl Cumber Dance. *Southern Review* 28.1 (1992): 1–20.

———. *Praisesong for the Widow.* 1983. Reprint, New York: Dutton, 1984.

———. " 'Recreating Ourselves All Over the World': Interview with Paule Marshall." With Omolara Ogundipe-Leslie. In *Black Women's Writing: Crossing the Boundaries*, ed. Carol Boyce Davies. *Matatu: Zeitschrift für afrikanische Kultur und Gesellschaft* 3.6 (1989): 25–38.

———. *Reena and Other Stories.* New York: Feminist Press, 1983.

———. "Return of a Native Daughter: An Interview with Paule Marshall and Maryse Conde." With John Williams. *Sage* 3.2 (1986): 52–53.

———. "Shaping the World of My Art." *New Letters* 40.1 (1973): 97–112.

———. "Some Get Wasted." In John Henrik Clarke, ed., *Harlem, U.S.A.* Berlin: Seven Seas, 1974.

———. *Soul Clap Hands and Sing.* 1961. Reprint, Washington, D.C.: Howard University Press, 1988.

———. " 'Talk as a Form of Action': An Interview with Paule Marshall." With Sabine Brock. In *History and Tradition in Afro-American Culture*, ed. Gunter H. Lenz. Frankfurt: Campus, 1982. 194–206.

———. "To Be in the World." With Angela Elam. *New Letters* 62.4 (1996): 96–105.

Marshall, Paule, and Sarah E. Wright, Abbey Lincoln, and Alice Childress. "The Negro Woman in American Literature." *Freedomways* (First Quarter 1966): 8–25.

Martin, Tony. *Literary Garveyism: Garvey, Black Arts and the Harlem Renaissance.* Dover: Majority, 1983.

McCluskey, John, Jr. "And Called Every Generation Blessed: Theme, Setting, and Ritual in the Works of Paule Marshall." In *Black Women Writers (1950–1980): A Critical Evaluation*, ed. Mari Evans. Garden City: Anchor, 1984. 316–34.

McDowell, Deborah. "New Directions for Black Feminist Criticism." In *The New Feminist Criticism: Essays on Women, Literature, and Theory*, ed. Elaine Showalter. New York: Pantheon, 1985. 186–99.

McKay, Claude. *Banana Bottom*. 1933. Reprint, New York: Harper, 1961.

———. *Banjo: A Story without a Plot*. 1929. Reprint, New York: Harper, 1957.

———. "Boyhood in Jamaica." *Phylon* 14 (1953): 134–45.

———. *Constab Ballads*. London: Watts, 1912.

———. *The Dialect Poetry of Claude McKay*. Freeport, N.Y.: Books for Libraries, 1972.

———. "Garvey as a Negro Moses." *Liberator* 5 (April 1922): 8–9. Reprinted in Wayne F. Cooper, ed., *The Passion of Claude McKay: Selected Poetry and Prose, 1912–1948*. New York: Schocken, 1973.

———. *Gingertown*. 1932. Reprint, Freeport, N.Y.: Books for Libraries, 1972.

———. *Harlem: Negro Metropolis*. New York: Dutton, 1940.

———. *Home to Harlem*. 1928. Reprint, Boston: Northeastern University Press, 1987.

———. "Lest We Forget." *Jewish Frontier* 7 (Jan. 1940): 9–11.

———. *A Long Way from Home*. 1937. Reprint, New York: Harcourt, 1970.

———. *My Green Hills of Jamaica and Five Jamaican Short Stories*. Ed. Mervyn Morris. Kingston: Heinemann, 1979.

———. *The Negroes in America*. Trans. Robert J. Winter. Ed. A. L. McLeod. 1923. Reprint, Port Washington, N.Y.: Kennikat, 1979.

———. "A Negro Writer to His Critics." *New York Herald-Tribune Books*, March 6, 1932. Reprinted in Wayne F. Cooper, ed., *The Passion of Claude McKay: Selected Poetry and Prose, 1912–1948*. New York: Schocken, 1973.

———. "The New Day." *Interracial Review* 19 (Mar. 1946): 37.

———. *Powre above Powres: Trial By Lynching—Stories about Negro Life in North America*. Trans. Robert Winter. Ed. A. L. McLeod. Mysore, India: University of Mysore, 1977.

———. *Selected Poems of Claude McKay*. Intro. John Dewey. New York: Bookman, 1953.

———. *Selected Poems of Claude McKay*. With a biographical note by Max Eastman. 1953. Reprint, New York: Harcourt, 1981.

———. *Songs of Jamaica*. 1912. Reprint, Miami: Mnemosyne, 1969.

———. *Spring in New Hampshire*. London: Richards, 1920.

———. To William Stanley Braithwaite. 11 January 1916. William Stanley Braithwaite Papers, bMS Am 144 (75). Houghton Library, Harvard University.

McLeod, A. L. *Claude McKay: Centennial Studies*. Ed. A. L. McLeod. New Delhi: Sterling, 1992.

———. "Claude McKay, Alain Locke, and the Harlem Renaissance." *Literary Half-Yearly* 27.2 (1986): 65–75.

———. "Claude McKay as Historical Witness." In *Subjects Worthy of Fame: Essays on Commonwealth Literature in Honour of H. H. Anniah Gowda*, ed. A. L. McLeod. New Delhi: Sterling, 1989.

Mead, Margaret. *And Keep Your Powder Dry: An Anthropologist Looks at America.* New York: Morrow, 1942.

Melnick, Jeffrey, ed. *Race and the Modernist Artist.* New York: Oxford University Press, forthcoming.

Memmi, Albert. *The Colonizer and the Colonized.* Boston: Beacon, 1965.

Michael, S. "Children of the New Wave Immigration." In *Emerging Perspectives on the Black Diaspora*, ed. A. V. Bonnett and G. L. Watson. Lanham, Md.: University Press of America, 1990.

Miller, James A. "African-American Writing of the 1930s: A Prologue." In *Radical Revisions: Rereading 1930s Culture*, ed. Bill Mullen and Sherry Lee Linkon. Urbana: University of Illinois Press, 1996.

Miller, R. Baxter, ed. *Black American Literature and Humanism.* Lexington: University of Kentucky Press, 1981.

Mintz, Sidney, ed. *Slavery, Colonialism, and Racism.* New York: Norton, 1974.

Mitchell, Angelyn, ed. *Within the Circle: An Anthology of African American Literary Criticism from the Harlem Renaissance to the Present.* Durham: Duke University Press, 1994.

Mohr, Eugene V. *The Other Caribbean: Concerns of West Indian Writing.* Commonwealth of Puerto Rico: Department of Education, 1979.

Morrison, Toni. *The Bluest Eye.* New York: Washington Square Press, 1970.

———. *Tar Baby.* New York: Signet, 1981.

Mortimer, Delores M., and Roy S. Bryce-Laporte, eds. *Female Immigrants to the United States: Caribbean, Latin American, and African Experiences.* Washington, D.C.: Smithsonian, 1981.

Moynihan, Daniel, and Nathan Glazer, eds. *Beyond the Melting Pot.* Cambridge, Mass.: MIT Press, 1970.

Nahirny, Vladimir, and Joshua Fishman. "American Immigrant Groups: Ethnic Identification and the Problem of Generations." In *Theories of Ethnicity: A Classical Reader*, ed. Werner Sollors. New York: New York University Press, 1996. 266–81.

Naipaul, V. S. *Finding the Center: Two Narratives.* London: Deutsch, 1984.

———. *A House for Mr. Biswas.* 1961. Reprint, New York: Knopf, 1983.

Nankoe, Lucia, and Essa Reijmers. "To Keep the Memory of the Past Alive: A Theoretical Approach to the Novels of Black Women Writers." In *Crisis and Creativity in the New Literatures in English: Cross/cultures*, ed. Geoffrey V. Davis and Hena Maes-Jelinek. Amsterdam: Rodopi, 1990. 481–97.

Nazareth, Peter. "Colonial Institutions, Colonized People." *Busara* 6.1 (1974): 49–64.

———. "Paule Marshall's Timeless People." *New Letters* 40.1 (1973): 113–31.

Nelson, Emmanuel S. "Black America and the Anglophone Afro-Caribbean Literary Consciousness." *Journal of American Culture* 12.4 (1989): 53–58.

Nightingale, Peggy, ed. *A Sense of Place in the New Literatures in English.* Queensland: University of Queensland Press, 1986.

North, Michael. *The Dialect of Modernism: Race, Language, and Twentieth-Century Literature.* New York: Oxford University Press, 1994.

Nunez-Harrell, Elizabeth. "The Paradoxes of Belonging: The White West Indian Woman in Fiction." *Modern Fiction Studies* 31.2 (1985): 281–93.

Ogunyemi, Chikwenye Okonjo. "'The Old Order Shall Pass': The Examples of 'Flying Home' and 'Barbados.'" *Studies in Short Fiction* 20.1 (1983): 23–32.

———. "Womanism: The Dynamics of the Contemporary Black Female Novel in English." *Signs* 11.1 (1985): 63–80.

Olinder, Britta, ed. *A Sense of Place: Essays in Post-Colonial Literatures.* Gothenburg: Gothenburg University, 1984.

Osofsky, Gilbert. *Harlem: The Making of a Ghetto—Negro New York, 1890–1930.* 2nd ed. New York: Harper, 1971.

Ottley, Roi, and William J. Weatherby, eds. *The Negro in New York: An Informal Social History.* New York: Oceana, 1967.

Paquet, Sandra Pouchet. "Response to William Andrews' 'Toward a Poetics of Afro-American Autobiography.'" In *Afro-American Literary Study in the 1990s,* ed. Houston A. Baker Jr. and Patricia Redmond. Chicago: University of Chicago Press, 1989. 91–97.

———. "West Indian Autobiography." In *African American Autobiography: A Collection of Critical Essays,* ed. William L. Andrews. Englewood Cliffs, N.J.: Prentice, 1993. 196–211.

Park, Robert E. "Human Migration and the Marginal Man." In *Theories of Ethnicity: A Classical Reader,* ed. Werner Sollors. New York: New York University Press, 1996. 156–67.

Patterson, Harvey T. "American Democracy in the Canal Zone." *The Crisis* 20.2 (1920): 83–85.

Perry, Margaret. *Silence to the Drums: A Survey of the Literature of the Harlem Renaissance.* Westport, Conn.: Greenwood, 1976.

Pescatello, Ann M., ed. *Old Roots in New Lands: Historical and Anthropological Perspectives on Black Experiences in the Americas.* Westport, Conn.: Greenwood, 1977.

Pettis, Joyce. *Toward Wholeness in Paule Marshall's Fiction.* Charlottesville: University of Virginia Press, 1995.

Phaf, Ineke. "Women and Literature in the Caribbean." In *Unheard Words: Women and Literature in Africa, the Arab World, Asia, the Caribbean, and Latin America,* trans. Barbara Potter Fasting, ed. Mineke Schipper. London: Allison, 1985. 168–200.

Pollard, Velma. "Cultural Connections in Paule Marshall's *Praisesong for the Widow.*" *Caribbean Quarterly* 34 (1988): 58–70.

Portes, Alejandro, ed. *The New Second Generation.* New York: Russell Sage Foundation, 1996.

Powell, Colin L., with Joseph E. Persico. *My American Journey.* New York: Random, 1995.

Powell, Timothy B., ed. *Beyond the Binary: Reconstructing Cultural Identity in a Multicultural Context.* New Brunswick, N.J.: Rutgers University Press, 1999.

Pownall, David E. *Articles on Twentieth Century Literature: An Annotated Bibliography, 1954–1970.* New York: Kraus-Thompson, 1973.

Preibe, Richard. "The Search for Community in the Novels of Claude McKay." *Studies in Black Literature* 3 (Summer 1972): 22–30.

Prestianni, Vincent. "Bibliographical Scholarship on Three Black Writers." *Obsidian II* 5.1 (1990): 75–85.

Pryse, Marjorie, and Hortense Spillers, eds. *Conjuring: Black Women, Fiction, and Literary Tradition*. Bloomington: Indiana University Press, 1985.

Pyne-Timothy, Helen. "Perceptions of the Black Woman in the Work of Claude McKay." *CLA Journal* 19.2 (1975): 152–64.

Rahming, Melvin B. *The Evolution of the West Indian's Image in the Afro-American Novel*. Millwood, N.Y.: Associated Faculty, 1986.

Ramchand, Kenneth. "Claude McKay and *Banana Bottom*." *Southern Review* 4 (1970): 53–66.

———. *The West Indian Novel and Its Background*. 2nd ed. 1970. Reprint, London: Heinemann, 1983.

Rampersad, Arnold. *The Life of Langston Hughes*. Vol. I: *1902–1941*. New York: Oxford University Press, 1986.

Redding, J. Saunders. "The New Negro Poet in the Twenties." In *Modern Black Poets: A Collection of Critical Essays*, ed. Donald B. Gibson. Englewood Cliffs, N.J.: Prentice, 1973. 18–33.

Reid, Ira de Augustine. *The Negro Immigrant: His Background, Characteristics and Social Adjustment, 1899–1937*. 1939. Reprint, New York: Arno, 1969.

Reimers, David M. "New York City and Its People: An Historical Perspective up to World War II." In *Caribbean Life in New York City: Sociocultural Dimensions*, ed. Elsa M. Chaney and Constance R. Sutton. New York: Center for Migration Studies, 1987. 31–54.

Reyes, Angelita. "Politics and Metaphors of Materialism in Paule Marshall's *Praisesong for the Widow* and Toni Morrison's *Tar Baby*." In *Politics and the Muse: Studies in the Politics of Recent American Literature*, ed. Adam J. Sorkin. Bowling Green: Bowling Green State University Popular Press, 1989. 179–205.

Rhys, Jean. *Wide Sargasso Sea*. New York: Norton, 1967.

Roberts, Kimberley. "The Clothes Make the Woman: The Symbolics of Prostitution in Nella Larsen's *Quicksand* and Claude McKay's *Home to Harlem*." *Tulsa Studies in Women's Literature* 16.1 (1997): 107–30.

Rodriguez, Richard. *Days of Obligation: An Argument with My Mexican Father*. New York: Viking, 1992.

Romalis, Coleman. "Some Comments on Race and Ethnicity in the Caribbean." In *Ethnicity in the Americas*, ed. France Henry. The Hague: Mouton, 1976. 417–28.

Rush, Theressa Gunnels. *Black American Writers Past and Present: A Biographical and Bibliographical Dictionary*. Metuchen: Scarecrow, 1975. 513–15.

Sander, Reinhard W. *The Trinidad Awakening: West Indian Literature of the Nineteen-Thirties*. Westport, Conn.: Greenwood, 1988.

Schneider, Deborah. "A Search for Selfhood: Paule Marshall's *Brown Girl, Brownstones*." In *The Afro-American Novel since 1960*, ed. Peter Bruck and Wolfgang Karrer. Amsterdam: Gruner, 1982. 53–73.

Scruggs, Charles. "'All Dressed Up but No Place to Go': The Black Writer and His Audience during the Harlem Renaissance." *American Literature* 48 (Jan. 1977): 543–63.

Segal, Aaron. "The Caribbean Exodus in a Global Context: Comparative Migration Experiences." In *The Caribbean Exodus*, ed. Barry B. Levine. New York: Praeger, 1987. 44–66.

Shankman, Arnold M. *Ambivalent Friends: Afro-Americans View the Immigrant.* Westport, Conn.: Greenwood, 1982.

Shapiro, Lily J. "Patronage as Peculiar Institution: Charlotte Osgood Mason and the Harlem Renaissance." Senior honors thesis, History and Literature, Harvard University, 1993.

Singh, Amritjit. *Novels of the Harlem Renaissance: Twelve Black Writers, 1923–1933.* University Park: Pennsylvania State University Press, 1973.

Singh, Amritjit; Joseph T. Skerrett, Jr.; and Robert E. Hogan, eds. *Memory and Cultural Politics: New Approaches to American Ethnic Literatures.* Boston: Northeastern University Press, 1996.

Skerrett, Joseph T., Jr. "Paule Marshall and the Crisis of Middle Years." *Callaloo* 6.2 (1983): 68–74.

Smiley, Jane. "Caribbean Voices." *Chicago Tribune—Books* (6 Oct. 1991): 3.

Smith, Barbara. "Toward a Black Feminist Criticism." In *The New Feminist Criticism: Essays on Women, Literature, and Theory,* ed. Elaine Showalter. New York: Pantheon, 1985. 168–85.

Smith, Gary. "Black Protest Sonnet." *American Poetry* 2.1 (1984): 2–12.

Smith, Robert. "Claude McKay: An Essay in Criticism." *Phylon* 9 (1948): 270–73.

Smith, Robert P., Jr. "Rereading *Banjo*: Claude McKay and the French Connection." *CLA Journal* 30.1 (1986): 46–58.

Sollors, Werner. *Beyond Ethnicity: Consent and Descent in American Culture.* New York: Oxford University Press, 1986.

———. "Ethnicity." *Critical Terms for Literary Study.* Ed. Frank Lentricchia and Thomas McLaughlin. Chicago: University of Chicago Press, 1990.

———. *The Life Stories of Undistinguished Americans As Told by Themselves.* New York: Routledge, 1990.

———. "Literature and Ethnicity." In Stephan Thernstrom, ed., *Harvard Encyclopedia of American Ethnic Groups.* Cambridge, Mass.: Harvard University Press, 1980.

Sollors, Werner, ed. *The Invention of Ethnicity.* New York: Oxford University Press, 1989.

———. *Theories of Ethnicity: A Classical Reader.* New York: New York University Press, 1996.

Spillers, Hortense J. "Chosen Place, Timeless People: Some Figurations on the New World." In *Conjuring: Black Women, Fiction, and Literary Tradition,* ed. Hortense J. Spillers and Marjorie Pryse. Bloomington: Indiana University Press, 1985. 151–75.

Spillers, Hortense J., and Marjorie Pryse, eds. *Conjuring: Black Women, Fiction, and Literary Tradition.* Bloomington: Indiana University Press, 1985.

Stein, Judith. *The World of Marcus Garvey.* Baton Rouge, Louisiana State University Press, 1986.

Stoff, Michael. "Claude McKay and the Cult of Primitivism." In *The Harlem Renaissance Remembered,* ed. Arna Bontemps. New York: Dodd, 1972. 124–46.

Story, Ralph D. "Patronage and the Harlem Renaissance: You Get What You Pay for." *CLA Journal* 32.3 (1989): 284–95.

Sutton, Constance R. "The Caribbeanization of New York City and the Emergence of a Transnational Socio-cultural System." In *Caribbean Life in New York City: Sociocultural Dimensions*, ed. Elsa M. Chaney and Constance R. Sutton. New York: Center for Migration Studies, 1987. 15–30.

Sutton, Constance R., and Susan Makiesky-Barrow. "Migration and West Indian Racial and Ethnic Consciousness." In *Caribbean Life in New York City: Sociocultural Dimensions*, ed. Elsa M. Chaney and Constance R. Sutton. New York: Center for Migration Studies, 1987. 92–116.

Talbert, L. Lee. "The Poetics of Prophecy in Paule Marshall's *Soul Clap Hands and Sing*." *MELUS* 5.1 (1978): 49–56.

Taylor, Clyde. "Black Folk Spirit and the Shape of Black Literature." *Black World* 21 (1972): 31–40.

Thernstrom, Stephan, ed. *Harvard Encyclopedia of American Ethnic Groups*. Cambridge, Mass.: Harvard University Press, 1980.

Thurman, Wallace. *The Blacker the Berry*. 1929. New York: Arno, 1969.

Tillery, Tyrone. *Claude McKay: A Black Poet's Struggle for Identity*. Amherst: University of Massachusetts Press, 1992.

Troester, Rosalie Riegle. "Turbulence and Tenderness: Mothers, Daughters, and "Othermothers" in Paule Marshall's *Brown Girl, Brownstones*." *Sage* 1.2 (1984): 13–6.

Trotter, Joe William, Jr., ed. *The Great Migration in Historical Perspective: New Dimensions of Race, Class, and Gender*. Bloomington: Indiana University Press, 1991.

Turner, Darwin. "Introduction." In Paule Marshall, *Soul Clap Hands and Sing*. Washington, D.C.: Howard University Press, 1998.

Turner, W. Burghardt, and Joyce Moore Turner, eds. *Richard B. Moore, Caribbean Militant in Harlem: Collected Writings 1920–1972*. Bloomington: Indiana University Press, 1988.

Turpin, W. E. "Four Short Fiction Writers of the Harlem Renaissance." *CLA Journal* 11 (1967): 59–72.

Van Mol, Kay R. "Primitivism and Intellect in Toomer's *Cane* and McKay's *Banana Bottom*: The Need for an Integrated Black Consciousness." *Negro American Literature Forum* 10 (Summer 1976): 48–52.

Van Vechten, Carl. *Nigger Heaven*. New York: Knopf, 1926.

Wade-Gayles, Gloria. "The Truths of Our Mothers' Lives: Mother–Daughter Relationships in Black Women's Fiction." *Sage* 1.2 (1984): 8–12.

Wagner, Jean. *Black Poets of the United States: From Paul Laurence Dunbar to Langston Hughes*. Trans. Kenneth Douglas. Urbana: University of Illinois Press, 1973.

Walcott, Derek. *Another Life*. New York: Farrar, Straus and Giroux, 1973.

———. *Collected Poems: 1948–1984*. New York: Farrar, 1986.

———. *Omeros*. New York: Farrar, 1990.

Wall, Cheryl. "Paris and Harlem: Two Cultural Capitals." *Phylon* 35 (March 1974): 64–73.

Wall, Cheryl, ed. *Changing Our Own Words: Essays on Criticism, Theory, and Writing by Black Women*. New Brunswick, N.J.: Rutgers University Press, 1989.

Walrond, Eric. *Tropic Death*. New York: Boni, 1926.

Waniek, Marilyn Nelson. "Paltry Things: Immigrants and Marginal Men." *Callaloo* 6.2 (1983): 46–56.

Warren, Stanley. "Claude McKay as an Artist." *Negro History Bulletin* 40.2 (1977): 685–87.

——. "A New Poem by Claude McKay." *Crisis* 85.1 (1978): 33.

Washington, Mary Helen. Afterword. *Brown Girl, Brownstones.* Old Westbury: Feminist Press, 1981. 311–24.

Waters, Mary C. "Ethnic and Racial Identities of Second-Generation Black Immigrants in New York City." In *The New Second Generation*, ed. Alejandro Portes. New York: Russell Sage Foundation, 1996. 171–96.

——. *Ethnic Options: Choosing Identities in America.* Berkeley: University of California Press, 1990.

——. "The Intersection of Race, Ethnicity and Class: Second Generation West Indians in the United States." Race, Ethnicity and Urban Poverty Workshop, Center for the Study of Urban Inequality, Northwestern University. Evanston, Illinois, 5 Dec. 1991.

Watkins-Owens, Irma. *Blood Relations: Caribbean Immigrants and the Harlem Community, 1900–1930.* Bloomington: Indiana University Press, 1996.

Weisbrot, Robert. *Father Divine and the Struggle for Racial Equality.* Urbana: University of Illinois Press, 1983.

West, Dorothy. *The Living Is Easy.* 1948. Reprint, New York: Feminist Press, 1982.

Wilentz, Gay. *Binding Cultures: Black Women Writers in Africa and the Diaspora.* Bloomington: Indiana University Press, 1992.

Williams, Sherley Anne. "Solidarity Is Not Silent." *Belles Lettres: A Review of Books by Women* 7.2 (1991–1992): 2–3.

Willis, Susan. *Specifying: Black Women Writing the American Experience.* Madison: University of Wisconsin Press, 1987.

Wintz, Cary D. *Black Culture and the Harlem Renaissance.* Houston: Rice University Press, 1988.

Woldemikael, T. M. *Becoming Black American: Haitian and American Institutions in Evanston, Illinois.* New York: AMS, 1989.

Woods, Gregory. "Gay Re-Readings of the Harlem Renaissance Poets." *Journal of Homosexuality* 26.2–3 (1993): 127–42.

Yaeger, Patricia, and Beth Kowaleski-Wallace, eds. *Refiguring the Father: New Feminist Readings of Patriarchy.* Carbondale: Southern Illinois University Press, 1989.

Index

Mason, Charlotte Osgood, 34
McCarran-Walter Act, 13
McDowell, Deborah, 154–55*n18*
McKay, Claude, 5, 10, 28, 115, 119, 120, 145; and relationship to Harlem Renaissance, 9, 46–47, 53, 154*n16*, 164*n4;* on African American/African Caribbean interaction in Harlem, 20; biographical history, 29–35; contribution to *The New Negro,* 26; sexual orientation of, 33, 159*n16*, 163*n70;* attitude about vernacular poetry, 34–35, 159–60*n22;* attitude toward Constabulary, 40; in New York, 41–47; use of sonnet, 42–47; and Communism, 51–52, 163–64*n1;* in Russia, 52; and relationship to American expatriate writers in Paris, 52; in Morocco, 53; in Marseilles, 53; depictions of female characters, 60–62, 72–74, 75–76, 78–83; ideas about relationship between art and propaganda, 65–66; fictional commentary on Garveyism, 67–68; on Africa as inspiration for *Banana Bottom,* 74–75; as the "marginal man," 83–84; controversy surrounding birthdate of, 158*n2*, 159*n7;* familial background, 158*n5;* and attitude toward Booker T. Washington, 160*n35*
McKay family: Hannah Ann McKay (mother), 29–30, 158*n5;* Thomas Francis McKay (father), 29–30; Rachel McKay (sister), 30; Uriah Theodore McKay (brother), 30–32
"Metropolis" (Lang), 62
"A Midnight Woman to the Bobby" (McKay), 38
Milosz, Czeslaw, 103
Montego Bay, 31
Moore, Richard B., 7, 170–71*n24*
Morrison, Toni, 56, 89; and depictions of African Caribbeaners, 146; *The Bluest Eye,* 171*n38; Tar Baby,* 173*n18*
Mortimer, Delores, 9
"Mulatto" (McKay), 61
"The Mulatto Girl" (McKay), 61
Mulattoes: McKay's attitudes toward, 61; McKay's definition of, 165*n18*
My American Journey (Powell), 7–8, 151
My Green Hills of Jamaica (McKay), 29, 33, 75, 78, 165*n11*, 167*n43*

"My House" (McKay), 50–51, 109, 157*n35*

Nahirny, Vladmir, 105
Naipaul, V. S., 148; *A House for Mr. Biswas,* 109, 163*n69*, 170*n21*
Nanny: and role in Jamaican folklore, 172*n11*
National Negro Congress: resolution to mediate intraracial strife, 27
National Urban League, 12, 22
"Near-White" (McKay), 61
Négritude, 44; influence of McKay on, 161*n45*
"The Negro Artist and the Racial Mountain" (Hughes), 66; aesthetic ideology of, 166*n29*
Negro World: newspaper of United Negro Improvement Association, 68
"A Negro Writer to His Critics" (McKay), 66
The Negroes in America (McKay), 57
"Nellie White" (McKay), 36
The New Negro (Locke), 24, 26, 46–47
New York Times: July 1998 series on the "new immigration," 150
Nigger Heaven (Van Vechten), 54; McKay's familiarity with, 164*n6*, 164*n7*

"O Word I Love to Sing" (McKay), 42
Omi, Michael, 3
Opportunity: A Journal of Negro Life: "Special Caribbean Issue," 12, 22–28; McKay's contribution to the "Special Issue," 50
The Orchid House (Allfrey), 132, 175*n5*
"Outcast" (McKay), 29, 49–50, 84

Panama Canal: patterns of segregation in construction of, 14–15; relation to Caribbean immigration to the United States, 14–16; as depicted in fiction of Walrond, 15–16
"Panama Money," 14; as described by Marshall, 101
Pankhurst, Sylvia, 47–48, 57
Paquet, Sandra Pouchet, 97, 170*n21*
Park, Robert: on the "Marginal Man," 83, 152
Plantation School authors: use of dialect among, 63

Heather Hathaway is an Assistant Professor of English at Marquette University. She received her B.A. in English and American Studies from Wesleyan University, and her Ph.D. in the History of American Civilization from Harvard University.